Mathematics

Class 12 (CBSE & CUET Exam 2025-26)
Part-2

Concept-clearing notes and
formulae with examples

By Pavitra Gupta
B.E.

Preface

It gives me great pleasure in presenting this book. This book is second part of my book 'MATHEMATICS for class XII (CBSE & CUET): Concept-clearing notes and formulae with examples'.

Also, it is paperback printed version of my digital book 'MATHEMATICS for class 12 (CBSE & CUET): Concept-clearing notes and formulae with examples Part-2'.

Part-1 book contained seven chapters. In continuation of it, Part-2 book contains chapter-8 to 14. Both these parts, together, complete the syllabus prescribed by CBSE for class 12 Mathematics and the syllabus of CUET entrance test for undergraduate programmes. Some topics, which are marked by an asterisk (*) in this book, are not in the CBSE syllabus for session 2025-26 (released in April 2025). However, these topics have been covered for CUET, state boards or other exams.

Part-1 book has been appreciated for complete list of formulae in it and for the ways the concepts have been explained with easy examples. The same structure has been followed in this part.

It's my endeavour to keep the content as simple as possible to make it easy to understand. For the students to remember the formulae easily, a formula is written first, and then it is explained, if needed, with the help of well labelled figure. After that, an example is given to know how to apply it.

These books are written just like a student makes notes in the class to remember the things easily. It makes the books very helpful to learn and remember all concepts even though they do not contain questions for practice. Also, they become very useful while revising for exams.

I hope the students will be able to understand each and every concept comfortably through these books.

Pavitra Gupta

Table of Contents

*Asterisk (*) marked article (if any) is **not** in CBSE 2025-26 syllabus.*

*Asterisk (*) marked article (if any) is **not** in CBSE 2025-26 syllabus.*

---

*Asterisk (*) marked article (if any) is **not** in CBSE 2025-26 syllabus.*

*Asterisk (*) marked article (if any) is **not** in CBSE 2025-26 syllabus.*

*Asterisk (*) marked article (if any) is **not** in CBSE 2025-26 syllabus.*

Chapter-8   Integrals

1   Concept of Integrals

The reverse process of differentiation is called as **Integration** *(or* **anti differentiation***).*

i.e., if derivative of a function $f(x)$ with respect to x is $F(x)$, then we say that

antiderivative (or integral) of $F(x)$ with respect to x is $f(x)$.
(**Note carefully f and F**).

- Symbolically, $\int F(x)dx$ is read as integral of $F(x)$ with respect to x.

  Here, $F(x)$ is called integrand, and x is variable of integration.

- If $\dfrac{d}{dx}\left[f(x)\right] = F(x)$, then $\int F(x)dx = f(x)$

  (**Notice lower case and upper case in letter f**)

<u>**Example**</u>

$\because$ Derivative of $sin\ x$ with respect to x is $cos\ x$

$$\text{i.e.,}\ \frac{d}{dx}(sin\ x)\ =\ cos\ x$$

We write its converse as:

Antiderivative (or integral) of $cos\ x$ with respect to x is $sin\ x$.
If we add an arbitrary constant C to $sin\ x$, then also its derivative is $cos\ x$.

$$\text{i.e.,}\ \frac{d}{dx}(sin\ x + C)\ =\ cos\ x$$

Thus, integration of $cos\ x$ with respect to x is $sin\ x + C$.

So, in general, we write $\int cos\ x\ dx\ =\ sin\ x\ + C$

$$\text{where C is an arbitrary constant}$$

- Similarly, we can obtain integrals of some other functions just by knowing whose derivatives they are. By using these integrals as formulae, integrals of other functions can be obtained.

- When we find the integral of a function $F(x)$, we **add an arbitrary constant C** in the result (as shown in the above example).
  This is an indefinite integral, which is symbolically written as
  $\int F(x)dx.$

- If the function is integrated on an interval $[a,b]$, then it becomes definite integral.

Symbolically, it is written as $\int_a^b F(x)dx$. There is **no arbitrary constant** in it.

Here, a is called **lower limit**, and b is called **upper limit** of the integral.

- If $\int F(x)dx = f(x)$

  then $\int_a^b F(x)dx = f(b) - f(a)$

Example

Indefinite integral of $cos\ x$ is $sin\ x + C$

i.e., $\int cos\ x\ dx = sin\ x + C$

$\therefore$ Definite integral of $cos\ x$ in the interval $[0,\frac{\pi}{2}]$ is written as

$$\int_0^{\frac{\pi}{2}} cos\ x\ dx = sin\frac{\pi}{2} - sin\ 0 = 1$$

2 Indefinite Integrals

Following integrals are found as antiderivatives (i.e., by knowing whose derivatives they are). By using these integrals as formulae, integrals of other functions can be obtained.

2.1 Integrals directly from anti derivative method

Following are the integrals, which are obtained directly from the formulas of differentiation just by reversing them.

(i) $\int x^n\ dx = \frac{x^{n+1}}{n+1} + C$

  $\rightarrow \int dx = x + C$

(ii) $\int \frac{1}{x}\ dx = log\ |x| + C$

(iii) $\int e^x dx = e^x + C$

(iv) $\int a^x dx = \frac{a^x}{log\ a} + C$

(v) $\int sin\ x\ dx = -cos\ x + C$

(vi) $\int cos\ x\ dx = sin\ x + C$

(vii) $\int sec^2\ x\ dx = tan\ x + C$

(viii) $\int cosec^2\ x\ dx = -cot\ x + C$

(ix) $\int sec\ x . tan\ x\ dx = sec\ x + C$

---

*Asterisk (*) marked article (if any) is **not** in CBSE 2025-26 syllabus.*

(x) $\quad \int cosec\, x\,.cot\, x\, dx\; =\; -\,cosec\, x\; +\; C$

(xi) $\quad \int \dfrac{1}{\sqrt{1-x^2}}\, dx\; =\; sin^{-1}x\; +\; C$

$$=\; -\,cos^{-1}x\; +\; C$$

(xii) $\quad \int \dfrac{1}{1+x^2}\, dx\; =\; tan^{-1}x\; +\; C$

$$=\; -\,cot^{-1}x\; +\; C$$

(xiii) $\quad \int \dfrac{1}{x\sqrt{x^2-1}}\, dx\; =\; sec^{-1}x\; +\; C$

$$=\; -\,cosec^{-1}x\; +\; C$$

2.2 Properties of integrals

(i) $\int ku\,.dx = k\int u\,.dx$

where k is any real number, and u is a function of x

<u>Example</u>

Find the integral, $\int 5x^{-3}\,.dx$

Solution

$$\int 5x^{-3}\,.dx = 5\int x^{-3}\,.dx = 5\left(\dfrac{x^{-2}}{-2}\right)+C$$

[applying formula no.(i) of article 2.1]

<u>Example</u>

Find the integral, $\int -2\sin x\,.dx$

Solution

$$\int -2\sin x\,.dx = -2\int \sin x\,.dx = -2(-\cos x)+C$$

[applying formula no.(v) of article 2.1]

$$= 2\cos x + C$$

(ii) $\int (u \pm v)\, dx = \int u\, dx \pm \int v\, dx$

i.e., Terms of integrands can be integrated separately.

<u>Example</u>

Find the integral, $\displaystyle\int \left(\dfrac{4}{3}x^3 - 2\sin x\right).dx$

Solution

$$\int \left(\dfrac{4}{3}x^3 - 2\sin x\right).dx = \int \dfrac{4}{3}x^3\,.dx - \int 2\sin x\,.dx$$

$$= \dfrac{4}{3}\int x^3\,.dx - 2\int \sin x\,.dx$$

$$= \dfrac{4}{3}\times\dfrac{x^4}{4} - 2(-\cos x)+C$$

[applying formula no.(i) and (v) of article 2.1]

$$= \dfrac{x^4}{3} + 2\cos x + C$$

2.3 Integration by Substitution

Usually, we make a substitution for a function whose derivative also occurs in the integrand (in multiplication with dx) as shown in the situations below in the table. However, it takes a little practice to find out a suitable substitution in different situations.

FORMS	METHOD
(i) $\int [f(x)]^n f'(x)\,dx$ OR $\int [g(f(x))]^n f'(x)\,dx$ (ii) $\int \dfrac{f'(x)}{[f(x)]^n}\,dx$ OR $\int \dfrac{f'(x)}{[g(f(x))]^n}\,dx$	Put $f(x) = t$ and $f'(x)\,dx = dt$

<u>Example</u>

To find the integral $\int sec^2 x \cdot \tan x\, dx$, we observe that $sec^2 x$ is derivative of $\tan x$.

If we take $\tan x$ as $f(x)$, then $f'(x) = sec^2 x$.

So, it is the of form $\int [f(x)]^n f'(x)\, dx$, where $n = 1$

$\therefore$ put $\tan x = t$ $\ldots\ldots\ldots\ldots$ (i)

Differentiating both sides w.r.t. t ,

we get $sec^2 x \dfrac{dx}{dt} = 1 \Rightarrow sec^2 x\, dx = dt$

$\therefore$ The given integral becomes

$$\int sec^2 x \cdot \tan x\, dx = \int \tan x \cdot sec^2 x\, dx = \int t\, dt$$

$$= \frac{t^2}{2} + C$$

$$\left(\text{Applying the formula } \int x^n\, dx = \frac{x^{n+1}}{n+1} + C, \text{ given in art2.1}\right)$$

$$= \frac{\tan^2 x}{2} + C \quad \text{(converting back } t \text{ into } x \text{ using eqn. (i))}$$

<u>Example</u>

To find the integral $\int 2x \cdot \sin x^2\, dx$, we observe that x^2 is present inside the sine function, and its derivative is $2x$.

If we take x^2 as $f(x)$, then $f'(x) = 2x$.

So, it is of the form $\int [g(f(x))]^n \, f'(x) \, dx$, where $n = 1$

$\therefore$ Put $x^2 = t$ ....(i)

Differentiating both sides w.r.t. t,

we get $2x \dfrac{dx}{dt} = 1 \Rightarrow 2x \, dx = dt$

$\therefore$ The given integral becomes

$$\int 2x \cdot \sin x^2 \, dx = \int \sin t \, dt$$
$$= -\cos t + C$$

(Applying the formula $\int \sin x \, dx = -\cos x + C$, given in art2.1)

$$= -\cos x^2 + C \quad \text{(converting back } t \text{ into } x \text{ using eqn.(i))}$$

Example

To find the integral $\int \dfrac{\sec^2 x}{\tan x} \, dx$, we observe that $\sec^2 x$ is derivative of $\tan x$.

If we take $\tan x$ as $f(x)$, then $f'(x) = \sec^2 x$.

So, it is the form $\int \dfrac{f'(x)}{[f(x)]^n} \, dx$, where $n = 1$

$\therefore$ Put $\tan x = t$ ....(i)

Differentiating both sides w.r.t. t,

we get $\sec^2 x \dfrac{dx}{dt} = 1 \Rightarrow \sec^2 x \, dx = dt$

$\therefore$ The given integral becomes

$$\int \dfrac{\sec^2 x}{\tan x} \, dx = \int \dfrac{1}{t} \, dt$$
$$= \log|t| + C$$

(Applying the formula $\int \dfrac{1}{x} \, dx = \log|x| + C$ given in art2.1)

$$= \log|\tan x| + C \quad \text{(converting back } t \text{ into } x \text{ using eqn.(i))}$$

Example

To find the integral $\int \dfrac{1}{x \, \mathrm{cosec} \, (\log x)} \, dx$ we observe that $\log x$ is present inside the cosecant function, and its derivative is $\dfrac{1}{x}$.

If we take $log\ x$ as $f(x)$, then $f'(x) = \frac{1}{x}$.

So, it is of the form $\displaystyle\int \frac{f'(x)}{[g(f(x))]^n}\ dx$, where $n = 1$

$\therefore$ Put $log\ x = t$ $\ldots\ldots\ldots$ (i)

Differentiating both sides w.r.t. t,

we get $\frac{1}{x} \cdot \frac{dx}{dt} = 1 \ \Rightarrow\ \frac{1}{x}\ dx = dt$

$\therefore$ The given integral becomes

$$\int \frac{1}{x\ cosec\ (log\, x)}\ dx \ =\ \int \frac{1}{cosec\ t}\ dt$$

$$=\ \int sin\, t\ dt\ =\ -\cos t\ +\ C$$

[Applying the formula $\int sin\, x\ dx = -\cos x\ +\ C$

given in art2.1]

$$=\ -\cos\,(log\ x)\ +\ C$$

- Using substitution method, we can find integration of $tan\ x$, $cot\ x$, $sec\ x$, and $cosec\ x$, and then they can be used as formulae.

  - $\int tan\, x\ dx\ =\ log\ |sec\ x|\ +\ C$
  $$=\ -log\ |cos\ x|\ +\ C$$

  - $\int cot\, x\ dx\ =\ log\ |sin\ x|\ +\ C$
  $$=\ -log\ |cosec\ x|\ +\ C$$

  - $\int sec\, x\ dx\ =\ log\ |sec\ x + tan\ x|\ +\ C$
  $$=\ log\left|tan\left(\frac{\pi}{4} + \frac{x}{2}\right)\right|\ +\ C$$

  - $\int cosec\, x\ dx\ =\ log\ |cosec\ x - cot\ x|\ +\ C$
  $$=\ log\left|tan\frac{x}{2}\right|\ +\ C$$

<u>Explanation</u>

(i) $\int tan\, x\ dx = \displaystyle\int \frac{sin\, x}{cos\, x}\ dx$

$$\left[\,Put\quad cos\ x = t\right.$$
$$\left.and\quad -sin\ x\ dx = dt\,\right]$$

$$=\ -\int \frac{1}{t}\ dt$$

$=\ -log|\,t\,| + C$ (Applying formula: $\int \frac{1}{x}\ dx = log\ |x| + C$,

given in art2.1)

$$=\ -log|cos\ x|\ +\ C$$

$$= \log|\sec x| + C$$

(ii) $\displaystyle \int \cot x \; dx = \int \frac{\cos x}{\sin x} \; dx$

$$\left[\begin{array}{l} \text{Put} \quad \sin x = t \\ \text{and} \quad \cos x \, dx = dt \end{array} \right]$$

$$= \int \frac{1}{t} \; dt$$

$$= \log|t| + C \quad \left(\text{Applying formula:} \int \frac{1}{x} \, dx = \log|x| + C, \right.$$
$$\left. \text{given in art2.1}\right)$$

$$= \log|\sin x| + C$$
$$= -\log|\operatorname{cosec} x| + C$$

(iii) $\displaystyle \int \sec x \; dx = \int \sec x \times \frac{\sec x + \tan x}{\sec x + \tan x} \; dx$

$$= \int \frac{\sec^2 x + \sec x \tan x}{\sec x + \tan x} \; dx$$

$$\left[\begin{array}{l} \text{Put} \quad \sec x + \tan x = t \\ \text{And} \quad (\sec x . \tan x + \sec^2 x)dx = dt \end{array} \right]$$

$$= \int \frac{1}{t} \; dt$$

$$= \log|t| + C \quad \left(\text{Applying formula:} \int \frac{1}{x} \, dx = \log|x| + C, \right.$$
$$\left. \text{given in art2.1}\right)$$

$$= \log|\sec x + \tan x| + C$$

(iv) $\displaystyle \int \operatorname{cosec} x \; dx = \int \operatorname{cosec} x \times \frac{\operatorname{cosec} x - \cot x}{\operatorname{cosec} x - \cot x} \; dx$

$$= \int \frac{\operatorname{cosec}^2 x - \operatorname{cosec} x \cot x}{\operatorname{cosec} x - \cot x} \; dx$$

$$\left[\begin{array}{l} \text{Put} \quad \operatorname{cosec} x - \cot x = t \\ \text{and} \quad (-\operatorname{cosec} x . \cot x + \operatorname{cosec}^2 x) \, dx = dt \end{array} \right]$$

$$= \int \frac{1}{t} \; dt$$

$$= \log|t| + C \quad \left(\text{Applying formula:} \int \frac{1}{x} \, dx = \log|x| + C, \right.$$
$$\left. \text{given in art2.1}\right)$$

$$= \log|\operatorname{cosec} x - \cot x| + C$$

- We can use all the formulae of integrals discussed in this chapter if, in the given integral, there is a linear expression in place of variable x, but we must divide the whole result by the coefficient of x in that linear expression. (See examples below).

- It is because, the same result is obtained if we solve the given integral by substituting linear expression in it. (See examples below).

<u>Example</u>

(i) To find $\int (4 - 3x)^{-2}\, dx$,

we can use formula $\int x^n\, dx = \dfrac{x^{n+1}}{n+1} + C$

But we have to divide the result by -3, which is the coefficient of x in $4 - 3x$.

$$\therefore \int (4 - 3x)^{-2}\, dx = \frac{(4-3x)^{-2+1}}{(-2+1)\,(-3)} + C = \frac{(4-3x)^{-1}}{3} + C$$

We can obtain the same result if we substitute $4 - 3x = t$

and $-3dx = dt$ or $dx = \dfrac{dt}{-3}$ as follows:

$$\int (4 - 3x)^{-2}\, dx = \int \frac{t^{-2} dt}{-3} = -\frac{1}{3}\int t^{-2} dt$$

$$= -\frac{1}{3}\left(\frac{t^{-1}}{-1}\right) + C = \frac{(4-3x)^{-1}}{3} + C$$

(ii) To find $\int \sin(2x + 3)dx$,

we can use formula $\int \sin x\, dx = -\cos x + C$

But we have to divide the result by 2, which is the coefficient of x in $2x + 3$.

$$\therefore \int \sin(2x + 3)dx = \frac{-\cos(2x+3)}{2} + C$$

We can obtain the same result if substitute $2x + 3 = t$

and $2dx = dt$ or $dx = \dfrac{dt}{2}$ as follows:

$$\int \sin(2x + 3)dx = \int \frac{\sin t\, dt}{2} = \frac{1}{2}\int \sin t\, dt$$

$$= \frac{1}{2}(-\cos t) + C = \frac{-\cos(2x+3)}{2} + C$$

2.4 Integration of some Trigonometric Functions

2.4.1 Higher powers of sine and cosine

2.4.1.1 Odd powers:

- To integrate odd powers of $sin\,x$ and $cos\,x$, first separate their power 1 to convert into even powers, and then we convert sin^2x and cos^2x according to the basic formula, $sin^2\theta + cos^2\theta = 1$:

  (i) $sin^2\theta = 1 - cos^2\theta$ (ii) $cos^2\theta = 1 - sin^2\theta$

  See examples below.

Example

(i) $\int \sin^3 x \, dx = \int \sin^2 x \cdot \sin x \, dx$ (separating power 1)

$$\left[\text{ use formula } \sin^2\theta = 1 - \cos^2\theta \right]$$

$$= \int (1 - \cos^2 x) \cdot \sin x \, dx$$

$$\left[\text{ Put } \quad \cos x = t \right.$$
$$\left. \text{and} \quad -\sin x \, dx = dt \right]$$

$$= \int (1 - t^2) \cdot (-dt)$$

$$= \int (-1 + t^2) \, dt$$

$$= -t + \frac{t^3}{3} + C$$

$$= -\cos x + \frac{\cos^3 x}{3} + C$$

(ii) $\int \cos^3 x \, dx = \int \cos^2 x \cdot \cos x \, dx$ (separating power 1)

$$\left[\text{ use formula } \cos^2\theta = 1 - \sin^2\theta \right]$$

$$= \int (1 - \sin^2 x) \cdot \cos x \, dx$$

$$\left[\text{ Put } \quad \sin x = t \right.$$
$$\left. \text{and} \quad \cos x \, dx = dt \right]$$

$$= \int (1 - t^2) \cdot dt$$

$$= t - \frac{t^3}{3} + C$$

$$= \sin x - \frac{\sin^3 x}{3} + C$$

(iii) $\int \sin^7 x \, dx = \int \sin^6 x \cdot \sin x \, dx$ (separating power 1)

$$= \int (\sin^2 x)^3 \cdot \sin x \, dx$$

$$\left[\text{ use formula } \sin^2\theta = 1 - \cos^2\theta \right]$$

$$= \int (1 - \cos^2 x)^3 \cdot \sin x \, dx$$

$$\left[\text{ Put } \quad \cos x = t \right.$$
$$\left. \text{and} \quad -\sin x \, dx = dt \right]$$

$$= \int (1 - t^2)^3 \cdot (-dt)$$

$$= -\int [1 - (t^2)^3 - 3t^2 + 3(t^2)^2] \, dt$$

$$\left[\text{ Using } (a - b)^3 = a^3 - b^3 - 3a^2 b + 3ab^2 \right]$$

$$= \int [-1 + t^6 + 3t^2 - 3t^4] \, dt$$

$$= -t + \frac{t^7}{7} + \frac{3t^3}{3} - 3\frac{t^5}{5} + C$$

$$= -\cos x + \frac{\cos^7 x}{7} + \cos^3 x - \frac{3\cos^5 x}{5} + C$$

Similarly, other odd powers of sine and cosine can be integrated.

- sin^3x and cos^3x can be integrated by using the following formulae also:
$$sin3A = 3\,sinA - 4\,sin^3A$$
and $\quad cos3A = 4\,cos^3A - 3\,cosA,\quad$ respectively.
See below:

(i) $sin3x = 3\,sinx - 4\,sin^3x$

$\Rightarrow sin^3x = \frac{1}{4}(3\,sinx - sin3x)$

$$\therefore \int sin^3x\,dx = \int \frac{1}{4}(3\,sinx - sin3x)\,dx$$

$$= \frac{3}{4}\int sinx\,dx - \frac{1}{4}\int sin3x\,dx$$

$$= \frac{3}{4}(-cosx) - \frac{1}{4}\left(\frac{-cos3x}{3}\right) + C$$

$$= -\frac{3}{4}cosx + \frac{1}{12}cos3x + C$$

(ii) $cos3x = 4\,cos^3x - 3\,cosx$

$\Rightarrow cos^3x = \frac{1}{4}(3\,cosx + cos3x)$

$$\therefore \int cos^3x\,dx = \int \frac{1}{4}(3\,cosx + cos3x)\,dx$$

$$= \frac{3}{4}\int cosx\,dx + \frac{1}{4}\int cos3x\,dx$$

$$= \frac{3}{4}\,sinx + \frac{1}{4}\left(\frac{sin3x}{3}\right) + C$$

$$= \frac{3}{4}\,sinx + \frac{1}{12}\,sin3x + C$$

2.4.1.2 Even powers:

- To integrate even powers of $sin\,x$ and $cos\,x$, we convert sin^2x and cos^2x according to half angle formulae:

(i) $sin^2\frac{\theta}{2} = \frac{1-cos\theta}{2}$ $\quad$ (ii) $cos^2\frac{\theta}{2} = \frac{1+cos\theta}{2}$

See examples below.

<u>Example</u>

(i) $\int sin^2x\,dx = \int \frac{1-cos\,2x}{2}\,dx$

$$\left[\text{ using formula } sin^2\frac{\theta}{2} = \frac{1-cos\theta}{2}\right]$$

$$= \int \frac{1}{2}\,dx - \int \frac{cos\,2x}{2}\,dx$$

$$= \frac{1}{2}\int dx - \frac{1}{2}\int cos\,2x\,dx$$

$$= \frac{x}{2} - \frac{1}{2}\cdot\frac{sin\,2x}{2} + C$$

$$= \frac{x}{2} - \frac{sin\,2x}{4} + C$$

(ii) $\int \cos^2 x\, dx = \int \dfrac{1+\cos 2x}{2}\, dx$

$$\left[\text{ using formula } \cos^2\frac{\theta}{2} = \frac{1+\cos\theta}{2}\right]$$

$$= \int \frac{1}{2}\, dx + \int \frac{\cos 2x}{2}\, dx$$

$$= \frac{1}{2}\int dx + \frac{1}{2}\int \cos 2x\, dx$$

$$= \frac{x}{2} + \frac{1}{2}\cdot\frac{\sin 2x}{2} + C$$

$$= \frac{x}{2} + \frac{\sin 2x}{4} + C$$

(iii) $\int \sin^6 x\, dx = \int (\sin^2 x)^3\, dx$

$$= \int \left(\frac{1-\cos 2x}{2}\right)^3 dx$$

$$\left[\text{using formula } \sin^2\frac{\theta}{2} = \frac{1-\cos\theta}{2}\right]$$

$$= \frac{1}{8}\int (1 - \cos^3 2x - 3\cos 2x + 3\cos^2 2x)\, dx$$

Now $\cos^3 2x$ can be integrated as explained in odd powers and $\cos^2 2x$ can be integrated as explained above in (ii).

So, we write: $\cos^3 2x = \dfrac{1}{4}(3\cos 2x + \cos 6x)$

and $\qquad\qquad \cos^2 2x = \dfrac{1+\cos 4x}{2}$

$$\therefore\ \int \sin^6 x\, dx = \frac{1}{8}\int \left[1 - \frac{1}{4}(3\cos 2x + \cos 6x) - 3\cos 2x\right.$$

$$\left. +3\frac{1+\cos 4x}{2}\right] dx$$

On simplifying like terms, we get

$$\int \sin^6 x\, dx = \frac{1}{8}\int \left(\frac{5}{2} - \frac{15}{4}\cos 2x + \frac{3}{2}\cos 4x - \frac{1}{4}\cos 6x\right) dx$$

$$= \frac{1}{8}\left[\frac{5}{2}x - \frac{15}{4}\cdot\frac{\sin 2x}{2} + \frac{3}{2}\cdot\frac{\sin 4x}{4} - \frac{1}{4}\cdot\frac{\sin 6x}{6}\right] + C$$

$$= \frac{5}{16}x - \frac{15}{64}\cdot\sin 2x + \frac{3}{64}\cdot\sin 4x - \frac{1}{192}\cdot\sin 6x + C$$

Similarly, other even powers of sine and cosine can be integrated.

2.4.2 Higher powers of tan and cot

- To integrate higher powers of $\tan x$ and $\cot x$, first separate their power 2, and then we convert $\tan^2 x$ and $\cot^2 x$ according to the basic formulae as follows:

$$\sec^2\theta - \tan^2\theta = 1 \quad\text{and}\quad \operatorname{cosec}^2\theta - \cot^2\theta = 1$$

i.e., we write $\tan^2\theta = \sec^2\theta - 1$

$$\text{or}\qquad \cot^2\theta = \operatorname{cosec}^2\theta - 1$$

Example

$$\int tan^7x \, dx = \int tan^5x . tan^2x \, dx \quad \text{(separating power 2)}$$
$$[\text{ use formula } tan^2\theta = sec^2\theta - 1 \text{ }]$$
$$= \int tan^5x . (sec^2x - 1)dx$$
$$= \int (tan^5x . sec^2x - tan^5x)dx$$
$$= \int tan^5x . sec^2x \, dx - \int tan^5x dx$$

Now, separate power 2 in the second integral to obtain

$$\int tan^7x \, dx = \int tan^5x . sec^2x \, dx - \int tan^3x . tan^2x dx$$
$$[\text{use formula } tan^2\theta = sec^2\theta - 1 \text{ in second integral}]$$
$$= \int tan^5x . sec^2x \, dx - \int tan^3x . (sec^2x - 1)dx$$
$$= \int tan^5x . sec^2x \, dx - \int tan^3x . sec^2x \, dx + \int tan^3x \, dx$$

Now, separate power 2 in the third integral to obtain

$$\int tan^7x \, dx = \int tan^5x . sec^2x \, dx - \int tan^3x . sec^2x \, dx$$
$$+ \int tan x . tan^2x \, dx$$
$$[\text{use formula } tan^2\theta = sec^2\theta - 1 \text{ in third integral}]$$
$$= \int tan^5x . sec^2x \, dx - \int tan^3x . sec^2x \, dx$$
$$+ \int tan x . (sec^2x - 1) \, dx$$
$$= \int tan^5x . sec^2x \, dx - \int tan^3x . sec^2x \, dx$$
$$+ \int tan x . sec^2x - \int tanx \, dx$$
$$[\text{Put } tan x = t \text{ in } 1^{st}, 2^{nd} \text{ and } 3^{rd} \text{ integrals}$$
$$\text{and} \quad sec^2x \, dx = dt \text{ }]$$
$$= \int t^5 dt - \int t^3 dt + \int t \, dt - \int tanx \, dx$$
$$= \frac{t^6}{6} - \frac{t^4}{4} + \frac{t^2}{2} - log|secx| + C$$
$$= \frac{tan^6x}{6} - \frac{tan^4x}{4} + \frac{tan^2x}{2} - log|secx| + C$$

Similarly, other powers of *tan* and *cot* can be integrated.

2.5 Integration by Partial Fractions

A rational function can be expressed as a sum of simpler rational functions by the method of partial fraction. After that, integration can be carried out by already known methods and formulae.

- A function f is said to be a rational function if

  $f(x) = \dfrac{g(x)}{h(x)}$, where $g(x)$, the numerator and $h(x)$, the denominator both are polynomial functions and $h(x) \neq 0$.

- A rational function $f(x) = \dfrac{g(x)}{h(x)}$ may be a proper rational function or an improper rational function.

- If the **degree of g(x)** $\geq$ **degree of h(x)**, then $f(x)$ is **improper** rational function.
- If the **degree of g(x)** $<$ **degree of h(x)**, then $f(x)$ is **proper** rational function.

<u>**Example**</u>

In the rational expression $\dfrac{x^3 + x + 1}{x^2 - 1}$, the degree of numerator is 3, and the degree of denominator is 2.

degree of numerator $>$ degree of denominator

$\therefore$ It is an improper rational function.

<u>**Example**</u>

In the rational expression, $\dfrac{3x + 5}{x^3 - x^2 - x + 1}$ the degree of numerator is 1, and the degree of denominator is 3.

degree of numerator $<$ degree of denominator

$\therefore$ It is a proper rational function.

2.5.1 Partial Fractions

Given a function: $f(x) = \dfrac{g(x)}{h(x)}$

Step-1 Observe the degree of $g(x)$ & degree of $h(x)$.

- If **degree of g(x)** $\geq$ **degree of h(x)**, then it is an improper rational function.

  (i) Divide $g(x)$ by $h(x)$, and find the quotient $q(x)$ & remainder $r(x)$.

  (ii) Now the function $f(x) = \dfrac{g(x)}{h(x)}$ can be written as

  $$f(x) = q(x) + \dfrac{r(x)}{h(x)}, \text{ where } \dfrac{r(x)}{h(x)} \text{ will be a proper}$$

  rational function

- If **degree of g(x)** $<$ **degree of h(x)**, then it is already a proper rational function.

  $$f(x) = \dfrac{g(x)}{h(x)} = \dfrac{r(x)}{h(x)} \quad \text{i.e., } g(x) \text{ is taken as } r(x)$$

Step-2 We have to do partial fractions of $\dfrac{r(x)}{h(x)}$.

- To do this, first factorize $h(x)$.

  Here, we will discuss the partial fraction, where the factors of $h(x)$ can be combination of linear or

---

quadratic expressions or linear expressions with some positive integral powers .

Step-3 Now suppose $\dfrac{r(x)}{h(x)}$ as sum of fractions as follows:

(i) For each linear factor in *h(x)*, we add a fraction having that linear factor as its Denominator and a constant like A, B, C, D, etc., in its Numerator (Values of these constants are yet to be determined).
(See **situation-1** below)

(ii) For each Quadratic factor in *h(x)*, we add a fraction having that quadratic factor as its Denominator and a Linear expression like A x + B, C x + D, etc., in its Numerator. Values of A, B, C, D, etc., are yet to determined.
(See **situation-2** below)

(iii) For each linear factor with power n in *h(x)*, we add as many fractions as the power. Each fraction has that linear factor with unique power from 1 to n in its Denominator and a constant in its Numerator.
(See **situation-3** below)

Consider some of the situations as below.

<u>Situation-1</u> (All the factors of *h(x)* are linear expressions):

If all the factors of $h(x)$ are linear expressions, then we have situation as follows:

$$\frac{r(x)}{h(x)} = \frac{r(x)}{(Linear_1)(Linear_2)(Linear_3)}$$

We proceed as follows:

Let

$$\frac{r(x)}{(Linear_1)(Linear_2)(Linear_3)} = \frac{A}{(Linear_1)} + \frac{B}{(Linear_2)} + \frac{C}{(Linear_3)}$$

$$\dots\dots\dots\text{(i)}$$

[Here we are considering only 3 linear factors. However, $h(x)$ may have any number of factors. For each linear factor, we add a fraction having that linear factor as its Denominator and a constant like A, B, C, D, etc., in Numerator.]

Taking LCM on RHS of eqn.(i), it becomes:

$$\frac{r(x)}{(Linear_1)(Linear_2)(Linear_3)}$$

$$= \frac{A(Linear_2)(Linear_3)+B(Linear_1)(Linear_3)+C(Linear_1)(Linear_2)}{(Linear_1)(Linear_2)(Linear_3)}$$

$$\Rightarrow r(x) = A(Linear_2)(Linear_3) + B(Linear_1)(Linear_3)$$
$$+C(Linear_1)(Linear_2)$$

Now expand all brackets on RHS, and combine similar terms.

Compare the coefficients of similar terms on both sides to find equations in A, B and C.

Solve these equations to find A, B and C.

Put these values of A, B and C in eqn.**(i)** to get partial fractions of $\dfrac{r(x)}{h(x)}$.

Example (Situation-1)

Find the integral $\displaystyle\int \frac{x^3 + x + 1}{x^2 - 1}\, dx$

Solution:

Step-1: Here we observe that the degree of numerator is 3 and that of denominator is 2.

It means degree of numerator > degree of denominator

So, dividing $x^3 + x + 1$ by $x^2 - 1$, we write

$$\frac{x^3 + x + 1}{x^2 - 1} = x + \frac{2x + 1}{x^2 - 1}$$

Step-2: Now $\dfrac{2x + 1}{x^2 - 1}$ is a proper rational function. We have to do its partial fractions.

For partial fractions, denominators must be factorised.

∴ We factorise the denominator, and write:

$$\frac{2x + 1}{x^2 - 1} = \frac{2x + 1}{(x + 1)(x - 1)}$$

Step-3: Here, it has all linear factors in its denominator. So, we proceed as explained in **situation-1** before this example, and suppose

$$\frac{2x + 1}{(x + 1)(x - 1)} = \frac{A}{x + 1} + \frac{B}{x - 1} \quad \ldots\ldots(i)$$

$$\Rightarrow \quad \frac{2x + 1}{(x + 1)(x - 1)} = \frac{A(x - 1) + B(x + 1)}{(x + 1)(x - 1)}$$

$$\Rightarrow \quad 2x + 1 = (A + B)x - A + B$$

(Cancelling the denominators, and grouping like terms on RHS)

Now comparing coefficient of x and constant terms of both sides, we get

$$A + B = 2 \quad \text{and} \quad -A + B = 1$$

$$\Rightarrow \quad A = \frac{1}{2} \text{ and } \quad B = \frac{3}{2}$$

∴ eqn.(i) can be written as:

$$\frac{2x+1}{(x+1)(x-1)} = \frac{1}{2(x+1)} + \frac{3}{2(x-1)}$$

Step-4: So, the integral in our question becomes as follows and can be evaluated easily:

$$\int \frac{x^3+x+1}{x^2-1}\, dx = \int \left[x + \frac{2x+1}{(x+1)(x-1)} \right] dx$$

$$= \int x\, dx + \frac{1}{2}\int \frac{1}{(x+1)}\, dx + \frac{3}{2}\int \frac{1}{(x-1)}\, dx$$

$$\Big[\text{Integrals on RHS can be solved by using following formulae}$$

$$\text{given in art2.1, } \int x^n\, dx = \frac{x^{n+1}}{n+1} + C$$

$$\text{and } \int \frac{1}{x}\, dx = \log|x| + C \Big]$$

$$\therefore \quad \int \frac{x^3+x+1}{x^2-1}\, dx = \frac{x^2}{2} + \frac{1}{2}\log|x+1| + \frac{3}{2}\log|x-1| + C$$

$$= \frac{x^2}{2} + \frac{1}{2}\log|x+1| + \frac{1}{2}\log|x-1|^3 + C$$

$$= \frac{x^2}{2} + \frac{1}{2}\log|(x+1)(x-1)^3| + C$$

<u>Situation-2</u> (If a factor of $h(x)$ is quadratic expression):

If one factor of $h(x)$ is linear, and other is quadratic expression, then we have situation as follows:

$$\frac{r(x)}{h(x)} = \frac{r(x)}{(Linear)(Quadratic)}$$

We proceed as follows:

$$\text{Let } \frac{r(x)}{(Linear)(Quadratic)} = \frac{A}{(Linear)} + \frac{Bx+C}{(Quadratic)}$$

$$\cdots\cdots\cdots\text{(i)}$$

[For each linear factor, we add a fraction having that linear factor as its Denominator and a constant like A, B, C, D, etc., in its Numerator.

For each Quadratic factor, we add a fraction having that Quadratic factor as its Denominator and a Linear expression like B x + C, D x + E, etc., in the Numerator.]

Now proceed in similar manner as explained in ***situation-1*** to find the values of constants, and get partial fractions of $\dfrac{r(x)}{h(x)}$.

<u>Example (Situation-2)</u>

Find the integral $\displaystyle\int \frac{x}{(x^2+1)(x-1)}\, dx$

Solution:

Step-1: Here we observe that the degree of numerator is 1 and that of denominator is 3.

It means degree of numerator $<$ degree of denominator

So, it is already a proper rational function.

Step-2: Now we have to do its partial fractions.

For partial fractions, denominators must be factorised. But it is already in factorised form.

Step-3: Here, it has a linear factor and a quadratic factor in its denominator. So, we proceed as explained in **situation-2** before this example, and suppose

$$\frac{x}{(x^2+1)(x-1)} = \frac{A}{x-1} + \frac{Bx+C}{x^2+1} \quad \ldots\ldots(i)$$

$$\Rightarrow \quad \frac{x}{(x^2+1)(x-1)} = \frac{A(x^2+1)+(Bx+C)(x-1)}{(x^2+1)(x-1)}$$

$$\Rightarrow \quad x = (A+B)x^2 + (-B+C)x + A - C$$

(Cancelling the denominators, and grouping like terms on RHS)

Now comparing coefficient of x^2, x and constant terms on both sides, we get

$$A + B = 0 \quad \text{and} \quad -B+C = 1 \quad \text{and} \quad A - C = 0$$

Solving these equations for A, B & C, we get

$$A = \frac{1}{2}, \qquad B = -\frac{1}{2} \qquad \text{and} \qquad C = \frac{1}{2}$$

$\therefore \quad$ eqn.(i) can be written as:

$$\frac{x}{(x^2+1)(x-1)} = \frac{1}{2(x-1)} + \frac{-\frac{1}{2}x+\frac{1}{2}}{x^2+1}$$

$$\frac{x}{(x^2+1)(x-1)} = \frac{1}{2(x-1)} + \frac{-x+1}{2(x^2+1)}$$

Step-4: So, the integral in our question becomes as follows and can be evaluated easily:

$$\int \frac{x}{(x^2+1)(x-1)}\, dx = \frac{1}{2}\int \frac{1}{(x-1)}\, dx + \frac{1}{2}\int \frac{-x+1}{(x^2+1)}\, dx$$

$$= \frac{1}{2}\int \frac{1}{(x-1)}\, dx + \frac{1}{2}\int \frac{-x}{(x^2+1)}\, dx + \frac{1}{2}\int \frac{1}{(x^2+1)}\, dx$$

In the 2nd integral on RHS, substitute $x^2 + 1 = t$.

$$\text{and} \quad 2x\, dx = dt \quad \text{or} \quad x\, dx = \frac{dt}{2}$$

It becomes:

$$\int \frac{x}{(x^2+1)(x-1)}\,dx = \frac{1}{2}\int \frac{1}{(x-1)}\,dx - \frac{1}{4}\int \frac{1}{t}\,dt + \frac{1}{2}\int \frac{1}{(x^2+1)}\,dx$$

$$\left[\text{On RHS, integrals can be solved using following}\right.$$

$$\text{formulae, given in art2.1, } \int \frac{1}{x}\,dx = log\,|x| + C$$

$$\text{and} \quad \int \frac{1}{1+x^2}\,dx = tan^{-1}x + C\left.\right]$$

$$\Rightarrow \int \frac{x}{(x^2+1)(x-1)}\,dx = \frac{1}{2}log\,|x-1| - \frac{1}{4}log\,|t| + \frac{1}{2}\,tan^{-1}x + C$$

$$= \frac{1}{2}log\,|x-1| - \frac{1}{4}log\,|x^2+1| + \frac{1}{2}\,tan^{-1}x + C$$

Situation-3 (If factor of $h(x)$ has some power on a linear expression):
If any factor of $h(x)$ has an integral power of a linear expression, then we may have situation as follows:

$$\frac{r(x)}{h(x)} = \frac{r(x)}{(Linear_1)(Linear_2)^3}$$

We proceed as follows:
Let

$$\frac{r(x)}{(Linear_1)(Linear_2)^3}$$
$$= \frac{A}{(Linear_1)} + \frac{B}{(Linear_2)} + \frac{C}{(Linear_2)^2} + \frac{D}{(Linear_2)^3}$$
$$\dots\dots\dots\dots \textbf{(i)}$$

[For each linear factor without power, we add a fraction having that linear factor as its Denominator and a constant like A, B, C, D, etc., in the Numerator.

For each linear factor with power n, we add as many fractions as the power. Each fraction has that linear factor with unique power from 1 to n in its Denominator and a constant in its Numerator.]

Now proceed in similar manner as explained in *situation-1* to find the values of constants, and get partial fractions of $\dfrac{r(x)}{h(x)}$.

Example (Situation-3)

Find the integral $\displaystyle\int \frac{3x-2}{(x+1)^2\,(x+3)}\,dx$

Solution:
Step-1: Here we observe that the degree of numerator is 1 and that of denominator is 3.

It means degree of numerator $<$ degree of denominator

So, it is already a proper rational function.

Step-2: Now we have to do its partial fractions.

For partial fractions denominators must be factorised, and it is already in factorised form.

Step-3: Here, it has all linear factors in its denominator with one factor having power 2. So, we suppose

$$\frac{3x-2}{(x+1)^2\,(x+3)} = \frac{A}{(x+1)} + \frac{B}{(x+1)^2} + \frac{C}{(x+3)} \quad \ldots\ldots\text{(i)}$$

$$\Rightarrow \quad \frac{3x-2}{(x+1)^2\,(x+3)} = \frac{A\,(x+1)(x+3) + B\,(x+3) + C\,(x+1)^2}{(x+1)^2\,(x+3)}$$

$$\Rightarrow \quad 3x-2 = (A+C)\,x^2 + (4A+B+2C)\,x + 3A+3B+C$$

(Cancelling the denominators, and grouping like terms on RHS)

Now comparing coefficient of x and constant terms on both sides, we get

$$A+C=0, \qquad 4A+B+2C=3, \qquad 3A+3B+C=-2$$

$$\Rightarrow \quad A=\frac{11}{4}, \qquad B=-\frac{5}{2} \qquad \text{and} \qquad C=-\frac{11}{4}$$

$\therefore$ eqn.(i) can be written as:

$$\frac{3x-2}{(x+1)^2\,(x+3)} = \frac{11}{4(x+1)} - \frac{5}{2(x+1)^2} - \frac{11}{4(x+3)}$$

Step-4: So, the integral in our question becomes as follows and can be evaluated easily:

$$\int \frac{3x-2}{(x+1)^2\,(x+3)}\,dx = \frac{11}{4}\int \frac{1}{(x+1)}\,dx - \frac{5}{2}\int \frac{1}{(x+1)^2}\,dx - \frac{11}{4}\int \frac{1}{(x+3)}\,dx$$

$$= \frac{11}{4}\int \frac{1}{(x+1)}\,dx - \frac{5}{2}\int (x+1)^{-2}\,dx - \frac{11}{4}\int \frac{1}{(x+3)}\,dx$$

$$\left[\text{Integrals on RHS can be solved by using formulae,}\right.$$

$$\text{given in art2.1, } \int x^n\,dx = \frac{x^{n+1}}{n+1} + C$$

$$\left. \text{and } \int \frac{1}{x}\,dx = log\,|x| + C\right]$$

$$\therefore \int \frac{3x-2}{(x+1)^2\,(x+3)}\,dx = \frac{11}{4}\,log\,|x+1| - \frac{5}{2}\cdot\frac{(x+1)^{-1}}{-1} - \frac{11}{4}\,log\,|x+3| + C$$

$$= \frac{11}{4}\,log\,\left|\frac{x+1}{x+3}\right| + \frac{5}{2(x+1)} + C$$

Let us tabulate proper rational functions discussed above and their forms in partial fractions (see next page).

S.N.	Proper rational functions	Partial Fractions
1)	$\dfrac{r(x)}{(Linear_1)(Linear_2)(Linear_3)}$	$\dfrac{A}{(Linear_1)} + \dfrac{B}{(Linear_2)} + \dfrac{C}{(Linear_3)}$
2)	$\dfrac{r(x)}{(Linear)(Quadratic)}$	$\dfrac{A}{(Linear)} + \dfrac{Bx+C}{(Quadratic)}$
3)	$\dfrac{r(x)}{(Linear_1)(Linear_2)^3}$	$\dfrac{A}{(Linear_1)} + \dfrac{B}{(Linear_2)} + \dfrac{C}{(Linear_2)^2} + \dfrac{D}{(Linear_2)^3}$

2.6 Integration by Parts

- This method is used to integrate product of functions.
- Every product of functions cannot be integrated by this method as there may not exist any function whose derivative is the given product.

To integrate the product of the functions $u = f(x)$ and $v = g(x)$, we use the following formula, which is called as **integration by parts**:

- $\int (u.v)dx = u.\int v\,dx - \int \left(\frac{d}{dx}(u)\int v\,dx\right)dx$

- We can remember it by marking one of the functions as 1st function and other as 2nd, and then write it as

$$\int (1st).(2nd)dx$$

$$= (1st).\int (2nd)dx - \int \left(\frac{d}{dx}(1st)\int (2nd)dx\right)dx$$

- To integrate by parts, the proper choice of 1st and 2nd functions matters a lot.
- Usually, to choose 1st and 2nd functions, we write the following letters in sequence:

I L A T E

Here, each letter stands for a kind of function as follows:

I → Inverse trigonometry

L → Logarithm

A → Algebra

T → Trigonometry

E → Exponent

From the given product of functions, the function which comes first in the above sequence is taken as 1st function and other as 2nd function.

<u>Example</u>

Find the integral $\int x \sin 3x \, dx$

Solution

Here the two functions are x and $\sin 3x$ i.e., **Algebra** and **Trigonometry**, respectively. Using the sequence ILATE, we can take algebra i.e., x the first function and trigonometry the second.

Now apply the rule

$$\int (1st).(2nd)dx = (1st).\int(2nd)dx$$
$$-\int\left(\frac{d}{dx}(1st)\int(2nd)dx\right)dx$$

we write   1st as x

      And   2nd as $\sin 3x$

$\therefore \int x \sin 3x \, dx = x . \int \sin 3x \, dx$

$$-\int\left(\frac{d}{dx}(x)\int(\sin 3x)dx\right)dx$$

$$= x.\left(\frac{-\cos 3x}{3}\right) - \int\left(1.\left(\frac{-\cos 3x}{3}\right)\right)dx$$

[*See* 'Integration by Substitution' to solve $\int \sin 3x \, dx$ and $\int \cos 3x \, dx$, and how to use formulae $\int \sin x \, dx = -\cos x + C$ and $\int \cos x \, dx = \sin x + C$]

$$= \frac{-x . \cos 3x}{3} + \frac{1}{3}\int \cos 3x \, dx$$

$$= \frac{-x . \cos 3x}{3} + \frac{\sin 3x}{9} + C$$

- Using substitution method, partial fraction method, or integration by parts method, we can find some important integrals and can use them as formulae. These are as follows:

  ○ $\int \dfrac{1}{x^2 - a^2} \, dx = \dfrac{1}{2a} \log \left|\dfrac{x-a}{x+a}\right| + C$

  ○ $\int \dfrac{1}{a^2 - x^2} \, dx = \dfrac{1}{2a} \log \left|\dfrac{a+x}{a-x}\right| + C$

- $\int \dfrac{1}{a^2 + x^2}\, dx = \dfrac{1}{a} \tan^{-1}\dfrac{x}{a} + C$

- $\int \dfrac{1}{\sqrt{a^2 - x^2}}\, dx = \sin^{-1}\dfrac{x}{a} + C$

- $\int \dfrac{1}{\sqrt{a^2 + x^2}}\, dx = \log\left|x + \sqrt{x^2 + a^2}\right| + C$

- $\int \dfrac{1}{\sqrt{x^2 - a^2}}\, dx = \log\left|x + \sqrt{x^2 - a^2}\right| + C$

- $\int \sqrt{a^2 - x^2}\, dx = \dfrac{x}{2}\sqrt{a^2 - x^2} + \dfrac{a^2}{2}\sin^{-1}\dfrac{x}{a} + C$

- $\int \sqrt{a^2 + x^2}\, dx = \dfrac{x}{2}\sqrt{a^2 + x^2}$
$\qquad\qquad + \dfrac{a^2}{2}\log\left|x + \sqrt{a^2 + x^2}\right| + C$

- $\int \sqrt{x^2 - a^2}\, dx = \dfrac{x}{2}\sqrt{x^2 - a^2}$
$\qquad\qquad - \dfrac{a^2}{2}\log\left|x + \sqrt{x^2 - a^2}\right| + C$

Let us list all important formulae to be used in the integrals found by using methods discussed above (see next page).

2.7 Formulae of Indefinite Integrals

Here we list all important formulae to be used in the integrals found by using methods discussed above:

1) $\int x^n \, dx = \dfrac{x^{n+1}}{n+1} + C$

$$\rightarrow \quad \int dx = x + C$$

2) $\displaystyle\int \dfrac{1}{x} \, dx = \log |x| + C$

3) $\int e^x dx = e^x + C$

4) $\int a^x dx = \dfrac{a^x}{\log a} + C$

5) $\int \sin x \, dx = -\cos x + C$

6) $\int \cos x \, dx = \sin x + C$

7) $\int \tan x \, dx = \log |\sec x| + C$
$$= -\log |\cos x| + C$$

8) $\int \cot x \, dx = \log |\sin x| + C$
$$= -\log |\operatorname{cosec} x| + C$$

9) $\int \sec x \, dx = \log |\sec x + \tan x| + C$
$$= \log \left| \tan \left(\dfrac{\pi}{4} + \dfrac{x}{2} \right) \right| + C$$

10) $\int \operatorname{cosec} x \, dx = \log |\operatorname{cosec} x - \cot x| + C$
$$= \log \left| \tan \dfrac{x}{2} \right| + C$$

11) $\int \sec^2 x \, dx = \tan x + C$

12) $\int \operatorname{cosec}^2 x \, dx = -\cot x + C$

13) $\int \sec x . \tan x \, dx = \sec x + C$

14) $\int \operatorname{cosec} x . \cot x \, dx = -\operatorname{cosec} x + C$

15) $\displaystyle\int \dfrac{1}{\sqrt{1 - x^2}} \, dx = \sin^{-1} x + C$
$$= -\cos^{-1} x + C$$

---

16) $\int \dfrac{1}{1+x^2}\, dx = tan^{-1}x + C$

$$= -cot^{-1}x + C$$

17) $\int \dfrac{1}{x\sqrt{x^2-1}}\, dx = sec^{-1}x + C$

$$= -cosec^{-1}x + C$$

18) $\int \dfrac{1}{x^2-a^2}\, dx = \dfrac{1}{2a} log\left|\dfrac{x-a}{x+a}\right| + C$

19) $\int \dfrac{1}{a^2-x^2}\, dx = \dfrac{1}{2a} log\left|\dfrac{a+x}{a-x}\right| + C$

20) $\int \dfrac{1}{a^2+x^2}\, dx = \dfrac{1}{a} tan^{-1}\dfrac{x}{a} + C$

21) $\int \dfrac{1}{\sqrt{a^2-x^2}}\, dx = sin^{-1}\dfrac{x}{a} + C$

22) $\int \dfrac{1}{\sqrt{a^2+x^2}}\, dx = log\left|x+\sqrt{x^2+a^2}\right| + C$

23) $\int \dfrac{1}{\sqrt{x^2-a^2}}\, dx = log\left|x+\sqrt{x^2-a^2}\right| + C$

24) $\int \sqrt{a^2-x^2}\, dx = \dfrac{x}{2}\sqrt{a^2-x^2} + \dfrac{a^2}{2} sin^{-1}\dfrac{x}{a} + C$

25) $\int \sqrt{a^2+x^2}\, dx = \dfrac{x}{2}\sqrt{a^2+x^2}$

$$+ \dfrac{a^2}{2} log\left|x+\sqrt{a^2+x^2}\right| + C$$

26) $\int \sqrt{x^2-a^2}\, dx = \dfrac{x}{2}\sqrt{x^2-a^2}$

$$- \dfrac{a^2}{2} log\left|x+\sqrt{x^2-a^2}\right| + C$$

2.8 Forms and Methods to Solve Integrals

Here we are tabulating some forms of integral, which can be integrated by specific methods (*some of these have been explained in earlier articles, and examples of other forms are given following this table*):

S.N.	FORMS	STEPS TO PROCEED
1)	**(a)** $\int [f(x)]^n \, f'(x) \, dx$ OR $\int [g(f(x))]^n \, f'(x) \, dx$ **(b)** $\displaystyle\int \frac{f'(x)}{[f(x)]^n} \, dx$ OR $\displaystyle\int \frac{f'(x)}{[g(f(x))]^n} \, dx$	(i) Put $f(x) = t$, *and* differentiate it to get $f'(x)\, dx = dt$ (ii) It will change the integral in terms of t. (iii) Now integral will get converted into easily solvable form, or any of the formulae given in article 2.7 will be applicable.
2)	**(a)** $\displaystyle\int \frac{1}{quadratic} \, dx$ **(b)** $\displaystyle\int \frac{1}{\sqrt{quadratic}} \, dx$ **(c)** $\int \sqrt{quadratic} \; dx$	(i) Make coeff. of x^2 unity. (ii) Convert quadratic into a perfect square. (iii) Now one of the formulae nos. (18) to (26) of article 2.7 will be applicable.
3)	**(a)** $\displaystyle\int \frac{linear}{quadratic} \, dx$ **(b)** $\displaystyle\int \frac{linear}{\sqrt{quadratic}} \, dx$ **(c)** $\int linear \sqrt{quadratic} \; dx$	(i) Let $linear = A\dfrac{d}{dx}(quadratic) + B$ (ii) Find the values of **A** and **B** by comparing coefficients and constants of both sides. (iii) Replace *linear* expression in the integral with the expression obtained in step(i), and substitute values of **A** & **B** in it. (iv) Separate the 2 terms in the numerator to obtain 2 integrals I_1 and I_2. (v) Put *quadratic* $= t$ in the integral I_1, and differentiate it to change dx into dt. (vi) I_2 will be in one of the forms in S.N.2. Solve it by the steps mentioned in S.N.2.

S.N.	FORMS	STEPS TO PROCEED
4)	**(a)** $\int linear_1 \sqrt{linear_2}\, dx$ **(b)** $\int \dfrac{linear_1}{\sqrt{linear_2}}\, dx$ **(c)** $\int \dfrac{1}{linear_1\sqrt{linear_2}}\, dx$	(i) Put $\sqrt{linear_2} = t$ or $linear_2 = t^2$, and differentiate it to change dx into dt. (ii) Find the value of x in terms of t from the above substituition. (iii) Put this value of x in $linear_1$, and convert the integral in terms of t. (iv) Simplify the integral. Now formula no.1 of article 2.7 will be applicable in forms (a) & (b) and formula no.18 to 20 in form (c).
5)	**(a)** $\int quadratic\sqrt{linear}\, dx$ **(b)** $\int \dfrac{quadratic}{\sqrt{linear}}\, dx$ **(c)** $\int \dfrac{1}{quadratic\,\sqrt{linear}}\, dx$	(i) Put $\sqrt{linear} = t$ or $linear = t^2$, and differentiate it to change dx into dt. (ii) Find the value of x in terms of t from it. (iii) Put this value of x in $quadratic$, and convert the integral in terms of t. (iv) Simplify the integral. Now formula no.1 of Article 2.7 will be applicable in form (a) & (b). (v) Solve form (c) by method in S.N.10 or by partial fractions.
6)	$\int \dfrac{1}{(linear)\sqrt{quadratic}}\, dx$	(i) Put $linear = \dfrac{1}{t}$, and differentiate it to change dx into dt. (ii) Find the value of x in terms of t from it. (iii) Put this value of x in $quadratic$. (iv) On simplifying, it will be converted into any of the other forms discussed above.

S.N.	FORMS	STEPS TO PROCEED
7)	$$\int \frac{x}{pure\ quad_1\ \sqrt{pure\ quad_2}}\ dx$$ $\rightarrow$ **Pure quadratic expression is in the form $ax^2 + c$.** **i.e., middle term of quadratic is absent.**	(i) Put $\sqrt{pure\ quad_2} = t$ or $pure\ quad_2 = t^2$, and differentiate it to change dx into dt. (ii) Find the value of x^2 in terms of t^2 from it. (iii) Put this value of x^2 in $quad_1$, and convert the integral in terms of t. (iv) On simplifying, the formula no.18 to 20 given in article2.7 will be applicable.
8)	$$\int \frac{1}{pure\ quad_1\ \sqrt{pure\ quad_2}}\ dx$$	(i) Put $x = \frac{1}{t}$, and differentiate it to change dx into dt. (ii) Put this value of x in both $quadratic$ (iii) Simplify it, and then integrate by the method in S.N.7
9)	(a) $$\int \frac{x^2 + a}{x^4 \pm k\,x^2 + a^2}\ dx$$ (b) $$\int \frac{x^2 - a}{x^4 \pm k\,x^2 + a^2}\ dx$$	(i) Divide numerator and denominator both by x^2 (ii) Convert quadratic in denominator into a perfect square by adding and subtracting $2a$ which will come as $(x \pm a/x)^2$ (iii) Put $x - \frac{a}{x} = t$ in form (a) & $x + \frac{a}{x} = t$ in from (b). Also differentiate it to change dx into dt. (iv) Now one of the formulae no.18,19 or 20 given in article2.7 will be applicable.
10)	$$\int \frac{1}{x^4 \pm k\,x^2 + a^2}\ dx$$	(i) Multiply numerator and denominator by $2a$ (ii) Add and subtract x^2 in the numerator. (iii) Separate the numerator as $(x^2 + a)$ and $(x^2 - a)$ (iv) Solve 2 terms by method in S.N.9

S.N.	FORMS	STEPS TO PROCEED
11)	$$\int \frac{x^2}{x^4 \pm kx^2 + a^2}\, dx$$	(i) Multiply numerator and denominator by 2 (ii) Add and subtract $2a$ in the numerator. (iii) Separate the numerator as (x^2+a) and (x^2-a) (iv) Solve 2 terms by the method in S.N.9
12)	$$\int \frac{1}{a\sin x + b\cos x + c}\, dx$$ OR $$\int \frac{1}{a + b\sin x}\, dx$$ OR $$\int \frac{1}{a + b\cos x}\, dx$$	(i) Put $\sin x = \dfrac{2\tan\frac{x}{2}}{1+\tan^2\frac{x}{2}}$ and $\cos x = \dfrac{1-\tan^2\frac{x}{2}}{1+\tan^2\frac{x}{2}}$, and then simplify. (ii) Put $\tan\frac{x}{2} = t$, and differentiate it to change dx into dt, and then convert the integral in terms of t. (iii) Now the integral will be in the form of earlier discussed form or can be easily integrated using the formulae.
13)	$$\int \frac{dx}{a + b\sin^2 x + c\cos^2 x + d\sin x.\cos x}$$ $\rightarrow$ **Any one or two of a, b, c, and d can be 0**	(i) Divide Numerator and Denominator both by $\cos^2 x$. It will change numerator to $\sec^2 x$ and denominator can be changed into quadratic of $\tan x$. (ii) Put $\tan x = t$ and by differentiating it, change dx into dt. (iii) It will convert the integral in terms of t, which will be in the form given in S.N.2(a), and then can be solved accordingly.
14)	**(a)** $\int \sin mx.\cos nx\, dx$ **(b)** $\int \cos mx.\cos nx\, dx$ **(c)** $\int \sin mx.\sin nx\, dx$	Use following trigonometry formulae, respectively, in **(a)**, **(b)**, and **(c)**: $2\sin A\cos B = \sin(A+B)+\sin(A-B)$ $2\cos A\cos B = \cos(A+B)+\cos(A-B)$ $2\sin A\sin B = \cos(A-B)-\cos(A+B)$ Now they can be integrated easily by the formulae given in art2.7

---

*Asterisk (*) marked article (if any) is **not** in CBSE 2025-26 syllabus.*

S.N.	FORMS	STEPS TO PROCEED
15)	**(a)** $\displaystyle\int \frac{1}{sin(x+a).sin(x+b)}\,dx$ **(b)** $\displaystyle\int \frac{1}{cos(x+a).cos(x+b)}\,dx$ **(c)** $\displaystyle\int \frac{1}{sin(x+a).cos(x+b)}\,dx$	(i) Multiply Numerator and Denominator both by $sin(b-a)$ in (a) & (b). (ii) Move $sin(b-a)$ of the denominator out of the integral. (iii) Add & subtract x in the argument of sine in numerator , i.e., write it as $sin(b - a + x - x)$. (iv) Rearrange this argument as $(x + b) - (x + a)$ i.e., write the argument in two terms, which are the arguments in the denominator, to get $sin\,[(x + b) - (x + a)]$. (v) Apply the formula, $sin(A–B)$ $= sinA\,cosB - cosA\,sinB.$ (vi) Now separate the terms in numerator, and then these terms can be easily integrated. For form (c), multiply Numerator and Denominator both by $cos(b-a)$, and do all the above steps (ii) to (vi) with the difference that now we have cos in the numerator, and we have to apply the formula, $cos(A–B) = cosA\,cosB–sinA\,sinB$ in step(v).
16)	$\displaystyle\int [\,f(x) + f\,'(x)\,].\,e^x\,dx$	In this form, we have sum of a function, $f(x)$ and its derivative, $f'(x)$ multiplied by e^x. (i) Separate it into 2 integrals as: $$\int f(x)e^x dx + \int f\,'(x)e^x dx$$ (ii) Solve 1st integral using 'By Parts' method as explained in article 2.6. For this take $f(x)$ as 1st function and e^x as 2nd. (iii) On solving 1st integral by Parts, the 2nd integral will cancel out.

Examples of forms in S.N. 1, in the above table, have been discussed earlier in the article 'Integration by Substitution' in this chapter.
Let's take examples of other forms given in this table.

<u>**Examples of forms in S.N. 2**</u>

<u>Example 2(a)</u>

Find the integral $\displaystyle\int \frac{1}{3\,x^2 + 13\,x - 10}\,dx$

Solution:

Let the given integral is **I** i.e.,

$$I = \int \frac{1}{3\,x^2 + 13\,x - 10}\,dx$$

It is of the form S.N.2(a). So, we proceed as follows:

Step-1: To make coefficient of x^2 unity, take out 3 from the denominator, and write it as:

$$\int \frac{1}{3\left(x^2 + \frac{13}{3}x - \frac{10}{3} \right)}\,dx$$

Step-2: To make perfect square from quadratic, we observe that coefficient of x is $\frac{13}{3}$. Multiply it by $\frac{1}{2}$ to obtain $\frac{13}{6}$, and then add & subtract its square $\left(\frac{13}{6}\right)^2$ in the quadratic.
After doing it, the integral becomes:

$$I = \int \frac{1}{3\left(x^2 + \frac{13}{3}x + \left(\frac{13}{6}\right)^2 - \left(\frac{13}{6}\right)^2 - \frac{10}{3} \right)}\,dx$$

$$\Rightarrow \quad I = \int \frac{1}{3\left[\left(x + \frac{13}{6}\right)^2 - \left(\frac{13}{6}\right)^2 - \frac{10}{3} \right]}\,dx$$

$$\Rightarrow \quad I = \frac{1}{3}\int \frac{1}{\left[\left(x + \frac{13}{6}\right)^2 - \frac{289}{36} \right]}\,dx$$

$$\Rightarrow \quad I = \frac{1}{3}\int \frac{1}{\left[\left(x + \frac{13}{6}\right)^2 - \left(\frac{17}{6}\right)^2 \right]}\,dx$$

Step-3: Now applying $\displaystyle\int \frac{1}{x^2-a^2}\, dx = \frac{1}{2a}\, log\left|\frac{x-a}{x+a}\right| + C$

$$\text{(Formula no.18 given above of article 2.7)}$$

We get

$$I = \frac{1}{3}\times\frac{1}{2\times\frac{17}{6}}\, log\left|\frac{x+\frac{13}{6}-\frac{17}{6}}{x+\frac{13}{6}+\frac{17}{6}}\right| + C_1$$

$$\Rightarrow \quad I = \frac{1}{17}\times log\left|\frac{6x-4}{6x+30}\right| + C_1$$

$$\Rightarrow \quad I = \frac{1}{17}\times log\left|\frac{2(3x-2)}{6(x+5)}\right| + C_1$$

$$\Rightarrow \quad I = \frac{1}{17}\times log\left|\frac{1}{3}\times\frac{(3x-2)}{(x+5)}\right| + C_1$$

$$\Rightarrow \quad I = \frac{1}{17}\times log\left|\frac{(3x-2)}{(x+5)}\right| + \frac{1}{17}\times log\frac{1}{3} + C_1$$

$$\Rightarrow \quad I = \frac{1}{17}\, log\left|\frac{3x-2}{x+5}\right| + C \qquad [\frac{1}{17}\, log\frac{1}{3} + C_1 = C\text{(new constant)}$$

Example 2(b)

Find the integral $\displaystyle\int \frac{1}{\sqrt{7-6x-x^2}}\, dx$

Solution:

Let the given integral is **I** i.e.,

$$I = \int \frac{1}{\sqrt{7-6x-x^2}}\, dx$$

It is of the form S.N.2(b). So, we proceed as follows:

Step-1: To make coefficient of x^2 unity, take out -ve sign from the quadratic expression , and write it as:

$$I = \int \frac{1}{\sqrt{-(x^2+6x-7)}}\, dx$$

Step-2: To make perfect square from quadratic, we observe that coefficient of x is 6. Multiply it by $\frac{1}{2}$ to obtain 3 , and then add & subtract its square, 3^2 in the quadratic.
After doing it, the integral becomes:

$$I = \int \frac{1}{\sqrt{-(x^2+6x+3^2-3^2-7)}}\, dx$$

$$\Rightarrow \quad I = \int \frac{1}{\sqrt{-[(x+3)^2-16]}}\, dx$$

$\Rightarrow \quad I = \int \dfrac{1}{\sqrt{16 - (x+3)^2}}\, dx$

$\Rightarrow \quad I = \int \dfrac{1}{\sqrt{4^2 - (x+3)^2}}\, dx$

Step-3: Now applying $\int \dfrac{1}{\sqrt{a^2 - x^2}}\, dx = sin^{-1}\dfrac{x}{a} + C$

(Formula no.21 given above of article 2.7)

We get

$I = sin^{-1}\left(\dfrac{x+3}{4}\right) + C$

Example 2(c)

Find the integral $\int \sqrt{x^2 + 4x + 6}\, dx$

Solution:

Let the given integral is **I** i.e.,

$I = \int \sqrt{x^2 + 4x + 6}\, dx$

It is of the form S.N.2(c). So, we proceed as follows:

Step-1: Here coefficient of x^2 is already unity, so we have to convert it into perfect square now.

Step-2: To make perfect square from quadratic, we observe that coefficient of x is 4. Multiply it by $\dfrac{1}{2}$ to obtain 2 , and then add & subtract its square, 2^2 in the quadratic.

After doing it, the integral becomes:

$I = \int \sqrt{x^2 + 4x + 2^2 - 2^2 + 6}\, dx$

$\Rightarrow \quad I = \int \sqrt{(x+2)^2 + 2}\, dx$

$\Rightarrow \quad I = \int \sqrt{\left(\sqrt{2}\right)^2 + (x+2)^2}\, dx$

Step-3: Now applying

$\int \sqrt{a^2 + x^2}\, dx = \dfrac{x}{2}\sqrt{a^2 + x^2} + \dfrac{a^2}{2} log\left|x + \sqrt{a^2 + x^2}\right| + C$

(Formula no.25 given above of article 2.7)

We get

$I = \dfrac{x+2}{2}\sqrt{\left(\sqrt{2}\right)^2 + (x+2)^2} + \dfrac{(\sqrt{2})^2}{2} log\left|x + 2 + \sqrt{\left(\sqrt{2}\right)^2 + (x+2)^2}\right| + C$

$\Rightarrow \quad I = \dfrac{x+2}{2}\sqrt{x^2 + 4x + 6} + log\left|x + 2 + \sqrt{x^2 + 4x + 6}\right| + C$

$$\Rightarrow \quad I = \frac{1}{17} \times log\left|\frac{2(3x-2)}{6(x+5)}\right| + C_1$$

$$\Rightarrow \quad I = \frac{1}{17} \times log\left|\frac{1}{3} \times \frac{(3x-2)}{(x+5)}\right| + C_1$$

$$\Rightarrow \quad I = \frac{1}{17} \times log\left|\frac{(3x-2)}{(x+5)}\right| + \frac{1}{17} \times log\frac{1}{3} + C_1$$

$$\Rightarrow \quad I = \frac{1}{17} log\left|\frac{3x-2}{x+5}\right| + C\;[\frac{1}{17}log\frac{1}{3}+C_1 = C \ldots\text{(new constant)}$$

<u>**Examples of forms in S.N. 3**</u>

<u>Example 3(a)</u>

Find the integral $\displaystyle\int \frac{5x-2}{1+2x+3x^2}\,dx$

Solution:

Let the given integral is **I** i.e.,

$$I = \int \frac{5x-2}{1+2x+3x^2}\,dx$$

It is of the form S.N.3(a). So, we proceed as follows:

Step-1: Let $5x - 2 = A\dfrac{d}{dx}(1+2x+3x^2) + B$

$$\Rightarrow \quad 5x - 2 = A(2+6x) + B \qquad \ldots\ldots\text{(i)}$$

$$\Rightarrow \quad 5x - 2 = 6Ax + (2A+B)$$

Step-2: Comparing coefficients of x and constants of both sides:

$6A = 5 \qquad$ and $\qquad 2A + B = -2$

Solving these equations, we get $A = \dfrac{5}{6}$ and $B = -\dfrac{11}{3}$

Step-3: Putting the value of **A** and **B** in eqn.(i), we get

$$5x - 2 = \frac{5}{6}(2+6x) - \frac{11}{3}$$

So, the given integral becomes:

$$I = \int \frac{\frac{5}{6}(2+6x) - \frac{11}{3}}{1+2x+3x^2}\,dx$$

Step-4: Now separate the 2 terms in the numerator to obtain 2 integrals:

$$I = \int \frac{\frac{5}{6}(2+6x)}{1+2x+3x^2}\,dx - \int \frac{\frac{11}{3}}{1+2x+3x^2}\,dx$$

$\Rightarrow \qquad I = \dfrac{5}{6}\displaystyle\int \dfrac{2+6x}{1+2x+3x^2}\,dx \;-\; \dfrac{11}{3}\displaystyle\int \dfrac{1}{1+2x+3x^2}\,dx$

Let $\quad I_1 = \dfrac{5}{6}\displaystyle\int \dfrac{2+6x}{1+2x+3x^2}\,dx$

And $\quad I_2 = -\dfrac{11}{3}\displaystyle\int \dfrac{1}{1+2x+3x^2}\,dx$

so that $\quad I = I_1 + I_2$

Step-5: To solve I_1, put $\;1+2x+3x^2 = t$

$$\Rightarrow \qquad (2+6x)\,dx = dt$$

$\therefore \qquad I_1 = \dfrac{5}{6}\displaystyle\int \dfrac{1}{t}\,dt$

$\qquad\qquad = \dfrac{5}{6}\,\log|t| + C_1 \qquad$ [using the formula no.2 of article 2.7]

$\Rightarrow \qquad I_1 = \dfrac{5}{6}\,\log|\,1+2x+3x^2\,| + C_1$

Step-6: To solve I_2, we have to make perfect square in the quadratic expression as explained in examples of S.N.2. So, we proceed as follows:

$I_2 = -\dfrac{11}{3}\displaystyle\int \dfrac{1}{1+2x+3x^2}\,dx$

$\Rightarrow \qquad I_2 = -\dfrac{11}{3}\displaystyle\int \dfrac{1}{3\left(\frac{1}{3}+\frac{2}{3}x+x^2\right)}\,dx \qquad$ [taking out 3, the coeff. of x^2]

$\Rightarrow \qquad I_2 = -\dfrac{11}{3}\displaystyle\int \dfrac{1}{3\left[x^2+\frac{2}{3}x+\left(\frac{1}{3}\right)^2-\left(\frac{1}{3}\right)^2+\frac{1}{3}\right]}\,dx$

$\left[\text{coeff of } x \text{ is } \dfrac{2}{3},\text{ and its half is } \dfrac{1}{3}.\text{ Adding \& subtracting } \left(\dfrac{1}{3}\right)^2\right]$

$\Rightarrow \qquad I_2 = -\dfrac{11}{3}\displaystyle\int \dfrac{1}{3\left[\left(x+\frac{1}{3}\right)^2-\left(\frac{1}{3}\right)^2+\frac{1}{3}\right]}\,dx$

$\Rightarrow \qquad I_2 = -\dfrac{11}{9}\displaystyle\int \dfrac{1}{\left(x+\frac{1}{3}\right)^2+\left(\frac{\sqrt{2}}{3}\right)^2}\,dx$

$\Rightarrow \qquad I_2 = -\dfrac{11}{9}\times\dfrac{1}{\sqrt{2}/3}\,\tan^{-1}\dfrac{x+\frac{1}{3}}{\sqrt{2}/3} + C_2$

$\Rightarrow \qquad I_2 = -\dfrac{11}{3\sqrt{2}}\,\tan^{-1}\dfrac{3x+1}{\sqrt{2}} + C_2 \qquad$ [using formula no.20 of art 2.7]

Step-7: Now $\;I = I_1 + I_2 \qquad$ (from step-4)

---

*Asterisk (*) marked article (if any) is **not** in CBSE 2025-26 syllabus.*

$$\therefore \quad I = \frac{5}{6} \log\left| 1 + 2x + 3x^2 \right| + C_1 - \frac{11}{3\sqrt{2}} \tan^{-1} \frac{3x+1}{\sqrt{2}} + C_2$$

[adding results of step-5 and step-6]

$$\Rightarrow \quad I = \frac{5}{6} \log\left| 1 + 2x + 3x^2 \right| - \frac{11}{3\sqrt{2}} \tan^{-1} \frac{3x+1}{\sqrt{2}} + C$$

[where, $C_1 + C_2 = C$]

Example 3(b)

Find the integral $\displaystyle\int \frac{x+2}{\sqrt{x^2 - 2x + 3}}\, dx$

Solution:

Let the given integral is **I** i.e.,

$$I = \int \frac{x+2}{\sqrt{x^2 - 2x + 3}}\, dx$$

It is of the form S.N.3(b). So, we proceed as follows:

Step-1: Let $\quad x + 2 = A\dfrac{d}{dx}\left(x^2 - 2x + 3\right) + B$

$$\Rightarrow \quad x + 2 = A(2x - 2) + B \qquad \dots\dots\dots(i)$$

$$\Rightarrow \quad x + 2 = 2Ax + (-2A + B)$$

Step-2: Comparing coefficients of x and constants of both sides:

$$2A = 1 \qquad \text{and} \qquad -2A + B = 2$$

Solving these equations, we get $\mathbf{A} = \dfrac{1}{2}$ and $\mathbf{B} = 3$

Step-3: Putting the value of **A** and **B** in eqn.(i), we get

$$x + 2 = \frac{1}{2}(2x - 2) + 3$$

So, the given integral becomes:

$$I = \int \frac{\frac{1}{2}(2x-2) + 3}{\sqrt{x^2 - 2x + 3}}\, dx$$

Step-4: Now separate the 2 terms in the numerator to obtain 2 integrals:

$$I = \int \frac{\frac{1}{2}(2x-2)}{\sqrt{x^2 - 2x + 3}}\, dx + \int \frac{3}{\sqrt{x^2 - 2x + 3}}\, dx$$

$$\Rightarrow \quad I = \frac{1}{2}\int \frac{2x-2}{\sqrt{x^2 - 2x + 3}}\, dx + 3\int \frac{1}{\sqrt{x^2 - 2x + 3}}\, dx$$

Let $\quad I_1 = \dfrac{1}{2}\displaystyle\int \frac{2x-2}{\sqrt{x^2 - 2x + 3}}\, dx$

And $\quad I_2 = 3\displaystyle\int \frac{1}{\sqrt{x^2 - 2x + 3}}\, dx$

---

so that $\ I = I_1 + I_2$

Step-5: To solve I_1 , put $\ x^2 - 2x + 3 = t$

$$\Rightarrow \qquad (2x - 2)\,dx = dt$$

$$\therefore \quad I_1 = \frac{1}{2}\int \frac{1}{\sqrt{t}}\ dt = \frac{1}{2}\int t^{-\frac{1}{2}}\ dt$$

$$= \frac{1}{2} \times \frac{t^{1/2}}{1/2} + C_1 \qquad \text{[using formula no.1 of art 2.7]}$$

$$\Rightarrow \quad I_1 = \sqrt{x^2 - 2x + 3} + C_1$$

Step-6: To solve I_2 , we have to make perfect square in the quadratic expression as explained in examples of S.N.2. So, we proceed as follows:

$$I_2 = 3\int \frac{1}{\sqrt{x^2 - 2x + 3}}\ dx$$

$$\Rightarrow \quad I_2 = 3\int \frac{1}{\sqrt{x^2 - 2x + 1^2 - 1^2 + 3}}\ dx$$

$$[\text{ coeff. of } x \text{ is 2, and its half is 1 . Adding \& subtracting } 1^2\,]$$

$$\Rightarrow \quad I_2 = 3\int \frac{1}{\sqrt{(x-1)^2 - 1^2 + 3}}\ dx$$

$$\Rightarrow \quad I_2 = 3\int \frac{1}{\sqrt{(x-1)^2 + \left(\sqrt{2}\right)^2}}\ dx$$

$$\Rightarrow \quad I_2 = \log \left| x - 1 + \sqrt{(x-1)^2 + \left(\sqrt{2}\right)^2} \right| + C_2$$

$$[\text{using the formula no.22 of article 2.7}]$$

$$\Rightarrow \quad I_2 = \log \left| x - 1 + \sqrt{x^2 - 2x + 3} \right| + C_2$$

Step-7: Now $\ I = I_1 + I_2 \qquad$ (from step-4)

$$\therefore\ I = \sqrt{x^2 - 2x + 3} + C_1 + \log\left| x - 1 + \sqrt{x^2 - 2x + 3}\right| + C_2$$

$$[\text{adding results of step-5 and step-6}]$$

$$\Rightarrow I = \sqrt{x^2 - 2x + 3} + \log\left| x - 1 + \sqrt{x^2 - 2x + 3}\right| + C \quad [C_1 + C_2 = C]$$

Example 3(c)

Find the integral $\ \int (x + 3)\sqrt{3 - 4x - x^2}\ dx$

Solution:

Let the given integral is **I** i.e.,

$$I = \int (x + 3)\sqrt{3 - 4x - x^2}\ dx$$

It is of the form S.N.3(c). So, we proceed as follows:

Step-1: Let $\ x + 3 = A\dfrac{d}{dx}\left(3 - 4x - x^2\right) + B$

$\Rightarrow \qquad x + 3 = A(-4 - 2x) + B \qquad \dots\dots\dots(i)$

$\Rightarrow \qquad x + 3 = -2Ax + (-4A + B)$

Step-2: Comparing coefficients of x and constants of both sides:

$$-2A = 1 \qquad \text{and} \qquad -4A + B = 3$$

Solving these equations, we get $A = -\dfrac{1}{2}$ and $B = 1$

Step-3: Putting the value of A and B in eqn.(i), we get

$$x + 3 = -\frac{1}{2}(-4 - 2x) + 1$$

So, the given integral becomes:

$$I = \int \left[-\frac{1}{2}(-4 - 2x) + 1 \right] \sqrt{3 - 4x - x^2}\ dx$$

Step-4: Now separate the 2 terms in the numerator to obtain 2 integrals:

$$I = \int \left[-\frac{1}{2}(-4 - 2x) \right] \sqrt{3 - 4x - x^2}\ dx + \int \sqrt{3 - 4x - x^2}\ dx$$

$$\Rightarrow \quad I = -\frac{1}{2}\int (-4 - 2x)\sqrt{3 - 4x - x^2}\ dx + \int \sqrt{3 - 4x - x^2}\ dx$$

Let $\quad I_1 = -\dfrac{1}{2}\int (-4 - 2x)\sqrt{3 - 4x - x^2}\ dx$

And $\quad I_2 = \int \sqrt{3 - 4x - x^2}\ dx$

so that $\quad I = I_1 + I_2$

Step-5: To solve I_1, put $3 - 4x - x^2 = t$

$$\Rightarrow \qquad (-4 - 2x)\ dx = dt$$

$$\therefore \qquad I_1 = -\frac{1}{2}\int \sqrt{t}\ dt = -\frac{1}{2}\int t^{\frac{1}{2}}\ dt$$

$$= -\frac{1}{2} \times \frac{t^{3/2}}{3/2} + C_1 \qquad \text{[using formula no.1 of art 2.7]}$$

$$\Rightarrow \quad I_1 = -\frac{1}{3}(3 - 4x - x^2)^{3/2} + C_1$$

Step-6: To solve I_2, we have to make perfect square in the quadratic expression as explained in examples of S.N.2. So, we proceed as follows:

$$I_2 = \int \sqrt{3 - 4x - x^2}\ dx$$

$$\Rightarrow \quad I_2 = \int \sqrt{-(x^2 + 4x - 3)}\ dx$$

$$\Rightarrow \quad I_2 = \int \sqrt{-(x^2 + 4x + 2^2 - 2^2 - 3)}\ dx$$

[Coeff of x is 4, and its half is 2 . Adding & subtracting 2^2]

$$\Rightarrow \quad I_2 = \int \sqrt{-[(x + 2)^2 - 7]}\ dx$$

$$\Rightarrow \quad I_2 = \int \sqrt{\left(\sqrt{7}\right)^2 - (x+2)^2} \; dx$$

$$\Rightarrow \quad I_2 = \frac{x+2}{2} \sqrt{\left(\sqrt{7}\right)^2 - (x+2)^2} + \frac{\left(\sqrt{7}\right)^2}{2} \sin^{-1}\left(\frac{x+2}{\sqrt{7}}\right) + C_2$$

[Using the formula no.24 of article 2.7]

$$\Rightarrow \quad I_2 = \frac{x+2}{2} \sqrt{3 - 4x - x^2} + \frac{7}{2} \sin^{-1}\left(\frac{x+2}{\sqrt{7}}\right) + C_2$$

$$\Rightarrow \quad I_2 = \log\left|x - 1 + \sqrt{x^2 - 2x + 3}\right| + C_2$$

Step-7: Now $I = I_1 + I_2$ (from step-4)

$$\therefore I = -\frac{1}{3}(3 - 4x - x^2)^{3/2} + C_1 + \frac{x+2}{2}\sqrt{3 - 4x - x^2} + \frac{7}{2}\sin^{-1}\left(\frac{x+2}{\sqrt{7}}\right) + C_2$$

[adding results of step-5 and step-6]

$$\Rightarrow I = -\frac{1}{3}(3 - 4x - x^2)^{3/2} + \frac{x+2}{2}\sqrt{3 - 4x - x^2} + \frac{7}{2}\sin^{-1}\left(\frac{x+2}{\sqrt{7}}\right) + C$$

[where, $C_1 + C_2 = C$]

<u>**Examples of forms in S.N. 4**</u>

<u>Example 4(a)</u>

Find the integral $\int (x + 3)\sqrt{x + 2}\; dx$

Solution:

Let the given integral be **I** i.e.,

$$I = \int (x + 3)\sqrt{x + 2}\; dx$$

It is of the form S.N.4(a). So, we proceed as follows:

Step-1): Let $\sqrt{x + 2} = t \quad \Rightarrow x + 2 = t^2$
$$\Rightarrow \quad dx = 2t\,dt$$

Step-2: $x + 2 = t^2 \quad \Rightarrow x = t^2 - 2$

Step-3: The given integral becomes:
$$I = \int (t^2 - 2 + 3)\, t \cdot 2t\,dt$$
$$\Rightarrow \quad I = 2\int (t^4 + t^2)\, dt$$

Step-4: $I = 2\int (t^4 + t^2)\, dt$

$$\Rightarrow \quad I = \frac{2t^5}{5} + \frac{2t^3}{3} + C \qquad \text{[Using formula no.1 of art2.7]}$$

$$\Rightarrow \quad I = \frac{2\left(\sqrt{x+2}\right)^5}{5} + \frac{2\left(\sqrt{x+2}\right)^3}{3} + C$$

$$\Rightarrow \quad I = \frac{2}{5}(x + 2)^{5/2} + \frac{2}{3}(x + 2)^{3/2} + C$$

<u>**Example 4(b)**</u>

Find the integral $\displaystyle\int \frac{x}{\sqrt{x+4}}\, dx$

Solution:

Let the given integral be **I** i.e.,

$$I = \int \frac{x}{\sqrt{x+4}}\, dx$$

It is of the form S.N.4(b). So, we proceed as follows:

Step-1: Let $\sqrt{x+4} = t \qquad \Rightarrow x+4 = t^2$
$$\Rightarrow \quad dx = 2\,t\,dt$$

Step-2: $x+4 = t^2 \quad \Rightarrow x = t^2 - 4$

Step-3: The given integral becomes:

$$I = \int \frac{t^2-4}{t}\, 2t\,dt$$

$$\Rightarrow \quad I = 2\int (t^2 - 4)\, dt$$

Step-4: $I = 2\int (t^2 - 4)\, dt$

$$\Rightarrow \quad I = \frac{2t^3}{3} - 8\,t + C \qquad\qquad \text{[Using formula no.1 of article 2.7]}$$

$$\Rightarrow \quad I = \frac{2\left(\sqrt{x+4}\right)^3}{3} - 8\,\sqrt{x+4} + C$$

$$\Rightarrow \quad I = \frac{2}{3}(x+4)^{3/2} - 8\,(x+4)^{1/2} + C$$

<u>**Example 4(c)**</u>

Find the integral $\displaystyle\int \frac{1}{(x-3)\sqrt{x+4}}\, dx$

Solution:

Let the given integral be **I** i.e.,

$$I = \int \frac{1}{(x-3)\sqrt{x+4}}\, dx$$

It is of the form S.N.4(c). So, we proceed as follows:

Step-1: Let $\sqrt{x+4} = t \qquad \Rightarrow x+4 = t^2$
$$\Rightarrow \quad dx = 2\,t\,dt$$

Step-2: $x+4 = t^2 \quad \Rightarrow x = t^2 - 4$

Step-3: The given integral becomes:

$$I = \int \frac{1}{(t^2-7)t}\, 2t\,dt$$

---

*Asterisk (*) marked article (if any) is **not** in CBSE 2025-26 syllabus.*

$$\Rightarrow \quad I = 2 \int \frac{1}{t^2 - 7} \, dt$$

Step-6: $I = 2 \int \frac{1}{t^2 - (\sqrt{7})^2} \, dt$

$$\Rightarrow \quad I = 2 \times \frac{1}{2\sqrt{7}} \log \left| \frac{t - \sqrt{7}}{t + \sqrt{7}} \right| \qquad \text{[Using formula no.18 of art2.7]}$$

$$\Rightarrow \quad I = \frac{1}{\sqrt{7}} \log \left| \frac{\sqrt{x+4} - \sqrt{7}}{\sqrt{x+4} + \sqrt{7}} \right| + C$$

<u>**Examples of forms in S.N. 5**</u>

<u>**Example 5(a)**</u>

Find the integral $\int (x^2 + 2x + 3) \sqrt{x+1} \, dx$

Solution:

Let the given integral be **I** i.e.,
$$I = \int (x^2 + 2x + 3) \sqrt{x+1} \, dx$$
It is of the form S.N.5(a). So, we proceed as follows:

Step-1: Let $\sqrt{x+1} = t \quad \Rightarrow x + 1 = t^2$
$$\Rightarrow \quad dx = 2t \, dt$$

Step-2: $x + 1 = t^2 \quad \Rightarrow x = t^2 - 1$

Step-3: The given integral becomes:
$$I = \int [(t^2 - 1)^2 + 2(t^2 - 1) + 3] \, t \cdot 2t \, dt$$

$$\Rightarrow \quad I = 2 \int t^2 (t^4 - 2t^2 + 1 + 2t^2 - 2 + 3) \, dt$$

Step-4: $I = 2 \int t^2 (t^4 + 2) \, dt$

$$\Rightarrow \quad I = 2 \int (t^6 + 2t^2) \, dt$$

$$\Rightarrow \quad I = \frac{2t^7}{7} + \frac{4t^3}{3} + C \qquad \text{[Using formula no.1 of article 2.7]}$$

$$\Rightarrow \quad I = \frac{2(\sqrt{x+1})^7}{7} + \frac{4(\sqrt{x+1})^3}{3} + C$$

$$\Rightarrow \quad I = \frac{2}{7}(x+1)^{7/2} + \frac{4}{3}(x+1)^{3/2} + C$$

<u>**Example 5(b)**</u>

Find the integral $\int \frac{x^2 + 2x + 3}{\sqrt{x+1}} \, dx$

Solution:

Let the given integral be **I** i.e.,
$$I = \int \frac{x^2 + 2x + 3}{\sqrt{x+1}} \, dx$$
It is of the form S.N.5(b). So, we proceed as follows:

Step-1: Let $\sqrt{x+1} = t \qquad \Rightarrow x+1 = t^2$
$$\Rightarrow \quad dx = 2\,t\,dt$$

Step-2: $x+1 = t^2 \quad \Rightarrow x = t^2 - 1$

Step-3: The given integral becomes:

$$I = \int \frac{(t^2-1)^2 + 2(t^2-1) + 3}{t}\, 2t\,dt$$

$$\Rightarrow \quad I = 2\int (t^4 - 2t^2 + 1 + 2t^2 - 2 + 3)\, dt$$

Step-4: $I = 2\int (t^4 + 2)\, dt$

$$\Rightarrow \quad I = \frac{2t^5}{5} + 4t + C \qquad\qquad \text{[Using formula no.1 of article 2.7]}$$

$$\Rightarrow \quad I = \frac{2\left(\sqrt{x+1}\right)^5}{5} + 4\sqrt{x+1} + C$$

$$\Rightarrow \quad I = \frac{2}{5}(x+1)^{5/2} + 4(x+1)^{1/2} + C$$

Example 5(c)

Find the integral $\displaystyle\int \frac{1}{(x^2 + 2x + 3)\sqrt{x+1}}\, dx$

Solution:

Let the given integral be **I** i.e.,

$$I = \int \frac{1}{(x^2 + 2x + 5)\sqrt{x+1}}\, dx$$

It is of the form S.N.5(c). So, we proceed as follows:

Step-1: Let $\sqrt{x+1} = t \qquad \Rightarrow x+1 = t^2$
$$\Rightarrow \quad dx = 2\,t\,dt$$

Step-2: $x+1 = t^2 \quad \Rightarrow x = t^2 - 1$

Step-3: The given integral becomes:

$$I = \int \frac{1}{[(t^2-1)^2 + 2(t^2-1) + 5]\,t} \cdot 2t\,dt$$

$$\Rightarrow \quad I = 2\int \frac{1}{t^4 - 2t^2 + 1 + 2t^2 - 2 + 5}\, dt$$

$$\Rightarrow \quad I = 2\int \frac{1}{t^4 + 4}\, dt$$

Now it is in the form given in S.N.10. So, we proceed accordingly.

Step-4: Multiply Numerator and Denominator both by 4

$$I = \frac{2}{4}\int \frac{4}{t^4 + (2)^2}\, dt$$

Step-5: Write 4 as $2 + 2$, and Add and subtract t^2 in the numerator

$$I = \frac{1}{2}\int \frac{2 + 2 + t^2 - t^2}{t^4 + (2)^2} \, dt$$

$$\Rightarrow \quad I = \frac{1}{2}\int \frac{t^2 + 2 - (t^2 - 2)}{t^4 + (2)^2} \, dt$$

Step-6: Now separate the two terms in the numerator to get two integrals

$$I = \frac{1}{2}\int \frac{t^2 + 2}{t^4 + (2)^2} \, dt \;-\; \frac{1}{2}\int \frac{t^2 - 2}{t^4 + (2)^2} \, dt$$

Step-7: Dividing Numerator and Denominator both by t^2 in both the integral, we get

$$I = \frac{1}{2}\int \frac{1 + \frac{2}{t^2}}{t^2 + \left(\frac{2}{t}\right)^2} \, dt \;-\; \frac{1}{2}\int \frac{1 - \frac{2}{t^2}}{t^2 + \left(\frac{2}{t}\right)^2} \, dt$$

Step-8: Adding and subtracting $2\times\sqrt{2}$ in the denominator, we get

$$\Rightarrow \quad I = \frac{1}{2}\int \frac{1 + \frac{2}{t^2}}{t^2 + \left(\frac{2}{t}\right)^2 + 2 - 2} \, dt \;-\; \frac{1}{2}\int \frac{1 - \frac{2}{t^2}}{t^2 + \left(\frac{2}{t}\right)^2 + 2 - 2} \, dt$$

$$\Rightarrow \quad I = \frac{1}{2}\int \frac{1 + \frac{2}{t^2}}{\left(t - \frac{2}{t}\right)^2 + 2} \, dt \;-\; \frac{1}{2}\int \frac{1 - \frac{2}{t^2}}{\left(t + \frac{2}{t}\right)^2 - 2} \, dt$$

$$\left[\text{ since } t^2 + \left(\frac{2}{t}\right)^2 - 2 = \left(t - \frac{2}{t}\right)^2 \text{ and } t^2 + \left(\frac{\sqrt{2}}{t}\right)^2 + 2 = \left(t + \frac{2}{t}\right)^2 \right]$$

Step-9: Put $t - \frac{2}{t} = u$ in the first integral

$$\Rightarrow \left(1 + \frac{2}{t^2}\right) dt = du$$

and $t + \frac{2}{t} = v$ in the second integral

$$\Rightarrow \left(1 - \frac{2}{t^2}\right) dt = dv$$

Step-10: The given integral becomes:

$$\Rightarrow \quad I = \frac{1}{2}\int \frac{1}{u^2 + (\sqrt{2})^2} \, du \;-\; \frac{1}{2}\int \frac{1}{v^2 - (\sqrt{2})^2} \, dv$$

$$\Rightarrow \quad I = \frac{1}{2}\times\frac{1}{\sqrt{2}} \tan^{-1}\left(\frac{u}{\sqrt{2}}\right) + C_1 \;-\; \frac{1}{2}\times\frac{1}{2\sqrt{2}}\log\left|\frac{v - \sqrt{2}}{v + \sqrt{2}}\right| + C_2$$

$$\left[\text{ applying formula no.20 of article2.7 in first integral and formula no.18 in the second.} \right]$$

$$\Rightarrow \quad I = \frac{1}{2\sqrt{2}} \tan^{-1}\left(\frac{t - \frac{2}{t}}{\sqrt{2}}\right) - \frac{1}{4\sqrt{2}}\log\left|\frac{t + \frac{2}{t} - \sqrt{2}}{t + \frac{2}{t} + \sqrt{2}}\right| + C$$

$$\left[\text{converting } u \text{ and } v \text{ back in terms of } t \text{ from step(iv)} \right]$$

$$\Rightarrow \quad I = \frac{1}{2\sqrt{2}} \, tan^{-1} \left(\frac{t^2 - 2}{\sqrt{2}\,t} \right) - \frac{1}{4\sqrt{2}} \log \left| \frac{t^2 + 2 - \sqrt{2}\,t}{t^2 + 2 + \sqrt{2}\,t} \right| + C$$

$$\Rightarrow \quad I = \frac{1}{2\sqrt{2}} \, tan^{-1} \left(\frac{x+1-2}{\sqrt{2}\,\sqrt{x+1}} \right) - \frac{1}{4\sqrt{2}} \log \left| \frac{x+1+ 2 - \sqrt{2}\,\sqrt{x+1}}{x+1+ 2 + \sqrt{2}\,\sqrt{x+1}} \right| + C$$

[converting t back in terms of x from step(i)]

$$\Rightarrow \quad I = \frac{1}{2\sqrt{2}} \, tan^{-1} \left(\frac{x-1}{\sqrt{2x+2}} \right) - \frac{1}{4\sqrt{2}} \log \left| \frac{x + 3 - \sqrt{2x+2}}{x + 3 + \sqrt{2x+2}} \right| + C$$

<u>Examples of form in S.N. 6</u>

<u>Example 6</u>

Find the integral $\displaystyle \int \frac{1}{x\,\sqrt{ax - x^2}} \, dx$

Solution:

Let the given integral be **I** i.e.,

$$I = \int \frac{1}{x\,\sqrt{ax - x^2}} \, dx$$

It is of the form S.N.6. So, we proceed as follows:

Step-1&2: Let $x = \dfrac{1}{t}$

$$\Rightarrow \quad dx = \frac{-1}{t^2} \, dt$$

Step-3: The given integral becomes:

$$I = \int \frac{1}{\frac{1}{t}\sqrt{a\left(\frac{1}{t}\right) - \left(\frac{1}{t}\right)^2}} \cdot \frac{-1}{t^2} \, dt$$

Step-4: $I = \displaystyle \int \frac{1}{\frac{1}{t}\sqrt{\frac{at-1}{t^2}}} \cdot \frac{-1}{t^2} \, dt$

$$\Rightarrow \quad I = - \int \frac{1}{\sqrt{at-1}} \, dt$$

$$\Rightarrow \quad I = - \int (at - 1)^{-\frac{1}{2}} \, dt$$

$$\Rightarrow \quad I = - \frac{(at-1)^{-\frac{1}{2}+1}}{\left(-\frac{1}{2}+1\right)a} + C$$

[using formula no.1 of art2.7 and
see 'Integration by Substitution' to know how to use it.]

$$\Rightarrow \quad I = -\frac{2}{a}(at - 1)^{\frac{1}{2}} + C$$

$$\Rightarrow \quad I = -\frac{2}{a}\left(a\frac{1}{x} - 1\right)^{\frac{1}{2}} + C$$

$$\Rightarrow \quad I = -\frac{2}{a}\sqrt{\frac{a-x}{x}} + C$$

Example 7

Find the integral $\displaystyle\int \frac{x}{(x^2+3)\sqrt{x^2-1}}\, dx$

Solution:

Let the given integral be **I** i.e.,

$$I = \int \frac{x}{(x^2+3)\sqrt{x^2-1}}\, dx$$

It is of the form S.N.7. So, we proceed as follows:

Step-1: Let $\sqrt{x^2-1} = t \Rightarrow x^2-1 = t^2$
$$\Rightarrow \quad 2x\,dx = 2t\,dt \Rightarrow \quad x\,dx = t\,dt$$

Step-2: $x^2-1 = t^2 \Rightarrow x^2 = t^2+1$

Step-3: The given integral becomes:

$$I = \int \frac{t}{(t^2+1+3)\,t}\,.\,dt$$

$$\Rightarrow \quad I = \int \frac{1}{(t^2+4)}\,.\,dt$$

Step-4: $I = \dfrac{1}{2}\,tan^{-1}\left(\dfrac{t}{2}\right)+C$ [applying formula no. 20 of art2.7]

$$\Rightarrow \quad I = \frac{1}{2}\,tan^{-1}\left(\frac{\sqrt{x^2-1}}{2}\right) + C$$

Example 8

Find the integral $\displaystyle\int \frac{1}{(x^2+3)\sqrt{x^2-1}}\, dx$

Solution:

Let the given integral be **I** i.e.,

$$I = \int \frac{1}{(x^2+3)\sqrt{x^2-1}}\, dx$$

It is of the form S.N.8. So, we proceed as follows:

Step-1:   Let $\quad x = \dfrac{1}{t}$

$$\Rightarrow \quad dx = \frac{-1}{t^2}\,dt$$

Step-2: The given integral becomes:

$$I = \int \frac{1}{\left[\left(\frac{1}{t}\right)^2 + 3\right]\sqrt{\left(\frac{1}{t}\right)^2 - 1}}\,.\,\frac{-1}{t^2}\,dt$$

---

*Asterisk (*) marked article (if any) is **not** in CBSE 2025-26 syllabus.*

Step-3: The given integral becomes:

$$ I = \int \frac{1}{\left[\frac{1+3\,t^2}{t^2}\right]\sqrt{\frac{1-t^2}{t^2}}} \cdot \frac{-1}{t^2}\, dt $$

$$ \Rightarrow \quad I = \int \frac{1}{\left[\frac{1+3\,t^2}{t^2}\right]\sqrt{\frac{1-t^2}{t^2}}} \cdot \frac{-1}{t^2}\, dt $$

$$ \Rightarrow \quad I = -\int \frac{t}{[1+3\,t^2]\sqrt{1-t^2}}\, dt $$

Now it is in the form given in S.N.7. So, it can be solved by putting $\sqrt{1-t^2} = z$, and proceeding in the same way as explained in the example 7 above. It is left as an exercise to do it yourself.

<u>**Examples of forms in S.N. 9**</u>

<u>**Example 9(a)**</u>

Find the integral $\displaystyle\int \frac{x^2+1}{x^4+x^2+1}\, dx$

Solution:

Let the given integral be **I** i.e.,

$$ I = \int \frac{x^2+1}{x^4+x^2+1}\, dx $$

It is of the form S.N.9(a). So, we proceed as follows:

Step-1: Dividing Numerator and Denominator both by x^2, we get

$$ I = \int \frac{1+\frac{1}{x^2}}{x^2+1+\frac{1}{x^2}}\, dx $$

$$ \Rightarrow \quad I = \int \frac{1+\frac{1}{x^2}}{x^2+\frac{1}{x^2}+1}\, dx $$

Step-2: Adding and subtracting $2\times 1 = 2$ in the denominator, we get

$$ \Rightarrow \quad I = \int \frac{1+\frac{1}{x^2}}{x^2+\frac{1}{x^2}-2+2+1}\, dx $$

$$ \Rightarrow \quad I = \int \frac{1+\frac{1}{x^2}}{\left(x-\frac{1}{x}\right)^2+3}\, dx \qquad \left[\text{since } x^2+\frac{1}{x^2}-2 = \left(x-\frac{1}{x}\right)^2\right] $$

Step-3: Put $x - \dfrac{1}{x} = t$

$$\Rightarrow \left(1 + \dfrac{1}{x^2}\right) dx = dt$$

Step-4: The given integral becomes:

$$\Rightarrow \quad I = \int \dfrac{1}{t^2 + 3} \, dx$$

$$\Rightarrow \quad I = \int \dfrac{1}{t^2 + \left(\sqrt{3}\right)^2} \, dx$$

$$\Rightarrow \quad I = \dfrac{1}{\sqrt{3}} \, tan^{-1}\left(\dfrac{t}{\sqrt{3}}\right) + C \qquad \text{[applying formula no. 20 of art2.7]}$$

$$\Rightarrow \quad I = \dfrac{1}{\sqrt{3}} \, tan^{-1}\left(\dfrac{x - \frac{1}{x}}{\sqrt{3}}\right) + C$$

$$\Rightarrow \quad I = \dfrac{1}{\sqrt{3}} \, tan^{-1}\left(\dfrac{x^2 - 1}{\sqrt{3}\, x}\right) + C$$

Example 9(b)

Find the integral $\displaystyle\int \dfrac{x^2 - 1}{x^4 + x^2 + 1} \, dx$

Solution:

Let the given integral be **I** i.e.,

$$I = \int \dfrac{x^2 - 1}{x^4 + x^2 + 1} \, dx$$

It is of the form S.N.9(b). So, we proceed as follows:

Step-1: Dividing Numerator and Denominator both by x^2, we get

$$I = \int \dfrac{1 - \frac{1}{x^2}}{x^2 + 1 + \frac{1}{x^2}} \, dx$$

$$\Rightarrow \quad I = \int \dfrac{1 + \frac{1}{x^2}}{x^2 + \frac{1}{x^2} + 1} \, dx$$

Step-2: Adding and subtracting $2 \times 1 = 2$ in the denominator, we get

$$\Rightarrow \quad I = \int \dfrac{1 - \frac{1}{x^2}}{x^2 + \frac{1}{x^2} + 2 - 2 + 1} \, dx$$

$$\Rightarrow \quad I = \int \dfrac{1 - \frac{1}{x^2}}{\left(x + \frac{1}{x}\right)^2 - 1} \, dx \qquad \left[\text{since } x^2 + \frac{1}{x^2} + 2 = \left(x + \frac{1}{x}\right)^2\right]$$

Step-3: Put $\;x + \dfrac{1}{x} = t$

$\Rightarrow \quad \left(1 - \dfrac{1}{x^2}\right) dx = dt$

Step-4: The given integral becomes:

$\Rightarrow \quad I = \displaystyle\int \dfrac{1}{t^2 - 1}\, dx$

$\Rightarrow \quad I = \displaystyle\int \dfrac{1}{t^2 - 1^2}\, dx$

$\Rightarrow \quad I = \dfrac{1}{2} \, log \left|\dfrac{t - 1}{t + 1}\right| + C \qquad$ [applying formula no. 18 of article 2.7]

$\Rightarrow \quad I = \dfrac{1}{2} \, log \left|\dfrac{x + \frac{1}{x} - 1}{x + \frac{1}{x} + 1}\right| + C$

$\Rightarrow \quad I = \dfrac{1}{2} \, log \left|\dfrac{x^2 - x + 1}{x^2 - x + 1}\right| + C$

Examples of forms in S.N. 10

Example 10

Find the integral $\displaystyle\int \dfrac{1}{x^4 + x^2 + 1}\, dx$

Solution:

Let the given integral be **I** i.e.,

$$I = \int \dfrac{1}{x^4 + x^2 + 1}\, dx$$

It is of the form S.N.10. So, we proceed as follows:

Step-1: Multiply Numerator and Denominator both by 2. We get

$$I = \dfrac{1}{2}\int \dfrac{2}{x^4 + x^2 + 1}\, dx$$

Step-2: Write 2 as 1+1 , and Add and subtract x^2 in the numerator

$$I = \dfrac{1}{2}\int \dfrac{1 + 1 + x^2 - x^2}{x^4 + x^2 + 1}\, dx$$

$$\Rightarrow \quad I = \dfrac{1}{2}\int \dfrac{x^2 + 1 - \left(x^2 - 1\right)}{x^4 + x^2 + 1}\, dx$$

Step-3: Now separate the two terms in the numerator to get two integrals

$$I = \dfrac{1}{2}\int \dfrac{x^2 + 1}{x^4 + x^2 + 1}\, dx - \dfrac{1}{2}\int \dfrac{x^2 - 1}{x^4 + x^2 + 1}\, dx$$

Step-4: Now these two integrals are in the forms in S.N. 9(a) & (b) respectively. So, they can be solved as explained in the examples 9(a) & 9 (b).

Here, it is left as an exercise to do it by yourself.

<u>**Examples of forms in S.N. 11**</u>

Example 11

Find the integral $\displaystyle \int \frac{x^2}{x^4 + x^2 + 1}\, dx$

Solution:

Let the given integral be **I** i.e.,

$$I = \int \frac{x^2}{x^4 + x^2 + 1}\, dx$$

It is of the form S.N.11. So, we proceed as follows:

Step-1: Multiply Numerator and Denominator both by 2. We get

$$I = \frac{1}{2} \int \frac{2x^2}{x^4 + x^2 + 1}\, dx$$

Step-2: Write $2x^2$ as $x^2 + x^2$, and add and subtract 1 in the numerator.

$$I = \frac{1}{2} \int \frac{x^2 + x^2 + 1 - 1}{x^4 + x^2 + 1}\, dx$$

$$\Rightarrow \quad I = \frac{1}{2} \int \frac{x^2 + 1 + \left(x^2 - 1\right)}{x^4 + x^2 + 1}\, dx$$

Step-3: Now separate the two terms in the numerator to get two integrals

$$I = \frac{1}{2} \int \frac{x^2 + 1}{x^4 + x^2 + 1}\, dx \; + \; \frac{1}{2} \int \frac{x^2 - 1}{x^4 + x^2 + 1}\, dx$$

Step-4: Now these two integrals are in the forms in S.N. 9(a) & (b) respectively. So, they can be solved as explained in the examples 9(a) & 9 (b).

Here, further procedure is left for readers as an exercise.

<u>**Examples of forms in S.N. 12**</u>

Example 12

Find the integral $\displaystyle \int \frac{1}{\sin x + \cos x + 1}\, dx$

Solution:

Let the given integral be **I** i.e.,

$$I = \int \frac{1}{\sin x + \cos x + 2}\, dx$$

It is of the form S.N.12. So, we proceed as follows:

Step-1: Put $\quad \sin x = \dfrac{2 \tan \frac{x}{2}}{1 + \tan^2 \frac{x}{2}}$ and $\cos x = \dfrac{1 - \tan^2 \frac{x}{2}}{1 + \tan^2 \frac{x}{2}}$

$$I = \int \frac{1}{\dfrac{2\,tan\,\frac{x}{2}}{1+tan^2\frac{x}{2}} + \dfrac{1-tan^2\frac{x}{2}}{1+tan^2\frac{x}{2}} + 2}\ dx$$

$$\Rightarrow \quad I = \int \frac{1+tan^2\frac{x}{2}}{2\,tan^2\frac{x}{2} + 1 - tan^2\frac{x}{2} + 2 + 2\,tan^2\frac{x}{2}}\ dx$$

$$\Rightarrow \quad I = \int \frac{sec^2\frac{x}{2}}{tan^2\frac{x}{2} + 2\,tan\frac{x}{2} + 3}\ dx$$

Step-2: Put $\quad tan\,\dfrac{x}{2} = t$

$$\Rightarrow \quad sec^2\,\frac{x}{2} \times \frac{1}{2}\ dx = dt$$

$$\Rightarrow \quad sec^2\,\frac{x}{2}\ dx = 2\,dt$$

Step-3: The integral becomes:

$$I = \int \frac{1}{t^2 + 2t + 3}\ dt$$

Now it is the form given in S.N. 2(a), and hence can be solved as explained in example 2(a).

Here, further procedure is left for readers as an exercise.

<u>**Examples of forms in S.N. 13**</u>

<u>**Example 13**</u>

Find the integral $\displaystyle\int \frac{1}{sin^2 x + cos^2 x + sin x \cos x}\ dx$

Solution:

Let the given integral be **I** i.e.,

$$I = \int \frac{1}{sin^2 x + cos^2 x + sin x \cos x}\ dx$$

It is of the form S.N.13. So, we proceed as follows:

Step-1: Divide Numerator and Denominator both by $cos^2 x$

$$I = \int \frac{\dfrac{1}{cos^2 x}}{\dfrac{sin^2 x}{cos^2 x} + \dfrac{cos^2 x}{os^2 x} + \dfrac{sin x \cos x}{cos^2 x}}\ dx$$

$$\Rightarrow \quad I = \int \frac{sec^2 x}{tan^2 x + 1 + tan\, x}\, dx$$

$$\Rightarrow \quad I = \int \frac{sec^2 x}{tan^2 x + an\, x + 1}\, dx$$

Step-2: Put $\quad tan\, x = t$

$$\Rightarrow \quad sec^2 x\, dx = dt$$

Step-3: $\quad I = \int \frac{1}{t^2 + t + 1}\, dx$

Now it is the form given in S.N. 2(a), and hence can be solved as explained in example 2(a).

Here, further procedure is left for readers as an exercise.

<u>Examples of forms in S.N. 14</u>

<u>Example 14</u>

Find the integral $\int \sin 3x.\cos 4x\, dx$

Solution:

Let the given integral be **I** i.e.,

$$I = \int \sin 3x.\cos 4x\, dx$$

It is of the form S.N.14(a). So, we proceed as follows:

Step-1: Using *2sinA cosB = sin(A+B)+sin(A − B),* the integral becomes:

$$I = \tfrac{1}{2}\int [\sin(3x + 4x) + \sin(3x - 4x)]\, dx$$

$$\Rightarrow \quad I = \tfrac{1}{2}\int [\sin 7x + \sin(-x)]\, dx$$

$$\Rightarrow \quad I = \tfrac{1}{2}\int [\sin 7x - \sin x]\, dx$$

$$\Rightarrow \quad I = \tfrac{1}{2}\left[\frac{-\cos 7x}{7} - (-\cos x)\right] + C$$

[using formula no.5 of art2.7, and see 'Integration by Substitution' to know how to use it.]

$$\Rightarrow \quad I = \frac{-\cos 7x}{14} + \frac{\cos x}{2} + C$$

Similarly, other forms of S.N.14 can be solved easily.

<u>Examples of forms in S.N. 15</u>

<u>Example 15(a)</u>

Find the integral $\int \dfrac{1}{\sin(x+a).\sin(x+b)}\, dx$

Solution:

Let the given integral be **I** i.e.,

$$I = \int \frac{1}{\sin(x+a).\sin(x+b)}\, dx$$

It is of the form S.N.15(a). So, we proceed as follows:

Step-1: Multiplying Numerator and Denominator both by $sin(b-a)$, the integral becomes:

$$I = \int \frac{1}{\sin(x+a).\sin(x+b)} \cdot \frac{sin(b-a)}{sin(b-a)}\, dx$$

Step-2: Move $sin(b-a)$ of the denominator out of the integral

$$\Rightarrow \quad I = \frac{1}{sin(b-a)} \int \frac{sin(b-a)}{\sin(x+a).\sin(x+b)}\, dx$$

Step-3: Add & subtract x in the argument of sine in numerator

$$\Rightarrow \quad I = \frac{1}{sin(b-a)} \int \frac{sin(b-a+x-x)}{\sin(x+a).\sin(x+b)}\, dx$$

Step-4: Rearrange this argument as $(x + b) - (x + a)$

$$\Rightarrow \quad I = \frac{1}{sin(b-a)} \int \frac{sin[(x+b)-(x+a)]}{\sin(x+a).\sin(x+b)}\, dx$$

Step-5: Apply formula, $\sin(A-B) = \sin A\cos B - \cos A\sin B$ in numerator

$$\Rightarrow \quad I = \frac{1}{sin(b-a)} \int \frac{sin(x+b).cos(x+a)-cos(x+b).sin(x+a)}{\sin(x+a).\sin(x+b)}\, dx$$

Step-6: Separate the terms in numerator into two terms, and integrate

$$\Rightarrow \quad I = \frac{1}{sin(b-a)} \int \left[\frac{\cancel{sin(x+b)}.\, cos(x+a)}{\sin(x+a).\, \cancel{sin(x+b)}} - \frac{cos(x+b).\cancel{sin(x+a)}}{\cancel{sin(x+a)}.\sin(x+b)} \right] dx$$

$$\Rightarrow \quad I = \frac{1}{sin(b-a)} \int \left[\cot(x+a) - \cot(x+b)\right] dx$$

$$\Rightarrow \quad I = \frac{1}{sin(b-a)}\, log|sin(x+a)| - log|sin(x+b)| + C$$

$$\text{[using formula no.8 in art2.7.]}$$

$$\Rightarrow \quad I = \frac{1}{sin(b-a)}\, log\left|\frac{sin(x+a)}{sin(x+b)}\right| + C$$

Similarly, other forms of S.N.15 can be solved easily.

Examples of forms in S.N. 16

Example 16

Find the integral $\int [\cos x - \sin x].e^x\, dx$

Solution:

Let the given integral be **I** i.e.,

$$I = \int [\cos x - \sin x].e^x\, dx$$

Here, we observe that derivative of $\cos x$ is $-\sin x$.

$\therefore$ it is of the form $\int [f(x) + f'(x)].e^x\, dx$ given in S.N.16,

where, $f(x) = \cos x$ and $f'(x) = -\sin x$

and hence we proceed as follows:

Step-1: Separating into 2 integrals

$$I = \int \cos x\, .e^x\, dx + \int [-\sin x].e^x\, dx$$

Step-2: Solving 1st integral by parts and keeping the 2nd without solving

$$I = \cos x \int e^x\, dx - \int \left(\frac{d}{dx}(\cos x) \int e^x\, dx\right) dx + \int [-\sin x].e^x\, dx$$

$$\Rightarrow \quad = \cos x.e^x - \int [-\sin x].e^x\, dx + \int [-\sin x].e^x\, dx$$

$$\Rightarrow \quad = \cos x.e^x + C$$

3 Definite Integrals

3.1 *Definite Integral as Limit of Sum

- Definite integral $\int_a^b f(x)dx$ can be calculated by the method of limit of sum using the following formula:

$$\int_a^b f(x)dx$$

$$= \lim_{h\to 0} h\, [f(a)+f(a+h)+f(a+2h)+f(a+3h)+\ldots+f(a+(n-1)h)]$$

where, $h = \dfrac{b-a}{n}$ and $h \to 0$, $n \to \infty$

- To simplify the limit, some formulae of limits may be required. These formulae are given in the chapter - 'Limits' of the book (part-1) for class XII.

- Mostly, one or more of the following formulae are also required :

    - Sum of First n natural numbers:

$$\sum_{k=1}^{n} k = 1+2+3+\ldots+n = \frac{n(n+1)}{2}$$

- Sum of Squares of First n natural numbers:

$$\sum_{k=1}^{n} k^2 = 1^2 + 2^2 + 3^2 + \ldots + n^2 = \frac{n(n+1)(2n+1)}{6}$$

- Sum of Cubes of First n natural numbers:

$$\sum_{k=1}^{n} k^3 = 1^3 + 2^3 + 3^3 + \ldots + n^3 = \left[\frac{n(n+1)}{2}\right]^2$$

Explanation

If f is a continuous function in closed interval $[a, b]$ and it has only positive values for every $x \in [a, b]$, then the area under the curve $y = f(x)$ bounded by x – axis can be found by the method of limit of sum, which is definite integral $\int_a^b f(x)dx$.

[**Note**: Here we are assuming that the values of function f are all positives for every $x \in [a, b]$, but the definite integral as limit of sum holds for every other function also.]

In the figure shown below, consider 2 thin rectangles MDBA and CLBA with width $x_2 - x_1 = h \Rightarrow x_2 = x_1 + h$ having points C and D on the curve $y = f(x)$.

Area of CLBA $= f(x_1).h$

Area of MDBA $= f(x_2).h = f(x_1 + h).h$

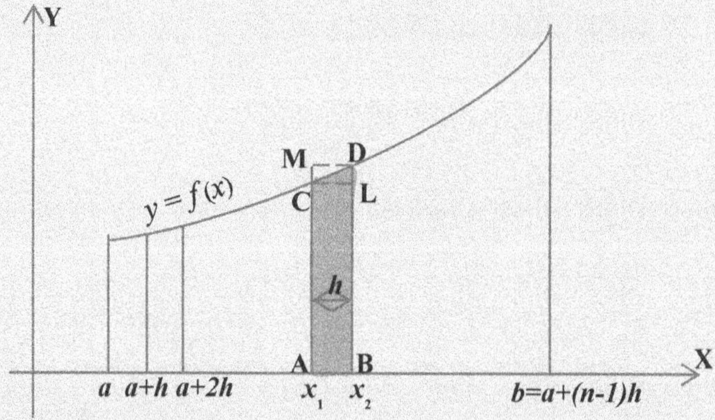

Magnitude of Area of shaded region CDBA will lie between these two areas.

If the width of rectangle is so thin that $h \to 0$, then
Area of MDBA will become equal to area of CLBA
i.e., $f(x_1 + h).h = f(x_1).h$

Since, area of shaded region CDBA is sandwiched between Area of CLBA and Area of MDBA

$\therefore$ Area of shaded region CDBA = Area of CLBA = Area of MDBA
$$= f(x_1).h$$

Now if divide the length of x- axis from a to b in n intervals of width h each

i.e., $\qquad nh = b - a \quad or \quad h = \dfrac{b-a}{n}$,

then area under the curve will be the sum of areas of rectangles at
$$x_1 = a, \ (a+h), (a+2h), (a+3h), \ldots, [a+(n-1)h]$$
$$[\text{ here, } b = a + (n-1)h\,]$$

$\therefore$ Area under the curve
$$= f(a).h + [\,f(a+h). \, h\,] + [\,f(a+2h). \, h\,] + [\,f(a+3h).h\,] + \ldots$$
$$+ [\,f(a+(n-1)h)\,].h$$
$$= h\,[\,f(a) + f(a+h) + f(a+2h) + f(a+3h) + \ldots + f(a+(n-1)h)]$$

Now, if $h \to 0$, then $n \to \infty$, and under these limits, the above sum becomes $\int_a^b f(x)dx$

$\therefore \ \int_a^b f(x)dx = \lim\limits_{h \to 0} h\,[\,f(a) + f(a+h) + f(a+2h) + f(a+3h) + \ldots$
$$+ f(a+(n-1)h)]$$

$\qquad$ where, $h = \dfrac{b-a}{n}$ and $h \to 0$, $n \to \infty$

Example

Find the integral $\int_1^4 (x^2 - x)\, dx$ as limit of sum.

Solution:

$\quad$ Here, $a = 1$, $b = 4$, $f(x) = x^2 - x$,

$\quad$ Let $\quad h = \dfrac{b-a}{n}$ $\qquad$ where $h \to 0$ and $n \to \infty$

$\Rightarrow \qquad h = \dfrac{4-1}{n} = \dfrac{3}{n} \quad \Rightarrow \qquad nh = 3$

Now $f(x) = x^2 - x$

$\Rightarrow \quad f(a) = f(1) = 1^2 - 1 = 0$

$\quad f(a+h) = f(1+h) = (1+h)^2 - (1+h) = h^2 + h$

$\quad f(a+2h) = f(1+2h) = (1+2h)^2 - (1+2h) = 2^2 h^2 + 2$

$\quad f(a+3h) = f(1+3h) = (1+3h)^2 - (1+3h) = 3^2 h^2 + 3h$

$\cdot$

$\cdot$

$\cdot$

$\quad f[a+(n-1)h] = f(1+(n-1)h) = [1+(n-1)h]^2 - [1+(n-1)h]$
$$= (n-1)^2 h^2 + (n-1)h$$

$\quad$ Definite integral as limit of sum is

$$\int_a^b f(x)dx = \lim_{h \to 0} h \, [f(a) + f(a+h) + f(a+2h) + f(a+3h) + \ldots$$
$$+ f(a + (n-1)h)]$$

$$\text{where, } h = \frac{b-a}{n} \text{ and } h \to 0 \, , \, n \to \infty$$

$$\therefore \int_1^4 (x^2 - x) \, dx = \lim_{h \to 0} h \, [f(1) + f(1+h) + f(1+2h) + f(1+3h) + \ldots$$
$$+ f(1 + (n-1)h)]$$

$$= \lim_{h \to 0} h \, [\, 0 + (h^2 + h) + (2^2 h^2 + 2h) + (3^2 h^2 + 3h) + \ldots$$
$$+ ((n-1)^2 h^2 + (n-1)h)]$$

$$= \lim_{h \to 0} h \, [\, (1^2 + 2^2 + 3^2 + \ldots + (n-1)^2)h^2$$
$$+ (1 + 2 + 3 + \ldots + (n-1))h \,]$$

[by grouping terms containing h^2 and h separately]

$$= \lim_{h \to 0} h \, [\, \frac{(n-1)\, n \, (2n-1)}{6} \, h^2 + \frac{(n-1)n}{2} \, h \,]$$

[using the formula of Sum of First n natural numbers:

$$\sum_{k=1}^{n} k = 1 + 2 + 3 + \ldots + n = \frac{n(n+1)}{2}$$

and Sum of Squares of First n natural numbers:

$$\sum_{k=1}^{n} k^2 = 1^2 + 2^2 + 3^2 + \ldots + n^2 = \frac{n(n+1)(2n+1)}{6}$$

also notice that we have $(n-1)$ terms instead of n]

$$= \lim_{h \to 0} [\, \frac{(n-1)\, n \, (2n-1)}{6} \, h^3 + \frac{(n-1)n}{2} \, h^2 \,]$$

[moving h inside the brackets]

$$= \lim_{h \to 0} [\, \frac{(nh-h)\, nh \, (2nh-h)}{6} + \frac{(nh-h)nh}{2} \,]$$

$$= \lim_{h \to 0} [\, \frac{(3-h)\, (3)\, (6-h)}{6} + \frac{(3-h)(3)}{2} \,]$$

$$= \frac{(3)\, (3)\, (6)}{6} + \frac{(3)(3)}{2}$$

$$= 9 + \frac{9}{2}$$

$$= \frac{27}{2}$$

3.2   Area Function

If f is a continuous function in closed interval $[a, b]$, then area function is defined as

$$A(x) = \int_a^x f(x)dx$$

- It is the area under the curve $y = f(x)$ bounded by x-axis from $x = a$ to x.

For Example, for the function $f(x) = x^2 - x$, $[-2, 4]$ the area function is

$$A(x) = \int_{-2}^{x} (x^2 - x)\, dx$$

$\therefore \quad \int_{-2}^{x} (x^2 - x)\, dx$ represent the area under the curve $y = x^2 - x$ bounded by x-axis from $x = -2$ to x

where $x \in [-2, 4]$.

3.3 Fundamental Theorems of Integral Calculus

3.3.1 First Fundamental Theorem of Integral Calculus

If f is a continuous function in closed interval $[a, b]$ and $A(x)$ is area function, then $A'(x) = f(x)$

i.e., $$\frac{d}{dx}\left[\int_{a}^{x} f(x)dx\right] = f(x)$$

For Example, $\dfrac{d}{dx}\left[\int_{-2}^{x} (x^2 - x)\, dx\right] = x^2 - x$

3.3.2 Second Fundamental Theorem of Integral Calculus

If f is a continuous function in closed interval $[a, b]$ and F is its antiderivative (i.e., integral), then

$$\int_{a}^{b} f(x)dx = [F(x)]_{a}^{b} = F(b) - F(a)$$

While applying these theorems, $f(x)$ should be well defined and continuous in the interval $[a, b]$.

<u>Example</u>

Evaluate $\int_{1}^{4} (x^2 - x)\, dx$ by the integrating the function.

Solution

Step-1: Find the integral of the function as discussed earlier in indefinite integral.

$$\int (x^2 - x)\, dx = \frac{x^3}{3} - \frac{x^2}{2} + C$$

[applying formula no.1 of article 2.7]

Step-2: Now first put the upper limit in the result and then the lower limit, and subtract the two answers (we can ignore constant C as it will be cancelled while subtracting).

$$\int_{1}^{4} (x^2 - x)\, dx = \left(\frac{x^3}{3} - \frac{x^2}{2}\right)\Big|_{1}^{4}$$

$$= \left(\frac{4^3}{3} - \frac{4^2}{2}\right) - \left(\frac{1^3}{3} - \frac{1^2}{2}\right)$$

$$= \frac{27}{2}$$

3.3.2.1 Solving definite integral by substitution:

In indefinite integral, we have seen that some integrals are solved by substitution method. If we use substitution method in definite integral, then integral can be evaluated further in two ways:

Method-1: First solve the integral without limits, and then convert the result back into the given variable. After that put limits in the result.

Method-2: Change the limits of the integral according to the substitution. It will not require conversion of the result back into the given variable.

<u>Example</u>

Evaluate the integral $\int_0^2 x\sqrt{x+2}\,dx$

Solution

Method-1:

Substituting $x+2=t$ or $x=t-2$

and differentiating it, we get $dx=dt$

$\therefore$ We solve the given integral without limits as

$$\int x\sqrt{x+2}\,dx = \int (t-2)\sqrt{t}\,dt = \int \left(t^{\frac{3}{2}} - 2t^{\frac{1}{2}}\right) dt$$

$$= \frac{2}{5}t^{\frac{5}{2}} - \frac{4}{3}t^{\frac{3}{2}} + C \quad \text{[applying formula no.1 of art2.7]}$$

$$= \frac{2}{5}(x+2)^{\frac{5}{2}} - \frac{4}{3}(x+2)^{\frac{3}{2}} + C$$

$$\therefore \int_0^2 x\sqrt{x+2}\,dx$$

$$= \left[\frac{2}{5}(x+2)^{\frac{5}{2}} - \frac{4}{3}(x+2)^{\frac{3}{2}}\right]_0^2$$

$$= \left[\frac{2}{5}(2+2)^{\frac{5}{2}} - \frac{4}{3}(2+2)^{\frac{3}{2}}\right] - \left[\frac{2}{5}(0+2)^{\frac{5}{2}} - \frac{4}{3}(0+2)^{\frac{3}{2}}\right]$$

$$= \left[\frac{2}{5}(4)^{\frac{5}{2}} - \frac{4}{3}(4)^{\frac{3}{2}}\right] - \left[\frac{2}{5}(2)^{\frac{5}{2}} - \frac{4}{3}(2)^{\frac{3}{2}}\right]$$

$$= \left[\frac{2}{5}(2^2)^{\frac{5}{2}} - \frac{4}{3}(2^2)^{\frac{3}{2}}\right] - \left[\frac{2}{5} \times 2^{2+\frac{1}{2}} - \frac{4}{3} \times 2^{1+\frac{1}{2}}\right]$$

$$= \left[\frac{2}{5}(2^5) - \frac{4}{3}(2^3)\right] - \left[\frac{2}{5} \times 2^2 \times 2^{\frac{1}{2}} - \frac{4}{3} \times 2 \times 2^{\frac{1}{2}}\right]$$

$$= \left[\frac{64}{5} - \frac{32}{3}\right] - \left[\frac{8\sqrt{2}}{5} - \frac{8\sqrt{2}}{3}\right]$$

$$= \frac{32}{15} - 8\sqrt{2}\left(\frac{3-5}{15}\right) = \frac{32+16\sqrt{2}}{15}$$

Method-2:

Substituting $x + 2 = t$ or $x = t - 2$
and differentiating it, we get $dx = dt$
Also, we change the limits by finding values of t from
$x + 2 = t$ at $x = 0$ and $x = 2$.

$\qquad$ At $x = 0$ we have $t = 2$

$\qquad$ At $x = 2$ we have $t = 4$

$\therefore$ We solve the given integral by changing the limits as follows:

$$\int_0^2 x\sqrt{x+2}\, dx = \int_2^4 (t-2)\sqrt{t}\, dt = \int_2^4 \left(t^{\frac{3}{2}} - 2t^{\frac{1}{2}}\right) dt$$

$$= \left[\frac{2}{5}t^{\frac{5}{2}} - \frac{4}{3}t^{\frac{3}{2}}\right]_2^4 \qquad \text{[applying formula no.1 of art2.7]}$$

$$= \left[\frac{2}{5}(4)^{\frac{5}{2}} - \frac{4}{3}(4)^{\frac{3}{2}}\right] - \left[\frac{2}{5}(2)^{\frac{5}{2}} - \frac{4}{3}(2)^{\frac{3}{2}}\right]$$

$$= \left[\frac{2}{5}(2^2)^{\frac{5}{2}} - \frac{4}{3}(2^2)^{\frac{3}{2}}\right] - \left[\frac{2}{5} \times 2^{2+\frac{1}{2}} - \frac{4}{3} \times 2^{1+\frac{1}{2}}\right]$$

$$= \left[\frac{2}{5}(2^5) - \frac{4}{3}(2^3)\right] - \left[\frac{2}{5} \times 2^2 \times 2^{\frac{1}{2}} - \frac{4}{3} \times 2 \times 2^{\frac{1}{2}}\right]$$

$$= \left[\frac{64}{5} - \frac{32}{3}\right] - \left[\frac{8\sqrt{2}}{5} - \frac{8\sqrt{2}}{3}\right]$$

$$= \frac{32}{15} - 8\sqrt{2}\left(\frac{3-5}{15}\right) = \frac{32+16\sqrt{2}}{15}$$

3.4   Properties of Definite Integrals

1) $\int_a^b f(x)\,dx \;=\; -\int_b^a f(x)\,dx$

2) $\int_a^a f(x)\,dx \;=\; 0$

3) $\int_a^b f(x)\,dx \;=\; \int_a^b f(t)\,dt$

4) $\int_a^b f(x)\,dx \;=\; \int_a^c f(x)\,dx \;+\; \int_c^b f(x)\,dx$

5) $\int_a^b f(x)\,dx \;=\; \int_a^b f(a+b-x)\,dx$

6) $\int_0^a f(x)\,dx \;=\; \int_0^a f(a-x)\,dx$

7) $\int_0^{2a} f(x)\,dx \;=\; \int_0^a f(x)\,dx \;+\; \int_0^a f(2a-x)\,dx$

8) $\int_0^{2a} f(x)\,dx \;=\; 2\int_0^a f(x)\,dx \;$; $\;if\; f(2a-x)=f(x)$

$$= 0 \qquad ;\; if\; f(2a-x)=-f(x)$$

9) $\int_{-a}^a f(x)\,dx = 2\int_0^a f(x)\,dx$; $if\; f(-x)=f(x)$ $i.e.,$

$$f(x)\; is\; even\; function$$

$$= 0 \qquad\qquad ;\; if\; f(-x)=-f(x)\; i.e.,$$
$$f(x)\; is\; odd\; function$$

- Property no.1 is applied when we need to interchange the lower and the upper limits. On interchanging the lower and the upper limits, the sign (+/-) of integral gets changed.
- Property no.2 is applied when the lower and the upper limits are same. In this case, the result is 0.
- Property no.3 is applied when we need to change the given variable into the required variable. On changing the variable both the limits remain same.
- Property no.4 is mostly applied if the function splits at a point. Let's understand application of property no.4 with an example.

Example

Evaluate $\int_2^8 |x - 5|\, dx$

Solution

Here, we have $f(x) = |x - 5| = \begin{cases} -(x - 5) & if \ \ x \le 5 \\ x - 5 & if \ \ x \ge 5 \end{cases}$

For a function which splits at a point like the given function, we use property no. 4 .

So, using $\int_a^b f(x)\, dx = \int_a^c f(x)\, dx + \int_c^b f(x)\, dx$, we write

$$\int_2^8 |x - 5|\, dx = \int_2^5 -(x - 5)\, dx + \int_5^8 (x - 5)\, dx$$

$$= \left(-\frac{x^2}{2} + 5x\right)\Big|_2^5 + \left(\frac{x^2}{2} - 5x\right)\Big|_5^8$$

[applying formula no.1 of article 2.7]

$$= \left(-\frac{5^2}{2} + 25\right) - \left(-\frac{2^2}{2} + 10\right) + \left(\frac{8^2}{2} - 40\right) - \left(\frac{5^2}{2} - 25\right)$$

$$= \frac{25}{2} - 8 - 8 + \frac{25}{2}$$

$$= 9$$

- To understand when to apply Property no.5 , let's consider the following example.

Example

Evaluate $\int_{\pi/6}^{\pi/3} \dfrac{1}{1 + \sqrt{\tan x}}\, dx$

Solution

Let $I = \int_{\pi/6}^{\pi/3} \dfrac{1}{1 + \sqrt{\tan x}}\, dx$ ………..…(i)

Here, we observe that the sum of lower and upper limits is $\dfrac{\pi}{2}$ which comes at y-axis in the quadrant system of angles. In such a case where the sum of lower and upper limits comes at x-axis or y-axis, we try to use property no. 5 .

So, using $\int_a^b f(x)\, dx = \int_a^b f(a + b - x)\, dx$

$$I = \int_{\pi/6}^{\pi/3} \frac{1}{1 + \sqrt{\tan x}}\, dx = \int_{\pi/6}^{\pi/3} \frac{1}{1 + \sqrt{\tan\left(\frac{\pi}{2} - x\right)}}\, dx$$

$$= \int_{\pi/6}^{\pi/3} \frac{1}{1 + \sqrt{\cot x}}\, dx$$

$$\Rightarrow I = \int_{\pi/6}^{\pi/3} \frac{\sqrt{\tan x}}{1 + \sqrt{\tan x}}\, dx$$ ………..…(ii)

Now add eqns. (i) and (ii) to get

$$2I = \int_{\pi/6}^{\pi/3} \frac{1+\sqrt{\tan x}}{1+\sqrt{\tan x}} \, dx$$

$$\Rightarrow 2I = \int_{\pi/6}^{\pi/3} dx$$

$$\Rightarrow 2I = x \Big|_{\pi/6}^{\pi/3} \qquad \text{[applying formula no.1 of article 2.7]}$$

$$\Rightarrow 2I = \frac{\pi}{3} - \frac{\pi}{6} = \frac{\pi}{6}$$

$$\Rightarrow I = \frac{\pi}{12}$$

- If the lower limit of the integral is 0, we think of applying Property no.6, 7 or 8. Also we note that property no.8 is modified and simplified version of property no.7.

  Let's take some examples to understand when to apply these properties.

<u>Example</u>

Evaluate $\int_0^\pi \dfrac{x \, \sin x}{1 + \cos^2 x} \, dx$

Solution

Let $I = \int_0^\pi \dfrac{x \, \sin x}{1 + \cos^2 x} \, dx \qquad \dots\dots\dots\dots (i)$

Here, lower limit is 0.

$\therefore$ We think of applying Property no.6 or 8

Here, $f(x) = \dfrac{x \, \sin x}{1 + \cos^2 x}$

To apply any of the property no.6 or 8, we notice that we have to replace x with 'upper limit minus x'. So, in this case we have to replace x with $(\pi - x)$.

$$\therefore \quad f(\pi - x) = \frac{(\pi - x) \, \sin(\pi - x)}{1 + \cos^2(\pi - x)}$$

$$\Rightarrow \quad f(\pi - x) = \frac{(\pi - x) \, \sin x}{1 + \cos^2 x}$$

$$\text{[since } \sin(\pi - x) = \sin x$$
$$\text{and } \cos^2(\pi - x) = [-\cos x]^2 = \cos^2 x]$$

Since $f(\pi - x)$ is neither equal to $f(x)$ nor $-f(x)$

$\therefore$ We can't apply property no.8, and hence apply property no. 6

So, using $\int_0^a f(x) \, dx = \int_0^a f(a - x) \, dx$, the given integral in eqn. (i) becomes

$$I = \int_0^\pi \frac{(\pi - x) \, \sin x}{1 + \cos^2 x} \, dx \qquad \dots\dots\dots\dots(ii)$$

Adding eqn.(i) and (ii), we get

$$2I = \int_0^\pi \left[\frac{x\,sinx}{1 + cos^2x} + \frac{(\pi - x)\,sinx}{1 + cos^2x} \right] dx$$

$$\Rightarrow \quad 2I = \int_0^\pi \frac{\pi\,sinx}{1 + cos^2x}\, dx$$

$$\Rightarrow \quad 2I = \pi \int_0^\pi \frac{sinx}{1 + cos^2x}\, dx$$

Now the function in the integral is $f(x) = \dfrac{sinx}{1 + cos^2x}$

$$\text{And} \quad f(\pi - x) = \frac{sin(\pi - x)}{1 + cos^2(\pi - x)}$$

$$\Rightarrow \quad f(\pi - x) = \frac{sinx}{1 + cos^2x}$$

$$= f(x)$$

Hence, we can apply prop no. 8 now.

So, using $\int_0^{2a} f(x)\, dx = 2 \int_0^a f(x)\, dx$; if $f(2a - x)\, dx = f(x)$, we have

$$\Rightarrow \quad 2I = 2\pi \int_0^{\frac{\pi}{2}} \frac{sinx}{1 + cos^2x}\, dx$$

$$\Rightarrow \quad I = \pi \int_0^{\frac{\pi}{2}} \frac{sinx}{1 + cos^2x}\, dx$$

Now we can solve it by substitution method.

Put $cos\,x = t \quad \Rightarrow \quad -sin\,x\,dx = dt$

Also, at $x = 0,\ t = 1$ and $x = \dfrac{\pi}{2},\ t = 0$

$$\therefore I = -\pi \int_1^0 \frac{1}{1 + t^2}\, dt$$

$$\Rightarrow I = -\pi\,(tan^{-1}t)\,\big|_1^0 \quad \text{[applying formula no. 16 or 20 of art2.7]}$$

$$\Rightarrow I = -\pi\,(tan^{-1}0 - tan^{-1}1)$$

$$\Rightarrow I = -\pi\left(0 - \frac{\pi}{4}\right)$$

$$\Rightarrow I = \frac{\pi^2}{4}$$

<u>Example</u>

Evaluate $\displaystyle\int_0^{\frac{\pi}{2}} \frac{sin^3x}{sin^3x + cos^3x}\, dx$

Solution

Let $I = \displaystyle\int_0^{\frac{\pi}{2}} \dfrac{sin^3 x}{sin^3 x + cos^3 x}\, dx$ $\qquad$ . . . . (i)

Here, lower limit is 0.

$\therefore$ We think of applying Property no.6 or 8

Here, $f(x) = \dfrac{sin^3 x}{sin^3 x + cos^3 x}$

To apply any of the property no.6 or 8, we notice that we have to replace x with 'upper limit minus x'. So, in this case we have to replace x with $(\frac{\pi}{2} - x\,)$.

$$\therefore \qquad f(\tfrac{\pi}{2} - x) = \dfrac{sin^3\left(\frac{\pi}{2} - x\right)}{sin^3\left(\frac{\pi}{2} - x\right) + cos^3\left(\frac{\pi}{2} - x\right)}$$

$$\Rightarrow \qquad f(\tfrac{\pi}{2} - x) = \dfrac{cos^3 x}{cos^3 x + sin^3 x}$$

$$[\text{ since } sin\left(\tfrac{\pi}{2} - x\right) = cos x \text{ and } cos\left(\tfrac{\pi}{2} - x\right) = sin x\,]$$

Since $f(\frac{\pi}{2} - x)$ is neither equal to $f(x)$ nor $-f(x)$

$\therefore$ We can't apply property no.8, and hence apply property no. 6

So, using $\int_0^a f(x)\, dx = \int_0^a f(a - x)\, dx$, the given integral in eqn. (i) becomes

$$I = \displaystyle\int_0^{\frac{\pi}{2}} \dfrac{cos^3 x}{sin^3 x + cos^3 x}\, dx \qquad . . . . (ii)$$

Adding eqn.(i) and (ii), we get

$$2I = \displaystyle\int_0^{\frac{\pi}{2}} \left[\dfrac{sin^3 x}{sin^3 x + cos^3 x} + \dfrac{cos^3 x}{sin^3 x + cos^3 x}\right] dx$$

$$\Rightarrow 2I = \displaystyle\int_0^{\frac{\pi}{2}} \dfrac{sin^3 x + cos^3 x}{sin^3 x + cos^3 x}\, dx$$

$$\Rightarrow 2I = \displaystyle\int_0^{\frac{\pi}{2}} dx$$

$$\Rightarrow 2I = x\, \Big|_0^{\frac{\pi}{2}} \qquad\qquad [\text{applying formula no.1 of article 2.7}]$$

$$\Rightarrow 2I = \tfrac{\pi}{2} - 0$$

$$\Rightarrow I = \tfrac{\pi}{4}$$

- Property no.9 is applied when the absolute values of lower and upper limits are same but opposite in sign. Also, the function should either be even or odd.

Example

Evaluate $\displaystyle\int_{-\frac{\pi}{2}}^{\frac{\pi}{2}} \frac{sin^3 x}{sin^4 x + cos^4 x}\, dx$

Solution

Let $\quad I = \displaystyle\int_{-\frac{\pi}{2}}^{\frac{\pi}{2}} \frac{sin^3 x}{sin^4 x + cos^4 x}\, dx \qquad \ldots\ldots\ldots\ldots (i)$

Here, lower limit is $-\frac{\pi}{2}$ and upper limit is $\frac{\pi}{2}$, which are opposite in sign but their absolute values are same, i.e., $\frac{\pi}{2}$. If the function is either even or odd, we can apply property no.9.

The given function is

$$f(x) = \frac{sin^3 x}{sin^4 x + cos^4 x}$$

To whether it is even or odd, we have to replace x with $-x$.

$$\therefore \qquad f(-x) = \frac{sin^3(-x)}{sin^4(-x) + cos^4(-x)}$$

$$\Rightarrow \qquad f(-x) = \frac{-sin^3 x}{sin^4 x + cos^4 x}$$

$$[\text{ since } sin(-x) = -sinx \text{ and } cos(-x) = cosx]$$

$$\Rightarrow \qquad f(-x) = -f(x)$$

It means $f(x)$ is an odd function, and we can apply property no.9.

So, using $\displaystyle\int_{-a}^{a} f(x)\, dx = 0$; if $f(-x) = -f(x)$.

$$\int_{-\frac{\pi}{2}}^{\frac{\pi}{2}} \frac{sin^3 x}{sin^4 x + cos^4 x}\, dx = 0$$

We have given some examples, just to clarify how to use the properties of definite integral. Once you are able to identify which property can be applied in the given integral, you can attempt complex questions also.

Chapter-9   Application of Integrals

1   Area bounded by the X – axis

Given: equation of curve $y = f(x)$, and ordinates $x = a$ and $x = b$.

Step-1   Draw the curve of given equation $y = f(x)$.
Also draw the lines $x = a$ and $x = b$.

Step-2   Consider an arbitrary vertical strip of height y and width dx (as shown in the figure)
Area of the elementary strip is $dA = y\,dx$

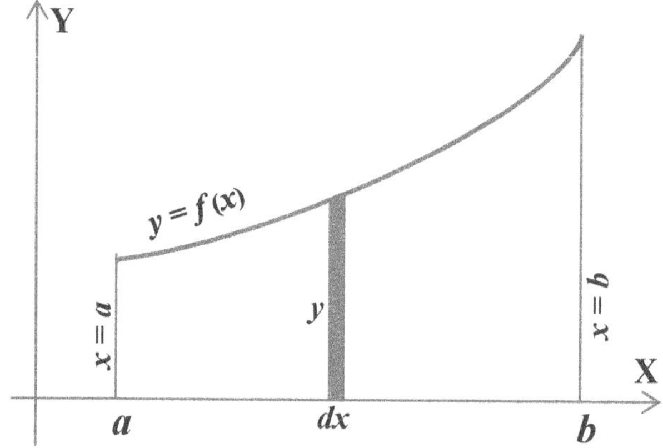

Step-3   Now the area bounded by the curve $y = f(x)$, X– axis and between the ordinates, $x = a$ and $x = b$ is given by

$$A = \int_a^b y\,dx$$

(*see* 'Area Function' in chapter-Integrals)

Step-4   It can be integrated if y is converted in term of x, and it is done by using equation of the curve $y = f(x)$.
∴ Put $y = f(x)$, and integrate to find the area.

→   If the position of the curve $y = f(x)$ is below the X-axis (as shown in the figure below), then

$$A = \left| \int_a^b y\,dx \right|$$

(∵ the value of this definite integral will come out to be negative, and area can't be negative.)

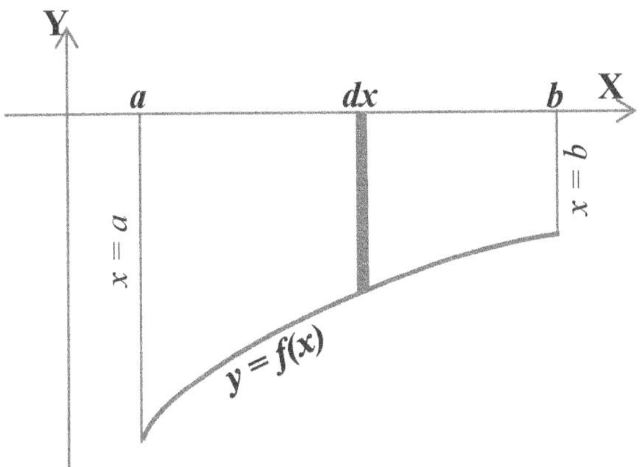

<u>**Example**</u>
Find the area of the region bounded by the curve $y^2 = x$ and the lines $x = 1$, $x = 4$ and the x-axis in the first quadrant.

Solution

Step-1: First we draw the curve $y^2 = x$.

We observe that it is an equation of parabola, which is in the form given in article 4.3.1 of this chapter.

We can draw a rough sketch just by knowing its axis of symmetry and the coordinates of its vertex.

Here, **axis of symmetry is X-axis** on the right side of Y-axis, and **vertex is (0,0)** (see table in article 4.3.1 of this chapter). So, the curve is as shown below. Also, we draw the lines $x = 1$ and $x = 4$.

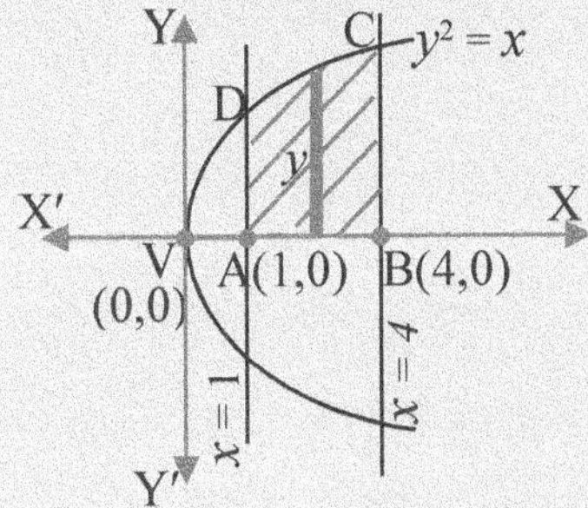

Now required area is the area ABCDA (shown by hatchings).

Step-2: Elementary rectangle in this region with base at x-axis has length y and breadth dx. So, its area $= ydx$.

Step-3: Now the required area is

$$\text{area of ABCDA} = \int_1^4 ydx$$

Step-4: Find y in terms of x from the equation of the curve,
$$y^2 = x.$$

i.e., $y = \pm\sqrt{x}$

but in the 1st quadrant y is positive.

$\therefore$ We take $\quad y = \sqrt{x}$, and Hence,

$$\text{area of ABCDA} = \int_1^4 y\,dx$$

$$= \int_1^4 \sqrt{x}\,dx = \int_1^4 x^{\frac{1}{2}}\,dx$$

$$= \left.\frac{x^{\frac{3}{2}}}{\frac{3}{2}}\right|_1^4 \qquad \left[\text{using } \int x^n\,dx = \frac{x^{n+1}}{n+1} + C,\right.$$

which is formula no.1 of article2.7
of chapter-Integrals]

$$= \left.\frac{2\,x^{\frac{3}{2}}}{3}\right|_1^4 = \frac{2}{3}\left(4^{\frac{3}{2}} - 1^{\frac{3}{2}}\right) = \frac{2}{3}\left(2^{2\times\frac{3}{2}} - 1^{\frac{3}{2}}\right) = \frac{14}{3}$$

- If the area above x-axis is bounded by two or more curves as shown in the following example, find the area under each curve, and add them.

Example

Find the area lying above x-axis and included between the circle $x^2 + y^2 = 32$ and the line $y = x$.

Solution

Step-1: We can draw the line $y = x$ by marking two or more points satisfying this equation.

$x^2 + y^2 = 32$ is a circle with centre $(0,0)$ and radius $\sqrt{32} = 4\sqrt{2}$ unit.

(See article4.2 in this chapter)

$\therefore$ With $(0,0)$ as centre, draw a circle of radius $= 4\sqrt{2}$ (roughly $4 \times 1.4 = 5.6$)

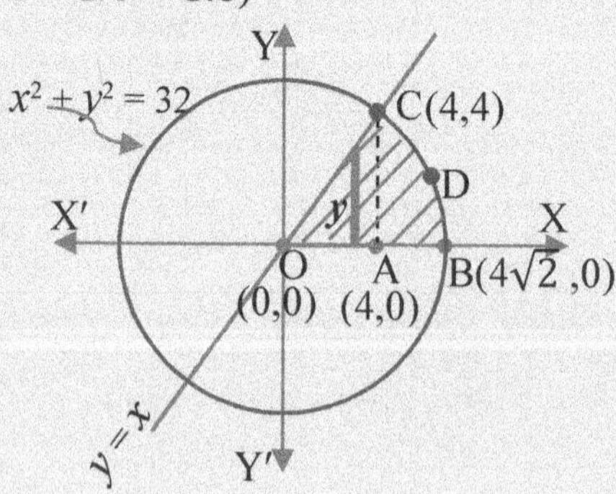

Also find the intersection of $y = x$ and $x^2 + y^2 = 32$ by solving them, and mark them on the figure.

If we put $y = x$ in $x^2 + y^2 = 32$, we find that $x = \pm 4$.

$\therefore$ Point of intersection in first quadrant is (4,4).

So, required area is area OABDCO (shown by hatchings)

Step-2: Elementary rectangle in this region with base at x-axis has length y and breadth dx. So, its area $= ydx$.

Step-3: Now required area is under the curve

$y = x$ from $x = 0$ to 4

and under $x^2 + y^2 = 32$ from $x = 4$ to $4\sqrt{2}$.

$\therefore$ Area of OABDCO $= \underbrace{\int_0^4 ydx}_{under\ y\ =\ x} + \underbrace{\int_4^{4\sqrt{2}} ydx}_{under\ x^2\ +\ y^2\ =\ 32}$

Step-4: Find y in terms of x from the equation $y = x$ for the first integral and from $x^2 + y^2 = 32$ for the second integral. i.e., put $y = x$ in the first integral

and put $y = \sqrt{32 - x^2}$ or $y = \sqrt{\left(4\sqrt{2}\right)^2 - x^2}$ in the second integral.

Hence, area of OABDCO

$$= \int_0^4 x\, dx + \int_4^{4\sqrt{2}} \sqrt{32 - x^2}\, dx$$

$$= \int_0^4 x\, dx + \int_4^{4\sqrt{2}} \sqrt{\left(4\sqrt{2}\right)^2 - x^2}\, dx$$

$$= \left(\frac{x^2}{2}\right)_0^4 + \left[\frac{x}{2}\sqrt{\left(4\sqrt{2}\right)^2 - x^2} + \frac{\left(4\sqrt{2}\right)^2}{2} sin^{-1}\frac{x}{4\sqrt{2}}\right]_4^{4\sqrt{2}}$$

[using formula no.1 and 25 of article2.7 of chapter- Integrals i.e., $\int x^n\, dx = \frac{x^{n+1}}{n+1} + C$

and $\int \sqrt{a^2 - x^2}\, dx = \frac{x}{2}\sqrt{a^2 - x^2} + \frac{a^2}{2}sin^{-1}\frac{x}{a} + C$]

$\Rightarrow$ area of OABDCO

$$= \frac{1}{2}(4^2 - 0^2) + \left[\frac{4\sqrt{2}}{2}\sqrt{\left(4\sqrt{2}\right)^2 - \left(4\sqrt{2}\right)^2} + \frac{\left(4\sqrt{2}\right)^2}{2} sin^{-1}\frac{4\sqrt{2}}{4\sqrt{2}}\right]$$

$$- \left[\frac{4}{2}\sqrt{\left(4\sqrt{2}\right)^2 - (4)^2} + \frac{\left(4\sqrt{2}\right)^2}{2} sin^{-1}\frac{4}{4\sqrt{2}}\right]$$

$$= 8 + [0 + 16\, sin^{-1}1] - \left[2\sqrt{16} + 16\, sin^{-1}\frac{1}{\sqrt{2}}\right]$$

$$= 8 + 16 \times \frac{\pi}{2} - \left[8 + 16 \times \frac{\pi}{4}\right]$$

$$= 8 + 8\pi - 8 - 4\pi$$

$$= 4\pi$$

---

2 Area bounded by the Y – axis

Given: equation of curve $y = f(x)$ and abscissa $y = c$ and $y = d$.
From this equation find x in terms of y i.e., $x = g(y)$

Step-1   Draw the curve of given equation $y = f(x)$.
Also draw the lines $y = c$ and $y = d$.

Step-2   Consider an arbitrary horizontal strip of length x and breadth dy (as shown in the figure).
The area of this elementary strip is $dA = x\,dy$

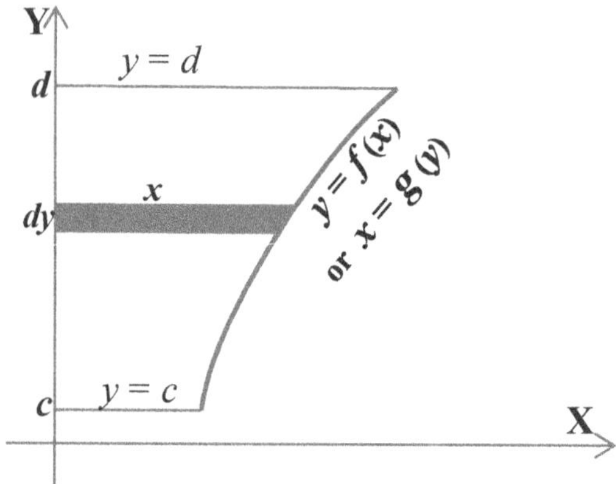

Step-3   Now area bounded by the curve $x = g(y)$, the Y – axis and between the lines, $y = c$ and $y = d$ is given by

$$A = \int_c^d x\,dy$$

(see 'Area Function' in chapter-Integrals)

Step-4   It can be integrated if x is converted in term of y, and it is done by using equation of the curve by writing x in terms of y as $x = g(y)$.
$\therefore$ Put $x = g(y)$, and integrate to find the area.

→ If position of the curve $x = g(y)$ is on left side of the Y-axis, then

$$A = \left| \int_c^d x\,dy \right|$$

($\because$ the value of this definite integral will come out to be negative, and area can't be negative)

> **<u>Example</u>**
> Find the area of the region bounded by the curve $x^2 = y$ and the lines $y = 1$, $y = 4$ and the y-axis in the first quadrant.
> **Solution**
> **Step-1:** First we draw the curve $x^2 = y$.
> We observe that it is an equation of parabola, which is in the form given in article 4.3.3 of this chapter.

---

*Asterisk (*) marked article (if any) is **not** in CBSE 2025-26 syllabus.*

We can draw a rough sketch just by knowing its axis of symmetry and the coordinates of its vertex.

Here, **axis of symmetry is Y-axis** above X-axis, and **vertex is (0,0)** (see table in article 4.3.1 of this chapter). So, the curve is as shown below. Also, we draw the lines $y=1$ and $y=4$.

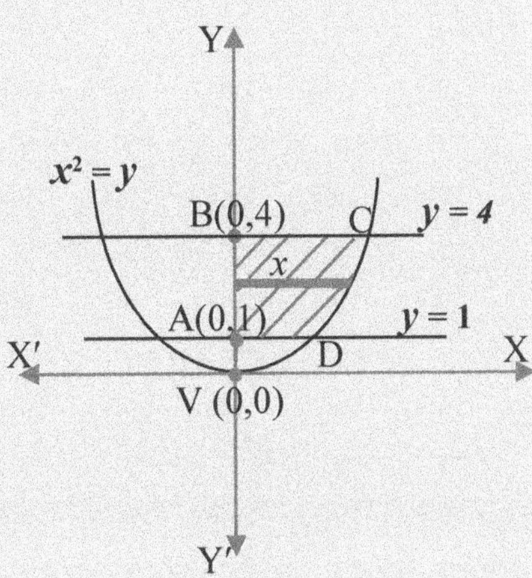

Now required area is area ABCDA (shown by hatchings)

Step-2: Elementary rectangle in this region with base at y-axis has length x and breadth dy. So, its area $= xdy$.

Step-3: Now the required area is

$$\text{area of ABCDA} = \int_1^4 x\,dy$$

Step-4: Find x in terms of y from the equation of the curve, $x^2 = y$.

i.e., $x = \pm\sqrt{y}$

but in the 1ˢᵗ quadrant x is positive.

$\therefore$ We take $x = \sqrt{y}$, and Hence,

$$\text{area of ABCDA} = \int_1^4 x\,dy$$

$$= \int_1^4 \sqrt{y}\,dy = \int_1^4 y^{\frac{1}{2}}\,dy$$

$$= \left.\frac{y^{\frac{3}{2}}}{\frac{3}{2}}\right|_1^4 \qquad \left[\text{using } \int x^n\,dx = \frac{x^{n+1}}{n+1} + C,\right.$$

$$\text{which is formula no.1 of article 2.7}$$
$$\text{of chapter-Integrals}]$$

$$= \left.\frac{2\,y^{\frac{3}{2}}}{3}\right|_1^4 = \frac{2}{3}\left(4^{\frac{3}{2}} - 1^{\frac{3}{2}}\right) = \frac{2}{3}\left(2^{2\times\frac{3}{2}} - 1^{\frac{3}{2}}\right) = \frac{14}{3}$$

---

3 *Area between two curves

Given two equations : $y = f(x)$ and $y = g(x)$

Step-1 Draw the curves for these equations.

Step-2 Find their points of intersections by solving them, and mark them on the curves.

(Suppose x – coordinates of these intersection points be $x = a, b, c$ in increasing order)

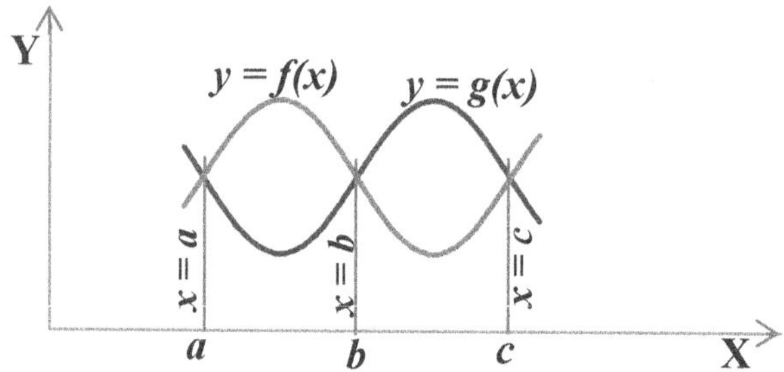

Step-3 Observe which curve is above and which is below between two successive intersection points.

(If $y = f(x)$ is above for $a < x < b$ and $y = g(x)$ is above for $b < x < c$, then it means $f(x) > g(x)$ for $a < x < b$ and $g(x) > f(x)$ for $b < x < c$)

Step-4 For each interval, subtract the area under the curve which is below from the area under the curve which is above, and then add them.

∴ For the case mentioned in step-3, the area between two curves is

$$A = \int_a^b [f(x) - g(x)]dx + \int_b^c [g(x) - f(x)]dx$$

<u>**Example**</u>

Find the area of the region bounded by the two parabolas $y = x^2$ and $y^2 = x$.

Solution

Step-1: First we draw the curve $y = x^2$ and $y^2 = x$.

We observe that they are equations of parabola, which are in the form given in article 4.3.1 and 4.3.3 respectively of this chapter. Here, $y^2 = x$ has **axis of symmetry at X-axis** on the right side of Y-axis, and its **vertex is (0,0)** (see table in article 4.3.1 of this chapter).

$y = x^2$ has **axis of symmetry at Y-axis** above X-axis, and its **vertex is (0,0)** (see table in article 4.3.3 of this chapter). So, their curves are as shown below.

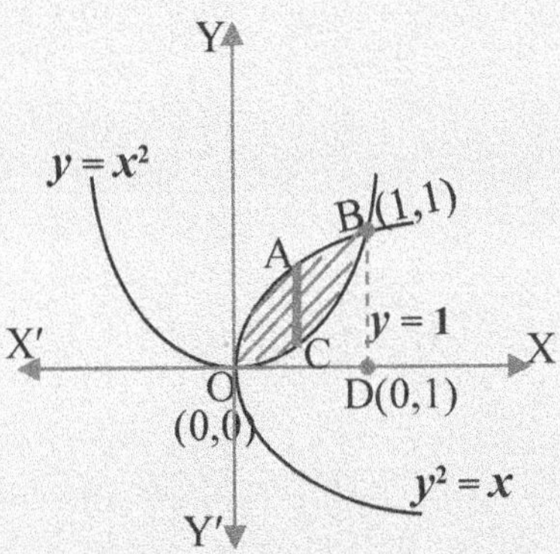

Step-2: To find their intersection points, we put $y = x^2$ in $y^2 = x$, and we get

$$x^4 = x \implies x^4 - x = 0 \implies x(x^3 - 1) = 0$$
$$x = 0 \text{ or } x^3 = 1 \implies x = 0 \text{ or } x = 1$$

Putting these values of x in $y = x^2$,

We get $y = 0$ or $x = 1$

$\therefore$ Intersection points are $O(0,0)$ and $B(1,1)$.

Mark these points on the figure.

Now required area is the area OABCO (shown by hatchings).

Step-3: We observe that between the intersection points O and B, the curve $y^2 = x$ is above the curve $y = x^2$.

$\therefore$ Area OABCO = (area under the curve $y^2 = x$ from $x = 0$ to 1)
$\qquad\qquad\qquad$ $-$ (area under the curve $y = x^2$ from $x = 0$ to 1)

Step-4: Now the required area is :

$$\text{area of OABCO} = \underbrace{\int_0^1 y\,dx}_{under\ y^2 = x} - \underbrace{\int_0^1 y\,dx}_{under\ y = x^2}$$

Find y in terms of x from the equation $y^2 = x$ for the first integral and from $y = x^2$ for the second integral.

i.e., put $y = \sqrt{x}$ in the first integral

and put $y = x^2$ in the second integral.

Hence, area of OABDCO $= \int_0^1 \sqrt{x}\,dx - \int_0^1 x^2\,dx$

$$= \int_0^1 x^{\frac{1}{2}}\,dx - \int_0^1 x^2\,dx$$

$$= \left(\frac{x^{\frac{3}{2}}}{\frac{3}{2}}\right)\Bigg|_0^1 - \left(\frac{x^3}{3}\right)\Bigg|_0^1 \qquad \text{[using formula no.1 of article2.7 of}$$

$$\text{chapter-Integrals: } \int x^n\,dx = \frac{x^{n+1}}{n+1} + C\,]$$

$\Rightarrow$ area of ABCDA

$$= \frac{2}{3}\left(1^{\frac{3}{2}} - 0^{\frac{3}{2}}\right) - \frac{1}{3}\left(1^3 - 0^3\right)$$

$$= \frac{2}{3} - \frac{1}{3} = \frac{1}{3}$$

4 Drawing some particular curves

4.1 Straight Line

- The equation in the form $A\,x + B\,y + C = 0$ is equation of straight line.
- Its curve can be drawn by finding coordinates of two points satisfying this equation (It has been done in lower classes).

4.2 Circle

- It can be drawn by knowing coordinates of its centre and its radius.
- Centre and radius can be obtained by writing & comparing the given equation with either standard equation or general equation of the circle.
  (*see* 'Standard Equation' and 'General Equation' below.)
- Mark the centre on the Cartesian plane.
  Open the compass equal to the radius, and draw the circle with the centre located above.

4.2.1 Standard Equation:

- $(x - h)^2 + (y - k)^2 = r^2$
  where, centre $= (\,h,\,k\,)$ and radius $= r$

4.2.2 General Equation:

- $x^2 + y^2 + 2gx + 2fy + c = 0$
  where, centre $= (\,-g,\,-f\,)$ and radius $= \sqrt{g^2 + f^2 - c}$

4.3 Parabola

- Its curve can be drawn by knowing its vertex, axis of symmetry and some points satisfying the equations.
- The above data can be obtained by writing & comparing the given equation with one of the four standard equations which are discussed below.
- Mark the vertex on the Cartesian plane, and draw axis of symmetry.
- Now mark some points satisfying the equation lying symmetrically on both sides of axis of symmetry. Join them to obtain parabolic curve.

There are 4 standard equations:

4.3.1   Equation: $y^2 = 4ax$, $a > 0$

Vertex (V)	$(0,0)$
Axis	X-axis or $y=0$ (right of Y-axis)
Focus (F)	$(a,0)$
Equation of Directrix	$x = -a$
Length of Latus Rectum	$4a$

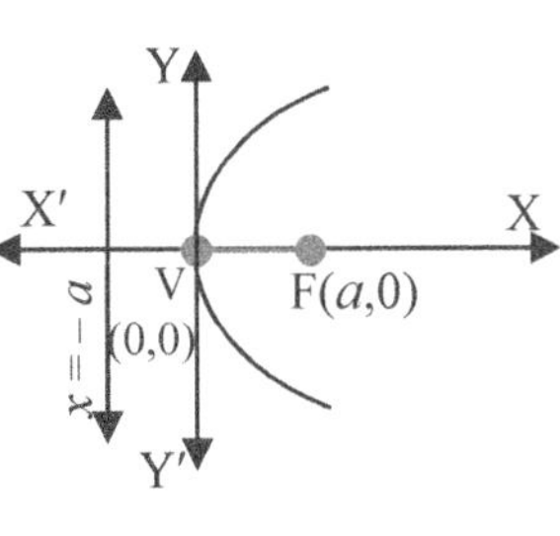

4.3.2   Equation: $y^2 = -4ax$, $a > 0$

Vertex (V)	$(0,0)$
Axis	X-axis or $y=0$ (left of Y-axis)
Focus (F)	$(-a,0)$
Equation of Directrix	$x = a$
Length of Latus Rectum	$4a$

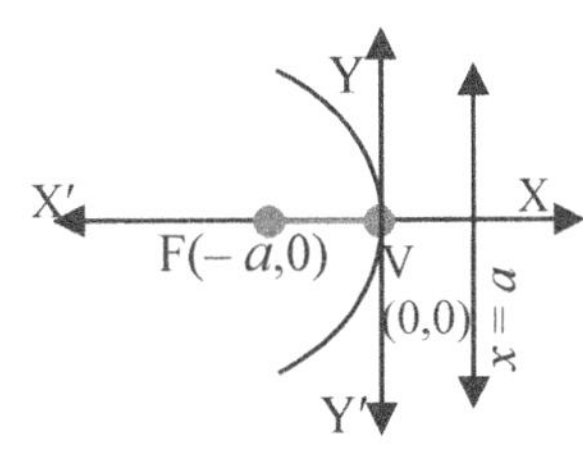

4.3.3   Equation: $x^2 = 4ay$, $a > 0$

Vertex	$(0,0)$
Axis	Y-axis or $x = 0$ (above X-axis)
Focus	$(0,a)$
Equation of Directrix	$y = -a$
Length of Latus Rectum	$4a$

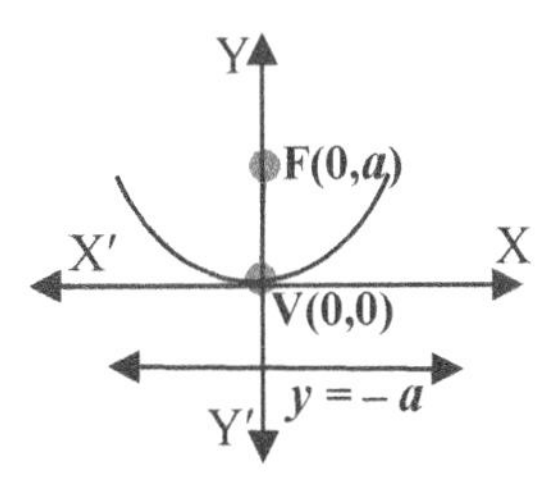

4.3.4 Equation: $x^2 = -4ay$, $a > 0$

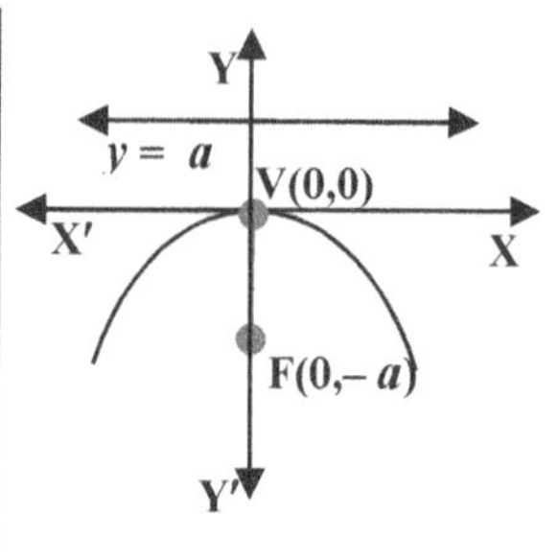

Vertex	$(0,0)$
Axis	Y-axis or $x = 0$ (below X-axis)
Focus	$(0, -a)$
Equation of Directrix	$y = a$
Length of Latus Rectum	$4a$

Chapter-10   Differential Equations

1   Differential Equation

An equation **containing derivatives** *of variables (dependent variables) of any order with respect to other variables (independent variables) is called a differential equation.*

- A differential equation which contains derivatives of only one dependent variable of any order with respect to only one independent variable is called an **ordinary differential equation**.

- Usually, we have dependent variable as y and independent variable as x.

  $\therefore$ Equations containing $\dfrac{dy}{dx}, \dfrac{d^2y}{dx^2}, \dfrac{d^3y}{dx^3}$, etc., are ordinary differential equations if they have only x and y as variables. (Remember, we can write these derivatives of y as y', y'', y''', etc., or y_1, y_2, y_3, etc.)

1.1   Order of Differential Equation

Order of the **highest order derivative** *present in the given differential equation is called as its order.*

Example

(i) $\dfrac{d^3y}{dx^3} + 3\left(\dfrac{d^2y}{dx^2}\right)^2 - 2\dfrac{dy}{dx} + sin\, y + x = 0$ has **order 3** because highest order derivative in it is $\dfrac{d^3y}{dx^3}$.

(ii) $\left(\dfrac{dy}{dx}\right)^2 + sin\left(\dfrac{dy}{dx}\right) = 0$ has **order 1** because highest order derivative in it is $\dfrac{dy}{dx}$.

1.2   Degree of Differential Equation

- Degree of a differential equation is defined only if it is polynomial in derivatives.

- If the degree is defined, **highest power of the highest order derivative** in the given differential equation is called its **degree**.

Example

$$\frac{d^3y}{dx^3} + 3\left(\frac{d^2y}{dx^2}\right)^2 - 2\left(\frac{d^3y}{dx^3}\right)^2 + sin\,y + x = 0 \quad \text{has } \textbf{degree 2}$$

because it is polynomial in derivatives and highest order of derivative in it is $\frac{d^3y}{dx^3}$ whose highest power is 2.

1.2.1 Polynomial in derivatives

- If the differential equation is algebraic in y', y'', y''' etc., and powers of y', y'', y''' etc., are non-negative integers, then it is polynomial in derivatives.

- If y', y'', y''' etc., are present as an argument of logarithm, trigonometry, inverse trigonometry, or exponent functions, etc., in the differential equation, then it is not polynomial in derivatives.

  i.e. If $log\left(\dfrac{dy}{dx}\right)$, $sin\left(\dfrac{dy}{dx}\right)$, $sin^{-1}\left(\dfrac{dy}{dx}\right)$, $e^{dy/dx}$,

  $\sqrt{\dfrac{dy}{dx}}$, $\left(\dfrac{dy}{dx}\right)^{\frac{3}{2}}$, etc., are present in the differential

  equation, then it is not polynomial in derivatives.

Example

(i) $\left(\dfrac{dy}{dx}\right)^2 + sin\left(\dfrac{dy}{dx}\right) = 0$ is not a polynomial in derivatives

because derivative, $\dfrac{dy}{dx}$ in it is present as argument of *sine* function which is a trigonometric and not an algebraic expression.

(ii) $\dfrac{d^3y}{dx^3} + 3\left(\dfrac{d^2y}{dx^2}\right)^2 - 2\sqrt{\dfrac{dy}{dx}} = 0$ is not a polynomial in

derivatives. Here, power of every derivative is not a non-negative integer because $\sqrt{\dfrac{dy}{dx}} = \left(\dfrac{dy}{dx}\right)^{\frac{1}{2}}$.

(iii) $\dfrac{d^3y}{dx^3} + 3\left(\dfrac{d^2y}{dx^2}\right)^2 - 2\dfrac{dy}{dx} + sin\,y + x = 0$ is a polynomial in

derivatives because all derivatives in it are present as algebraic expression, and power of every derivative in it is a non-negative integer.

2 Solution of Differential Equation

A function $y = f(x)$ will be a solution of the given differential equation if $y = f(x)$ satisfies that equation on substituting it in place of dependent variable y.

2.1 To check whether a function is a solution of the given differential equation

Given: (i) A function $y = f(x)$ and (ii) a differential equation.

Step-1 Differentiate the function $y = f(x)$ to obtain $\dfrac{dy}{dx}$. After that differentiate the result to obtain $\dfrac{d^2y}{dx^2}$ if order of differential equation is higher than 1. Continue to differentiate the result till we obtain the highest order derivative present in the differential equation.

Step-2 Put all these derivatives in LHS of given differential equation. Also use the given function $y = f(x)$, if needed, and simplify.

Step-3 Put all the derivatives in RHS of differential equation. Also use the given function $y = f(x)$, if needed, and simplify.

Step-4 If LHS = RHS, then $y = f(x)$ is a solution of the given differential equation.

If LHS $\neq$ RHS, then $y = f(x)$ is not a solution of the given differential equation.

Example

Verify that the function $y = x \sin x$ is a solution of the differential equation: $\quad x\,\dfrac{d^2y}{dx^2} + xy = 2\,\dfrac{dy}{dx} - 2\sin x$

Solution

Step-1: Here, the highest order derivative is 2 therefore, we must find $\dfrac{dy}{dx}$ and $\dfrac{d^2y}{dx^2}$ by differentiating the given function.

$$y = x \sin x \qquad \dots\dots(i)$$

$$\Rightarrow \quad \frac{dy}{dx} = x \cos x + \sin x \qquad \dots\dots(ii)$$

$$\Rightarrow \quad \frac{d^2y}{dx^2} = -x \sin x + \cos x + \cos x$$

$$= -x \sin x + 2\cos x \qquad \dots\dots(iii)$$

Step-2: LHS of given differential equation is

$$\mathbf{LHS} = x\,\frac{d^2y}{dx^2} + xy$$

$$= x\,(-x \sin x + 2\cos x) + x^2 \sin x$$

$$\dots\dots[\text{using eqn. (i) and (iii)}]$$

$$= 2x \cos x$$

Step-3: RHS of given differential equation is

$$\mathbf{RHS} = 2\,\frac{dy}{dx} - 2 \sin x$$

$$= 2\,(x \cos x + \sin x) - 2 \sin x \quad \dots\dots[\text{using eqn. (ii)}]$$

$$= 2\,x \cos x$$

Step-4: since LHS = RHS

$\therefore$ It is verified that $y = x\,sin\,x$ is a solution of the differential equation:

$$x\,\frac{d^2y}{dx^2} + xy = 2\,\frac{dy}{dx} - 2sin\,x$$

2.2 General Solution

The solution of differential equation, which **contains arbitrary constants** *is called the general solution (primitive).*

- Arbitrary constants are usually written as a, b, c, d, etc.
- Arbitrary constants are also called as **parameters.**
- The number of arbitrary constants in general solution of a differential equation is equal to its order.
  i.e.,

  $\rightarrow$ The number of arbitrary constants in differential equation of order 1 is 1, of order 2 is 2, of order 3 is 3, and so on.

2.3 Particular Solution

The solution which **does not contain any arbitrary constant** *is called the particular solution of the differential equation.*

- General solution represents family of curves while particular solution represents a single curve.

<u>**Example**</u>

Consider the differential equation $\frac{d^2y}{dx^2} + y = 0$.

And we are given two of its solutions as:

(i) $y = a\,sin\,(x + b)$ and (ii) $y = -3\,sin\,(x + \frac{\pi}{3})$

Both these solutions satisfy the given differential equation.
(We can verify them as explained in article 2.1 of this chapter)
$y = a\,sin\,(x + b)$ contains two arbitrary constants a and b, which can take any real values. So, this is a **general solution** and represents a family of curves.

$y = -3\,sin\,(x + \frac{\pi}{3})$ doesn't contain any arbitrary constant so,

this is a particular solution and represents only one curve.

3 *Formation of Differential Equation

Given: Equation of family of curves $y = f(x)$ which contains some arbitrary constants.

Forming Differential Equation:

Step-1 Observe the number of arbitrary constants (parameters) in the equation $y = f(x)$

Step-2 Differentiate the equation $y = f(x)$, and find $\dfrac{dy}{dx}, \dfrac{d^2y}{dx^2}$, etc.

Obtain the highest order derivative whose order is equal to the number of parameters.

→ If there is only one parameter, find only 1st order derivative,

i.e., $\dfrac{dy}{dx}$

→ If there are two parameters, find 1st and 2nd order derivatives,

i.e., $\dfrac{dy}{dx}$ and $\dfrac{d^2y}{dx^2}$

and so on.

Step-3 Eliminate all the parameters using the given equation,

$y = f(x)$ and the derivatives obtained in step-2.

Step-4 Equation obtained, after eliminating all the parameters, is the required differential equation.

Example

Form differential equation for the family of curves $y = e^{2x}(a + bx)$, where a and b are the parameters.

Solution

Step-1: Here, the number of arbitrary constants (parameters) are 2 i.e., a and b.

Step-2: So, in the required differential equation, 2 should be the highest order of the derivative, and hence, we must find $\dfrac{dy}{dx}$ and $\dfrac{d^2y}{dx^2}$.

Now given eqn. is:

$$y = e^{2x}(a + bx) \qquad \ldots \ldots \ldots (i)$$

Differentiating w.r.t. 'x'

$$\frac{dy}{dx} = 2e^{2x}(a + bx) + b\,e^{2x}$$

It is more convenient to write the eqn. in a concise way by using given eqn., if it is possible.

So, using eqn. (i) we can write:

$$\frac{dy}{dx} = 2y + b\,e^{2x} \qquad \ldots \ldots \ldots (ii)$$

Again differentiating w.r.t. 'x'

$$\frac{d^2y}{dx^2} = 2\frac{dy}{dx} + 2b\,e^{2x} \qquad \ldots \ldots \ldots (iii)$$

Now we can eliminate b from eqn. (iii) by using eqn.(ii).

From eqn.(ii) we have $b\,e^{2x} = \dfrac{dy}{dx} - 2y$

Putting it in eqn.(iii) to eliminate b, we get

$$\frac{d^2y}{dx^2} = 2\frac{dy}{dx} + 2\left(\frac{dy}{dx} - 2y\right)$$

$$\frac{d^2y}{dx^2} = 4\frac{dy}{dx} - 4y$$

$$\frac{d^2y}{dx^2} - 4\frac{dy}{dx} + 4y = 0$$

This is the required differential equation.

4   Methods to Solve Differential Equation

- 1st order and 1st degree differential equation can be written in the form:

$$\frac{dy}{dx} = F(x, y) \quad \text{where } F(x, y) \text{ is a function of } x \text{ and } y.$$

In this book, we will give methods to solve 1st order and 1st degree differential equation of the following types:

(i) Variable separable (ii) Homogeneous equation (iii) Linear differential equation.

4.1   Variable Separable

- A differential equation which can be written in the form:

$$\frac{dy}{dx} = f(x).\, g(y) \qquad \textit{is variable separable.}$$

where $f(x)$ is function of x only, and $g(y)$ is function of y only.

- It means we can separate variables x and y completely into different factors on RHS of equation: $\dfrac{dy}{dx} = F(x, y)$.

4.1.1   Procedure to solve variable separable differentiable equation:

Step-1 Write the given differential equation in the form $\dfrac{dy}{dx} = F(x, y)$

Step-2 Factorize $F(x, y)$ to convert it in the form $f(x).\, g(y)$ i.e., in two functions: one denoted by $f(x)$ which is a function of x only and other denoted by $g(y)$ which is a function of y only .

So, we have $\dfrac{dy}{dx} = f(x).\, g(y)$

Step-3 Now rearrange it so that dx and dy are on opposite sides of 'equal' sign and are in numerators. Shift $f(x)$ towards dx and $g(y)$ towards dy.

we get the equation in the form:

$$\frac{1}{g(y)}\, dy = f(x)\, dx$$

Step-4 Now integrate both sides to obtain the general solution:

$$\int \frac{1}{g(y)}\, dy = \int f(x)\, dx$$

<u>Example</u>

Solve the differential equation:

$$dy = (1 + x^2 + y^2 + x^2 y^2)\, dx$$

Solution

Step-1: Writing in the form, $\dfrac{dy}{dx} = F(x, y)$

$$dy = (1 + x^2 + y^2 + x^2 y^2)\, dx$$

$$\Rightarrow \quad \frac{dy}{dx} = 1 + x^2 + y^2 + x^2 y^2$$

Step-2: Factorising RHS

$$\frac{dy}{dx} = 1 + x^2 + y^2 + x^2 y^2$$

$$= (1 + x^2) + y^2(1 + x^2)$$

$$= (1 + y^2)(1 + x^2)$$

Step-3: Separating variables

$$\frac{1}{(1 + y^2)}\, dy = (1 + x^2)\, dx$$

Step-4: Integrating both sides,

$$\int \frac{1}{(1 + y^2)}\, dy = \int (1 + x^2)\, dx$$

$$\Rightarrow \quad tan^{-1}y = x + \frac{x^3}{3} + C$$

[using formula no.20 and formula no.1
of article 2.7 of chapter- Integral]

This is the required solution.

4.2 Homogeneous Differential Equation

Before defining homogeneous differential equation, we should know about homogeneous function of x and y.

4.2.1 Homogeneous Function

- A function $F(x, y)$ is homogeneous function of degree n if

$$F(\lambda x, \lambda y) = \lambda^n F(x, y), \quad \textit{where } \lambda \neq 0 \textit{ and is a constant}$$

or $F(x,y) = x^n \cdot g\left(\dfrac{y}{x}\right)$

or $F(x,y) = y^n \cdot h\left(\dfrac{x}{y}\right)$

Where $g\left(\dfrac{y}{x}\right)$ is a function of $\left(\dfrac{y}{x}\right)$, and $h\left(\dfrac{x}{y}\right)$ is a function of $\left(\dfrac{x}{y}\right)$.

4.2.2 Homogeneous Differential Equation

- A differential equation of the form $\dfrac{dy}{dx} = F(x, y)$ is a homogeneous differential equation if **$F(x, y)$ is homogeneous function of degree 0**.

$$\text{i.e.,} \quad F(\lambda x, \lambda y) = F(x, y)$$

$$\text{or} \quad F(x, y) = g\left(\dfrac{y}{x}\right)$$

$$\text{or} \quad F(x, y) = h\left(\dfrac{x}{y}\right)$$

where $g\left(\dfrac{y}{x}\right)$ is a function of $\left(\dfrac{y}{x}\right)$, and $h\left(\dfrac{x}{y}\right)$ is a function of $\left(\dfrac{x}{y}\right)$.

- If $F(x, y)$ is an algebraic expression having same degree in every term in the numerator and in the denominator, then the given equation is a homogeneous differential equation.

4.2.3 Procedure to check homogeneous differential equation

Step-1 Write given differential equation in the form $\dfrac{dy}{dx} = F(x, y)$

Step-2 Note down RHS as $F(x, y) = - - - -$

$$\text{(which is a function of } x \text{ and } y\text{)}$$

Step-3 Find $F(\lambda x, \lambda y) = - - - - -$

(i.e., put λx & λy in place of x & y respectively in $F(x, y)$)

Step-4 On simplifying, if we find that $F(\lambda x, \lambda y) = F(x, y)$, then we say that the given differential equation is homogeneous differential equation.

<u>Example</u>

Check whether the differential equation: $x^2 \dfrac{dy}{dx} = y^2 + 2xy$ is a homogeneous or not.

Solution

Step-1: Writing in the form, $\dfrac{dy}{dx} = F(x, y)$

$$x^2 \dfrac{dy}{dx} = y^2 + 2xy$$

$$\Rightarrow \quad \dfrac{dy}{dx} = \dfrac{y^2 + 2xy}{x^2}$$

Step-2: Let RHS as $F(x, y)$

$$\therefore \ F(x, y) = \dfrac{y^2 + 2xy}{x^2}$$

Step-3: Find $F(\lambda x, \lambda y)$

$$\Rightarrow \quad F(\lambda x, \lambda y) = \dfrac{\lambda^2 y^2 + 2\lambda x \lambda y}{\lambda^2 x^2}$$

Step-4: On simplifying,

$$F(\lambda x,\ \lambda y) = \frac{\lambda^2(y^2 + 2\,x\,y)}{\lambda^2 x^2}$$

$$\Rightarrow \qquad F(\lambda x,\ \lambda y) = \frac{y^2 + 2\,x\,y}{x^2}$$

$$\Rightarrow \qquad F(\lambda x,\ \lambda y) = F(x,\ y)$$

$\therefore$ Given differential eqn. is homogeneous differential equation.

$\rightarrow$ **In this question observe that** $F(x,\ y) = \dfrac{y^2 + 2\,x\,y}{x^2}$ **is an algebraic expression in which every term in the numerator and denominator has same degree (i.e., 2).**

$\therefore$ **It comes out to be a homogeneous differential equation.**

4.2.4 Procedure to solve homogeneous differential equation

- A given homogeneous equation can be written in one of the following forms:

  (i) $\dfrac{dy}{dx} = f\!\left(\dfrac{y}{x}\right)$. We call it as $\dfrac{y}{x}$ form

  (ii) $\dfrac{dx}{dy} = f\!\left(\dfrac{x}{y}\right)$. We call it as $\dfrac{x}{y}$ form

__Form-1__ ($\dfrac{y}{x}$ form): $\dfrac{dy}{dx} = f\!\left(\dfrac{y}{x}\right)$

Step-1 Write the given differential equation in the form

$$\frac{dy}{dx} = F(x,\ y) \qquad \text{------ (i)}$$

Step-2 Put $\dfrac{y}{x} = v$ or $y = v\,x$ ------ (ii)

Step-3 Differentiating equation (ii) w.r.t. 'x', we get

$$\frac{dy}{dx} = v + x\cdot\frac{dv}{dx} \qquad \text{------ (iii)}$$

Step-4 Using eqns. (ii) & (iii), y is eliminated from eqn. (i), and then eqn. (i) gets converted in the following form:

$$v + x\cdot\frac{dv}{dx} = F(x,\ v)$$

Step-5 Now simplify and rearrange this equation to separate the variables x and v as explained in variable separable method, and then integrate to obtain required solution.

- **A homogeneous differential equation which contains only algebraic terms can be represented in any of the form:**

$$\frac{dy}{dx} = f\!\left(\frac{y}{x}\right) \quad \text{or} \quad \frac{dx}{dy} = f\!\left(\frac{x}{y}\right)$$

__Example__

Solve the differential equation: $x^2 \dfrac{dy}{dx} = y^2 + 2xy$ given that $y = 1$ when $x = 1$.

Solution

Step-1: Writing in the form, $\dfrac{dy}{dx} = \mathbf{F}(x, y)$

$$x^2 \frac{dy}{dx} = y^2 + 2xy$$

$$\Rightarrow \quad \frac{dy}{dx} = \frac{y^2 + 2xy}{x^2} \qquad \ldots\ldots\ldots (i)$$

We observe that $\mathbf{RHS} = \dfrac{y^2 + 2xy}{x^2}$ is an algebraic expression in which every term in the numerator and denominator has same degree (i.e., 2).

$\therefore \qquad$ It is a homogeneous differential equation.

$\qquad$ We can represent it in any form $\dfrac{y}{x}$ or $\dfrac{x}{y}$.

Let's represent it in $\dfrac{y}{x}$ form by dividing numerator and denominator both by x^2.

$$\Rightarrow \quad \frac{dy}{dx} = \frac{\left(\frac{y}{x}\right)^2 + 2\frac{y}{x}}{1}$$

We can also proceed further from eqn.(i), without converting into the above form as follows.

Step-2: Let $\quad \dfrac{y}{x} = v \quad$ or $\quad y = vx \quad \text{-------} (ii)$

Step-3: Differentiating eqn.(ii) w.r.t. 'x', we get

$$\frac{dy}{dx} = v + x\frac{dv}{dx} \qquad \ldots\ldots\ldots (iii)$$

Step-4: using eqn.(ii) and (iii) , eqn.(i) becomes

$$v + x\frac{dv}{dx} = \frac{v^2x^2 + 2x.x}{x^2}$$

Step-5: Simplifying and rearranging the terms,

$$\Rightarrow \quad v + x\frac{dv}{dx} = \frac{x^2(v^2 + 2v)}{x^2}$$

$$\Rightarrow \quad v + x\frac{dv}{dx} = v^2 + 2v$$

$$\Rightarrow \quad x\frac{dv}{dx} = v^2 + v$$

$$\Rightarrow \quad \frac{1}{(v^2 + v)} dv = \frac{1}{x} dx$$

$\qquad$ Integrating both sides,

$$\int \frac{1}{v^2 + v} dv = \int \frac{1}{x} dx$$

Here LHS is of the form $\int \frac{1}{quadratic}\, dx$ and can be solved by the method as explained in article2.8 of chapter – Integral.

On RHS, we can apply the formula, $\int \frac{1}{x}\, dx = log\,|x| + C$, which is given in art2.7 of chapter – Integral.

So, we proceed as follows:

$$\int \frac{1}{v^2 + v + \left(\frac{1}{2}\right)^2 - \left(\frac{1}{2}\right)^2}\, dv = \int \frac{1}{x}\, dx$$

$$\Rightarrow \int \frac{1}{\left(v + \frac{1}{2}\right)^2 - \left(\frac{1}{2}\right)^2}\, dv = \int \frac{1}{x}\, dx$$

[Apply the formula $\int \frac{1}{x^2 - a^2}\, dx = \frac{1}{2a} log\left|\frac{x-a}{x+a}\right| + C$ on LHS and the formula, $\int \frac{1}{x}\, dx = log\,|x| + C$ on RHS, which are given in art2.7 of chapter – Integral]

$$\Rightarrow \frac{1}{2 \times \frac{1}{2}} log \left|\frac{v + \frac{1}{2} - \frac{1}{2}}{v + \frac{1}{2} + \frac{1}{2}}\right| = log\,|x| + C$$

$$\Rightarrow log\left|\frac{v}{v+1}\right| = log\,|x| + C$$

$$\Rightarrow log\left|\frac{\frac{y}{x}}{\frac{y}{x}+1}\right| = log\,|x| + C$$

$$\left[\text{putting back } v = \frac{y}{x} \text{ from eqn.(ii)}\right]$$

$$\Rightarrow log\left|\frac{y}{y+x}\right| = log\,|x| + log\,|C_1|$$

$$\left[\text{There will be some constant } C_1 \text{ such that } log\,|C_1| = C\right]$$

$$\Rightarrow log\left|\frac{y}{y+x}\right| = log\,|C_1 x|$$

$$\Rightarrow \left|\frac{y}{y+x}\right| = |C_1 x|$$

$$\Rightarrow \frac{y}{y+x} = \pm\, C_1 x$$

$$\Rightarrow \frac{y}{y+x} = K\,x \qquad\qquad \ldots\ldots\ldots(iv)$$

$$\left[\text{where } K = \pm\, C_1 \text{ is a new arbitrary constant.}\right]$$

Now given that $y = 1$ when $x = 1$. Putting these values in eqn.(iv), we can get value of K.

$$\therefore \quad \frac{1}{1+1} = K\,(1)$$

$$\Rightarrow \quad K = \frac{1}{2}$$

So, eqn.(iv) becomes

$$\frac{y}{y+x} = \frac{1}{2}\,x$$

$$\Rightarrow \quad 2y = xy + x^2$$

This is the required solution.

Form-2 ($\dfrac{x}{y}$ **form**): $\dfrac{dx}{dy} = F\left(\dfrac{x}{y}\right)$

Step-1 Write the given differential equation in the form

$$\frac{dx}{dy} = F(x, y) \qquad \text{------ (i)}$$

Step-2 Put $\dfrac{x}{y} = v$ or $x = vy$ $\qquad$ ------ (ii)

Step-3 Differentiating equation (ii) w.r.t. 'y' , we get

$$\frac{dx}{dy} = v + y.\frac{dv}{dy} \qquad \text{------ (iii)}$$

Step-4 Using eqns. (ii) & (iii) , x is eliminated from eqn. (i), and we proceed as follows:

$$v + y.\frac{dv}{dy} = F(y, v)$$

Step-5 Rearrange to separate the variables y and v as explained in variable separable method, and then integrate to obtain required solution.

<u>Example</u>

Solve the differential equation:

$$\left(1 + e^{\frac{x}{y}}\right) dx + e^{\frac{x}{y}}\left(1 - \frac{x}{y}\right) dy = 0$$

Solution

Step-1: Writing in the form, $\dfrac{dy}{dx} = F(x, y)$

$$\left(1 + e^{\frac{x}{y}}\right) dx + e^{\frac{x}{y}}\left(1 - \frac{x}{y}\right) dy = 0$$

$$\Rightarrow \quad \frac{dy}{dx} = \frac{-\left(1 + e^{\frac{x}{y}}\right)}{e^{\frac{x}{y}}\left(1 - \frac{x}{y}\right)} \qquad \text{........ .(i)}$$

Here, we can easily find that it is a homogeneous differential equation in the form, $\dfrac{dx}{dy} = f\left(\dfrac{x}{y}\right)$

So, we write eqn. (i) as

$$\frac{dx}{dy} = \frac{-e^{\frac{x}{y}}\left(1-\frac{x}{y}\right)}{1+e^{\frac{x}{y}}} \qquad \ldots\ldots\ldots(ii)$$

Step-2: Let $\quad \dfrac{x}{y} = v \quad$ or $\quad x = v\,y \quad$ ------(iii)

Step-3: Differentiating eqn.(ii) w.r.t. 'x', we get

$$\frac{dx}{dy} = v + y\frac{dv}{dy} \qquad \ldots\ldots\ldots(iv)$$

Step-4: using eqn.(iii) and (iv) , eqn.(ii) becomes

$$v + y\frac{dv}{dy} = \frac{-e^{v}(1-v)}{1+e^{v}}$$

Step-5: Simplifying and rearranging the terms,

$$y\frac{dv}{dy} = \frac{-e^{v}(1-v)}{1+e^{v}} - v$$

$$\Rightarrow \quad y\frac{dv}{dy} = \frac{-e^{v}(1-v)-v(1+e^{v})}{1+e^{v}}$$

$$\Rightarrow \quad y\frac{dv}{dy} = \frac{-e^{v}-v}{1+e^{v}}$$

$$\Rightarrow \quad \frac{1+e^{v}}{-e^{v}-v}\,dv = \frac{1}{y}\,dy$$

Integrating both sides,

$$-\int \frac{1+e^{v}}{e^{v}+v}\,dv = \int \frac{1}{y}\,dx$$

To solve LHS, substitute $\quad e^{v} + v = t$

$$\& \qquad (e^{v}+1)\,dv = dt$$

On substitution we get,

$$-\int \frac{1}{t}\,dt = \int \frac{1}{y}\,dx$$

[Apply the formula, $\int \dfrac{1}{x}\,dx = log\,|x| + C$ on both sides,

which is given in art 2.7 of chapter – Integral]

$$\Rightarrow \quad -log|\,t\,| = log\,|y| + C$$

$$\Rightarrow \quad -log|\,e^{v}+v| = log\,|y| + C$$

$$[\text{ putting back, } t = e^{v}+v\ ]$$

$$\Rightarrow \quad log\left|e^{\frac{x}{y}} + \frac{x}{y}\right| = -log\,|y| + C \qquad \ldots\ldots\ldots(v)$$

$$[\text{ putting back, } \tfrac{x}{y} = v \text{ from eqn.(iii)}]$$

Since in this equation all terms have log except constant term, we can convert constant C also in log to obtain a new constant say, $log\,|C_1|$

$\therefore$ We can write it as

$$\Rightarrow \quad log\left|e^{\frac{x}{y}} + \frac{x}{y}\right| = -log\,|y| + log\,|C_1|$$

$$\Rightarrow \quad log\left|e^{\frac{x}{y}} + \frac{x}{y}\right| = log\left|\frac{C_1}{y}\right|$$

$$\Rightarrow \quad e^{\frac{x}{y}} + \frac{x}{y} = \frac{\pm C_1}{y}$$

$$\Rightarrow \quad ye^{\frac{x}{y}} + x = K \text{ where } K = \pm C_1$$

This is the required solution.

4.3 Linear Differential Equation

- A differential equation in any of the two following forms **is a First Order Linear differential equation**:

(i) $\dfrac{dy}{dx} + P.y = Q$,

where P & Q *are constants or functions of* x

(ii) $\dfrac{dx}{dy} + P.x = Q$,

where P & Q *are constants or functions of* y

4.3.1 Procedure to solve linear differential equation

Form-1: $\qquad \dfrac{dy}{dx} + P.y = Q$

Step-1 Write the given differential equation in the form

$$\frac{dy}{dx} + P.y = Q \qquad\qquad ------(i)$$

where P & Q are constants or functions of x .

Step-2 Find a function of x called *Integrating Factor* , **I.F.** as

$$\textbf{I.F.} = e^{\int P dx} = ----$$

Step-3 If we multiply both sides of equation (i) by **I.F.** , it can be integrated.

However, we write the solution directly in the form:

$$y \times \textbf{(I.F.)} = \int Q \times (\textbf{I.F.})\,dx + C$$

Step-4 Now solve the integral on RHS to get the required solution.

<u>Example</u>

Solve the differential equation:

$(1 + x^2)\,dy + 2xy\,dx = cot\,x\,dx$, $(x \neq 0)$.

Solution

Step-1: Writing in the form, $\dfrac{dy}{dx} + P.y = Q$

$\qquad (1 + x^2)\,dy + 2xy\,dx = cot\,x\,dx$

$\Rightarrow \quad (1 + x^2)\, dy = cot\, x\, dx - 2xy\, dx$

$\Rightarrow \quad \dfrac{dy}{dx} = \dfrac{cot\, x - 2xy}{1 + x^2}$

$\Rightarrow \quad \dfrac{dy}{dx} = \dfrac{cot\, x}{1 + x^2} - \dfrac{2x\, y}{1 + x^2}$

$\Rightarrow \quad \dfrac{dy}{dx} + \dfrac{2x}{1 + x^2} y = \dfrac{cot\, x}{1+x^2}$

It is in the form $\dfrac{dy}{dx} + P.y = Q$

where $P = \dfrac{2x}{1+x^2}$ and $Q = \dfrac{cot\, x}{1+x^2}$ are both functions of x.

Step-2: Finding integrating factor, I.F.

$\text{I.F.} = e^{\int P dx}$

$\Rightarrow \quad \text{I.F.} = e^{\int \frac{2x}{1+x^2} dx}$

$$\text{Substitute } 1 + x^2 = t$$
$$\text{and } 2\, x\, dx = dt$$

$\Rightarrow \quad \text{I.F.} = e^{\int \frac{1}{t} dt}$

$= e^{log\, t} = t$

$\Rightarrow \quad \text{I.F.} = 1 + x^2$

Step-3: Writing solution of differential eqn.

Solution of given differential eqn. will be as follows.

$y\,(I.F.) = \int Q\,(I.F.)dx + C$

$\Rightarrow \quad y\,(1 + x^2) = \int \dfrac{cot\, x}{1+x^2}\,(1 + x^2)dx + C$

$\Rightarrow \quad y\,(1 + x^2) = \int cot\, x\, dx + C$

$\Rightarrow \quad y\,(1 + x^2) = log\,(sin\, x) + C$

This is the required solution.

<u>**Form-2:**</u> $\qquad \dfrac{dx}{dy} + P.x = Q$

Step-1 Write the given differential equation in the form

$\dfrac{dx}{dy} + P.x = Q \qquad\qquad ------ (i)$

where P & Q are constants or functions of y

Step-2 Find a function of y called *Integrating Factor* , **I.F.** as

$\text{I.F.} = e^{\int P dy} = ----$

Step-3 If we multiply both sides of equation (i) by **I.F.**, it can be integrated.

However, we write the solution directly in the form:

$$x \times (\text{I.F.}) = \int Q \times (\text{I.F.}) dy + C$$

Step-4 Now solve the integral on RHS to get the required solution.

Example

Solve the differential equation: $y\, dx + (x - y^2)\, dy = 0$.

Solution

Step-1: Writing in the form, $\dfrac{dx}{dy} + P.x = Q$

$$y\, dx + (x - y^2)\, dy = 0$$

$$\Rightarrow \quad \frac{dy}{dx} = \frac{-y}{x - y^2}$$

Observe that it can't be expressed in the form $\dfrac{dy}{dx} + P.y = Q$, where P & Q are constants or functions of x.

$\therefore$ We write it as:

$$\frac{dx}{dy} = \frac{x - y^2}{-y}$$

$$\Rightarrow \quad \frac{dx}{dy} = \frac{-x}{y} + y$$

$$\Rightarrow \quad \frac{dx}{dy} + \frac{1}{y} x = y$$

It is in the form $\dfrac{dx}{dy} + P.x = Q$

where $P = \dfrac{1}{y}$ and $Q = y$ are both functions of y.

Step-2: Finding integrating factor, I.F.

$$\text{I.F.} = e^{\int P dy}$$

$$\Rightarrow \quad \text{I.F.} = e^{\int \frac{1}{y} dy} = e^{\log y}$$

$$\Rightarrow \quad \text{I.F.} = y$$

Step-3: Writing solution of differential eqn.

Solution of given differential eqn. will be as follows.

$$x\,(I.F.) = \int Q\,(I.F.) dy + C$$

$$\Rightarrow \quad x\,y = \int y \cdot dy + C$$

$$\Rightarrow \quad x\,y = \int y^2\, dy + C$$

$$\Rightarrow \quad x\,y = \frac{y^3}{3} + C$$

This is the required solution.

Chapter-11   Vector Algebra

1   Basic Concepts

A quantity that needs **magnitude as well as direction,** *to be expressed, is called a vector quantity.*

- Geometrically, a vector is represented by an arrow whose head shows the direction of vector, and length indicates its magnitude.

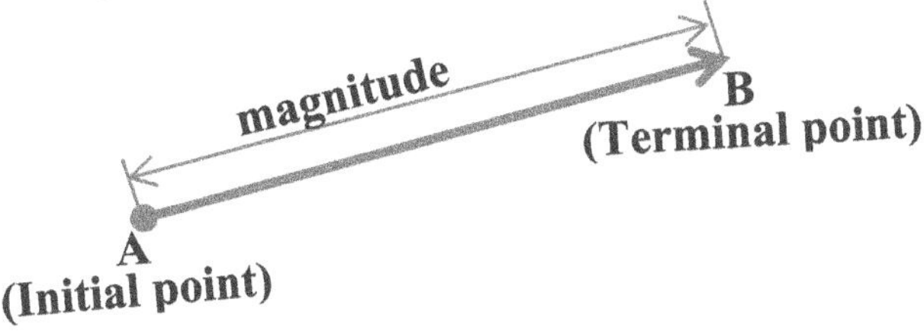

- The point from where this arrow starts is called *initial point*, and the point at which it ends is called *terminal point* of the vector.
- We can say that a directed line segment represents a vector.
- A vector from initial point A to terminal point B is denoted as $\overrightarrow{AB}$ and is read 'vector AB'
- It may also be denoted by a single letter as $\vec{a}, \vec{b}, \vec{c}$, etc., and read as 'vector a', 'vector b', 'vector c', etc.
- Magnitude of $\overrightarrow{AB}$ is denoted as $\left|\overrightarrow{AB}\right|$ or simply AB.
  Similarly, Magnitude of $\vec{a}$ is denoted as $|\vec{a}|$ or simply a.

    Magnitude of $\vec{b}$ is denoted as $|\vec{b}|$ or simply b.

    Magnitude of $\vec{c}$ is denoted as $|\vec{c}|$ or simply c.
- Since magnitude is distance between the initial and terminal points which can't be negative, the magnitude of a vector can't be negative.

    i.e., $\left|\overrightarrow{AB}\right| < 0$, $|\vec{a}| < 0$, etc., have no meaning.

Example

Represent a force of 40 N in the direction 30° east of north.

Solution

In the figure below, vector $\overrightarrow{AB}$ represent a force of 40 N in the direction 30° east of north.

The distance between two successive marks on AB represent a length of 10 N so that length of AB represents the magnitude of force, i.e., 40 N, and AB is making an angle of 30° with the north direction towards east.

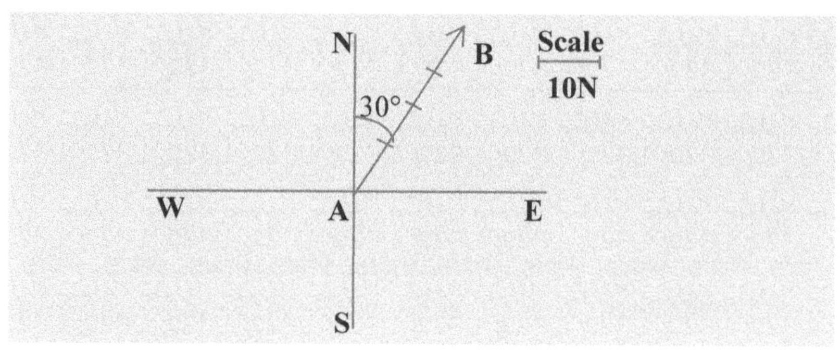

2 Types of Vectors

2.1 Zero Vector ($\vec{0}$)

A vector which has **same initial and terminal points** *is called zero vector.*

- It is denoted by $\vec{0}$.
- It has zero magnitude and no definite direction.
- We can say $\vec{0}$ **is just a point** which can't have any magnitude and direction.

2.2 Unit Vector (^)

A vector with **magnitude equal to 1,** *is called unit vector.*

- It is denoted by placing a cap (^) on a letter.

- $\hat{a}$ denotes unit vector in the direction of $\vec{a}$.

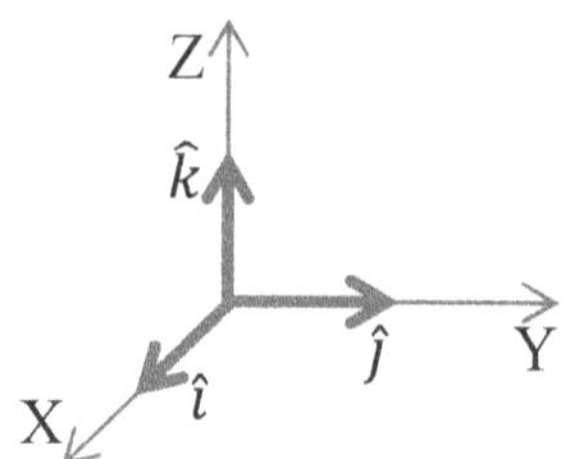

- $\hat{a} = \dfrac{\vec{a}}{|\vec{a}|}$

2.2.1 Unit vector along axes

We define unit vectors along axes as:

$\hat{i}$ = Unit vector in the positive direction of X-axis.

$\hat{j}$ = Unit vector in the positive direction of Y-axis.

$\hat{k}$ = Unit vector in the positive direction of Z-axis.

2.3 Coinitial Vectors

Two or more vectors having **same initial point,** *are called coinitial vectors.*

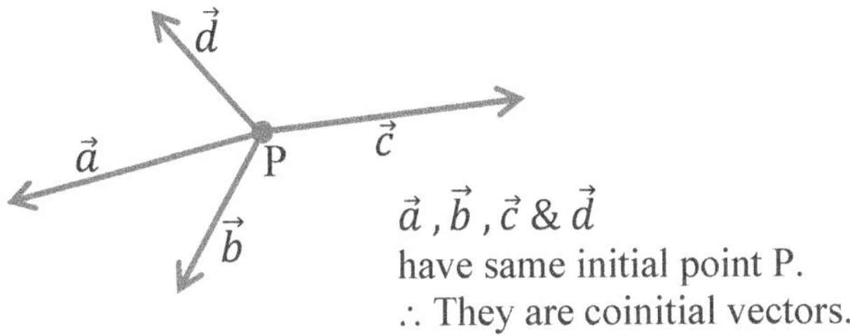

$\vec{a}, \vec{b}, \vec{c}$ & $\vec{d}$
have same initial point P.
∴ They are coinitial vectors.

2.4 Collinear Vectors

Two or more vectors, which are **parallel to the same line,** *are called collinear vectors.*

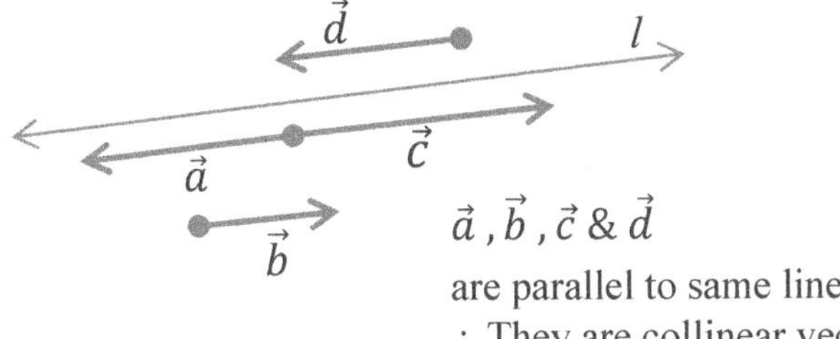

$\vec{a}, \vec{b}, \vec{c}$ & $\vec{d}$
are parallel to same line l.
∴ They are collinear vectors.

- They are either in same direction or opposite to each other.

2.5 Equal Vectors

Vectors having **same magnitude and same direction,** *are equal vectors.*

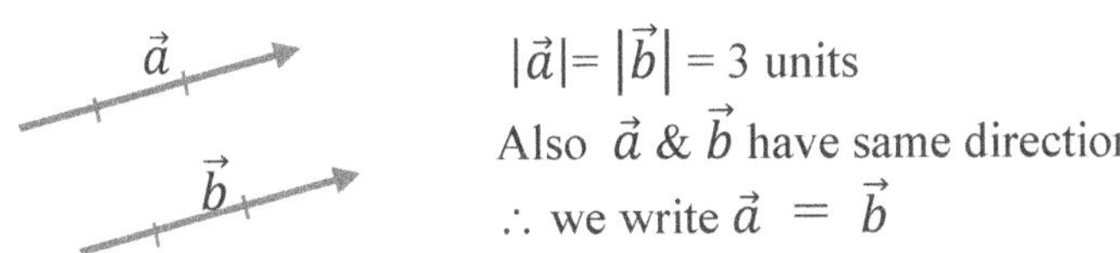

$|\vec{a}| = |\vec{b}| = 3$ units
Also $\vec{a}$ & $\vec{b}$ have same direction
∴ we write $\vec{a} = \vec{b}$

- They can have same or different initial points.

2.6 Negative Vector

A vector having **same magnitude** *as that of a given vector,* $\vec{a}$ *but* **opposite in direction** *is called negative vector of* $\vec{a}$.

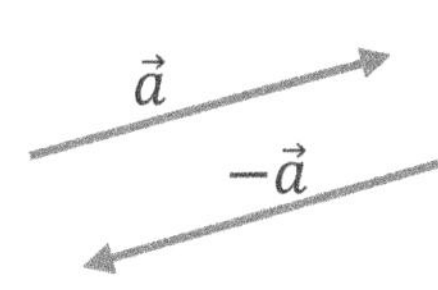

- Negative of $\vec{a}$ is written as $-\vec{a}$.

2.7 Free Vector

A vector, which can be displaced parallel to itself without change in its magnitude and direction, is called free vector.

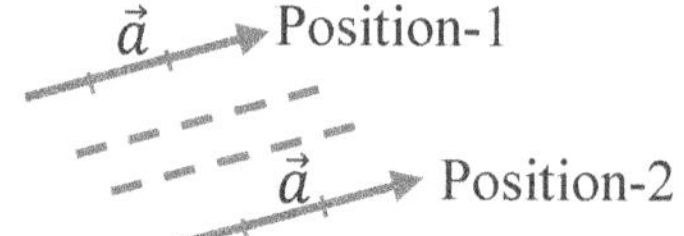

$\vec{a}$ is displaced parallel to itself from position-1 to position-2

3   Addition of Vectors

Vectors can be added using any of the following two laws:

(i) Triangle law   (ii) Parallelogram law

3.1   Addition by Triangle Law:

If 2 vectors are represented by 2 sides of a triangle (in magnitudes as well as in directions) such as the terminal point of one coincides with the initial point of other, then 3rd side of the triangle from initial point of first to the terminal point of the second, represents sum of these 2 vectors.

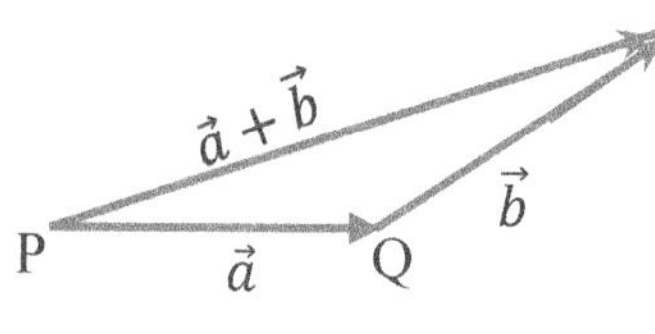

Terminal point of $\vec{a}$ (represented by side PQ) & initial point of $\vec{b}$ (represented by side QR) coincide at point Q.

$\therefore$ 3rd side PR represent $\vec{a}+\vec{b}$.

- The vector sum of 3 sides of a triangle taken in order is $\vec{0}$
  i.e., $\vec{a}+\vec{b}+\vec{c}=\vec{0}$ in the figure below.

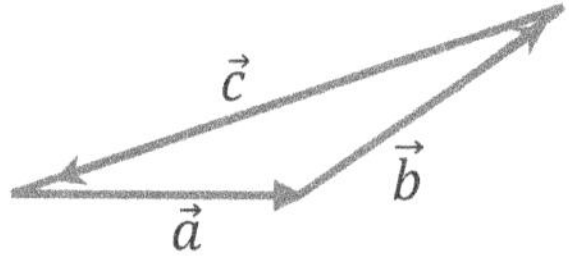

3.1.1   Procedure to add by triangle law

Given: Two vectors $\vec{a}$ & $\vec{b}$ as shown below:

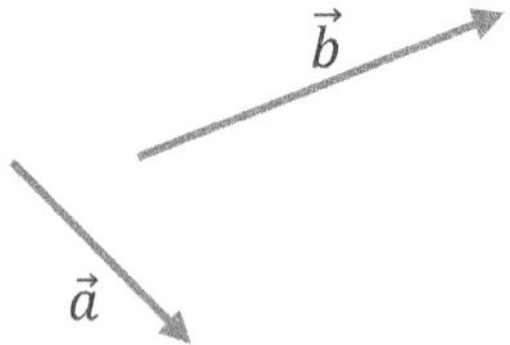

Step-1 Draw an arrow in the direction of $\vec{a}$, whose length is equal to $|\vec{a}|$.

Label its initial point and terminal point (say A and B respectively).

Step-2 From the head of $\overrightarrow{AB}$ i.e., from point B, draw another arrow in the direction of $\vec{b}$ with length $|\vec{b}|$. Its initial point is B. Label the terminal point (say C).

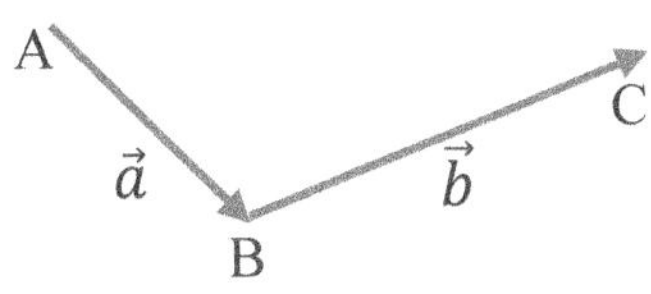

Step-3 Now Join A to C to form a triangle. The vector $\overrightarrow{AC}$ represents the sum $\left(\vec{a}+\vec{b}\right)$ with initial point A and terminal point C.

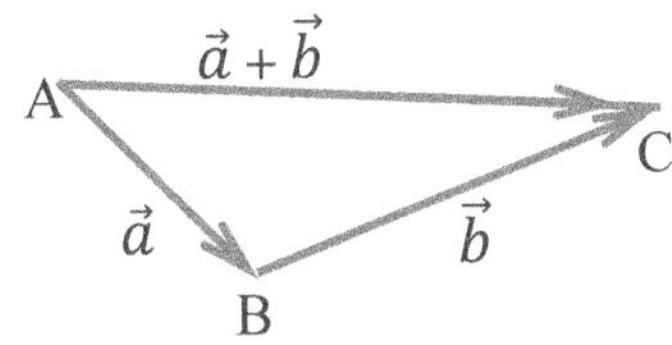

3.2   Addition by Parallelogram Law:

If 2 vectors are represented by 2 adjacent sides of a parallelogram (in magnitudes as well as in directions) with same initial point, then the diagonal of parallelogram which is coinitial with them, represents the sum of the given vectors.

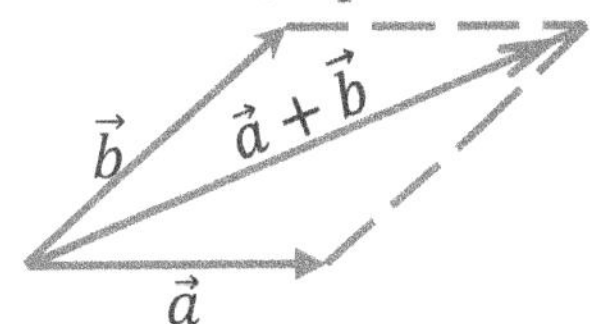

3.2.1   Procedure to add by parallelogram law

Given: Two vectors $\vec{a}$ & $\vec{b}$ as shown below:

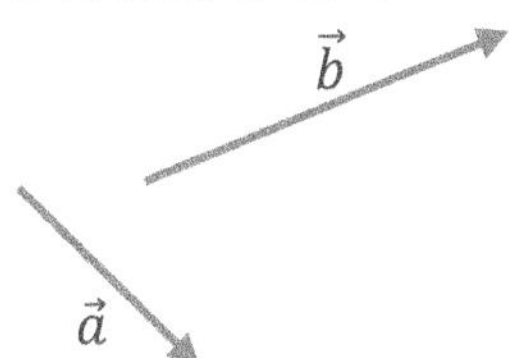

Step-1 Draw an arrow in the direction of $\vec{a}$, whose length is equal to $|\vec{a}|$. Label its initial point and terminal point (say A and B respectively).

Step-2 From the initial point of $\overrightarrow{AB}$ i.e., from point A, draw another arrow in the direction of $\vec{b}$ with length $|\vec{b}|$. Label the terminal point (say D).

---

*Asterisk (*) marked article (if any) is **not** in CBSE 2025-26 syllabus.*

Step-3 Now complete the parallelogram ABCD by drawing $BC \parallel AD$ and $DC \parallel AB$ as shown in the adjoining figure.

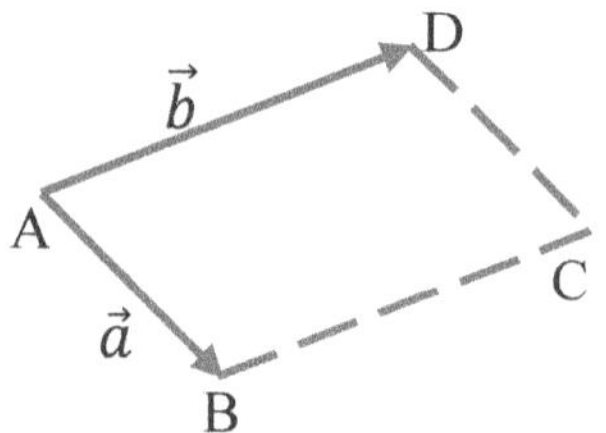

Step-4 Join A to C to obtain the diagonal AC. The vector $\overrightarrow{AC}$ represents the sum $\left(\vec{a} + \vec{b}\right)$ with initial point A and terminal point C.

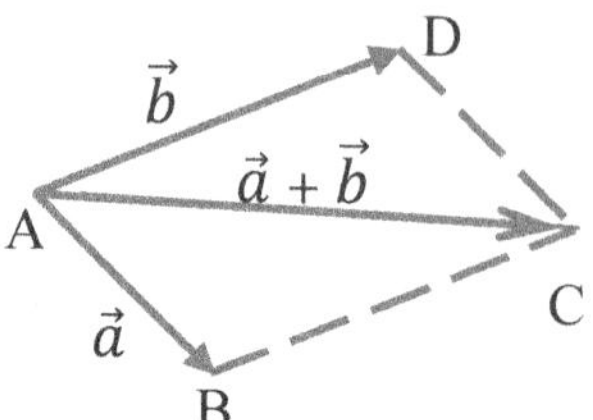

3.3 Properties of Vector addition

(i) **Commutative:** $\quad \vec{a} + \vec{b} = \vec{b} + \vec{a}$

(ii) **Associative:** $\quad \left(\vec{a} + \vec{b}\right) + \vec{c} = \vec{a} + \left(\vec{b} + \vec{c}\right)$

(iii) **Additive identity** of Vector Addition is $\vec{0}$ i.e., $\vec{a} + \vec{0} = \vec{a}$

4 Multiplication of a Vector by a scalar (λ)

When a vector $\vec{a}$ is multiplied by a scalar λ then it becomes $\lambda\vec{a}$.

(i) If λ is positive, then magnitude of new vector is λ times $|\vec{a}|$, and its direction is same as that of $\vec{a}$.

i.e., $|\lambda\vec{a}| = \lambda|\vec{a}|$, and direction of $\lambda\vec{a}$ is same as that of $\vec{a}$. (*See* figure below.)

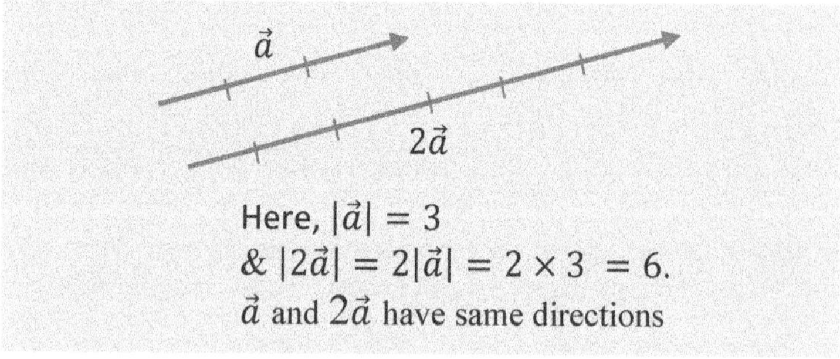

- From this we can conclude the formula: $\quad \hat{a} = \dfrac{\vec{a}}{|\vec{a}|}$

(ii) If λ is negative, then magnitude of new vector is $|\lambda|$ times $|\vec{a}|$, and its direction is opposite to $\vec{a}$.

i.e., $|\lambda\vec{a}| = |\lambda|\,|\vec{a}|$, and direction of $\lambda\vec{a}$ is opposite to that of $\vec{a}$. (*See* figure below.)

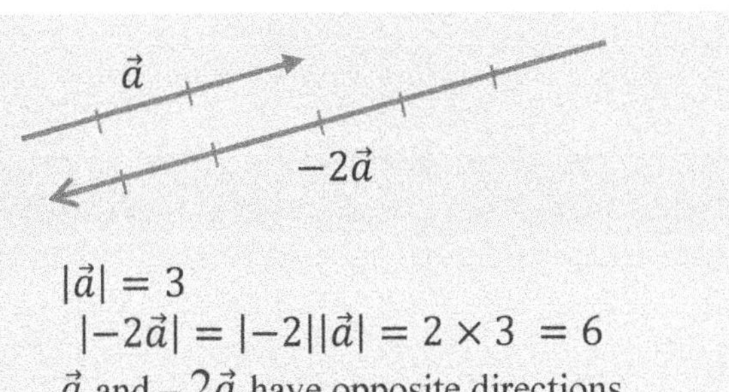

$$|\vec{a}| = 3$$
$$|-2\vec{a}| = |-2||\vec{a}| = 2 \times 3 = 6$$
$\vec{a}$ and $-2\vec{a}$ have opposite directions

(iii) From the above points (i) and (ii), we can conclude that

- If $\vec{a} = \lambda\,\vec{b}$ for some scalar λ, then $\vec{a}\ \&\ \vec{b}$ are collinear vectors. (i.e., they are either in same direction or opposite to each other.)

- Also, if $\vec{a}\ \&\ \vec{b}$ are collinear vectors, then $\vec{a} = \lambda\,\vec{b}$ for some scalar λ.

5 Position Vector of a Point

Vector from the origin to the point P(x, y, z), is known as the position vector of point P.

i.e., $\overrightarrow{OP}$ is position vector of point P.

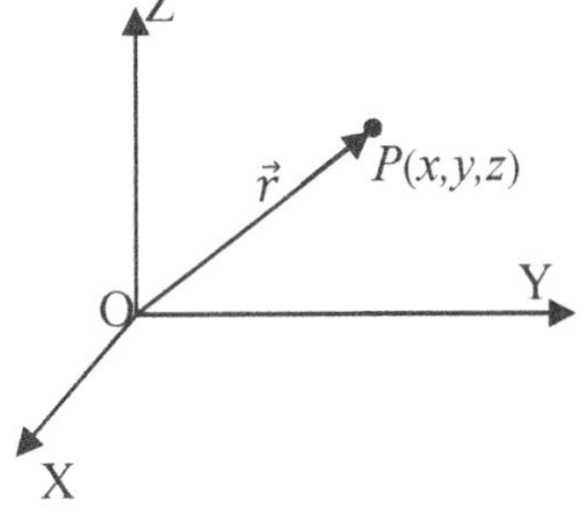

- Position vector is usually denoted by $\vec{r}$.

- In terms of components along X, Y and Z axes, position vector of P(x, y, z) can be found by parallelogram law of vector addition easily and that comes out to be,

$$\vec{r} = \overrightarrow{OP} = x\,\hat{\imath} + y\,\hat{\jmath} + z\,\hat{k}$$

- Magnitude of $\overrightarrow{OP}$ is
$$|\vec{r}| = \sqrt{x^2 + y^2 + z^2}$$

- $x, y,$ and z are called *scalar components* of $\vec{r}$.

- $x\,\hat{\imath},\ y\,\hat{\jmath}$ and $z\,\hat{k}$ are called *vector components* of $\vec{r}$.

- They are also termed as rectangular components of $\vec{r}$.

Example

Write the position vector of point A whose coordinates are (1,2,–3). Also find its magnitude.

Solution

Rectangular components of position vector of a point are its coordinates.

$\therefore$ Position vector of A is $\overrightarrow{OA} = \hat{\imath} + 2\hat{\jmath} - 3\hat{k}$.

And magnitude of $\overrightarrow{OA} = |\overrightarrow{OA}| = \sqrt{1^2 + 2^2 + (-3)^2} = \sqrt{14}$

5.1 Direction Angles of position vector

Angles made by a vector with positive directions of X, Y and Z-axes are called direction angles of the vector.

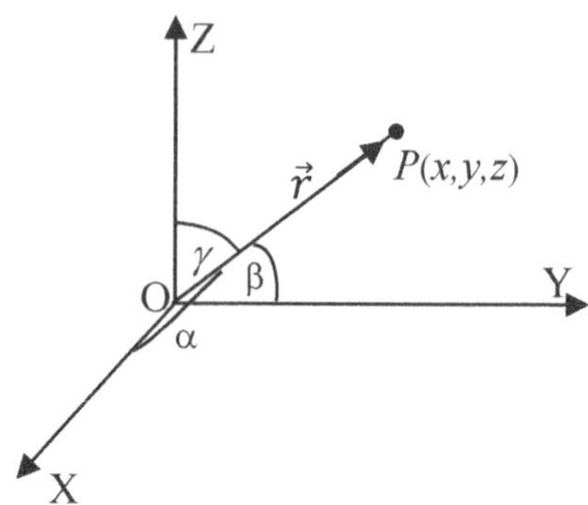

- Directional angles are, usually, denoted by α, β and γ respectively.
- α = angle made by the vector with +ve direction of X-axis.
  β = angle made by the vector with +ve direction of Y-axis.
  γ = angle made by the vector with +ve direction of Z-axis.

5.2 Direction Cosines (DCs) of position vector

Cosines of direction angles of a vector are called direction cosines of the vector.

i.e., *cos α, cos β, cos γ* are direction cosines of vector, where α, β and γ are direction angles.

- In short, we can write Direction Cosines as DCs.
- Direction Cosines are usually denoted by **l, m, n**
- $l^2 + m^2 + n^2 = 1$
- For a position vector $\vec{r} = x\hat{\imath} + y\hat{\jmath} + z\hat{k}$, if we draw perpendiculars on X, Y and Z-axis from its terminal point $P(x,y,z)$, we find that

$$l = \cos\alpha = \frac{x}{|\vec{r}|}$$

$$m = \cos\beta = \frac{y}{|\vec{r}|}$$

$$n = \cos\gamma = \frac{z}{|\vec{r}|}$$

Explanation

We can obtain direction cosines by drawing perpendiculars from point P on respective X, Y & Z-axes.

$$l = \cos\alpha = \frac{x}{|\vec{r}|} \qquad m = \cos\beta = \frac{y}{|\vec{r}|} \qquad n = \cos\gamma = \frac{z}{|\vec{r}|}$$

$$l^2 + m^2 + n^2 = \frac{x^2 + y^2 + z^2}{|\vec{r}|^2} = \frac{|\vec{r}|^2}{|\vec{r}|^2} = 1 \quad (\because \; x^2 + y^2 + z^2 = |\vec{r}|^2)$$

Example

Find the direction cosines of vector $\vec{r} = \hat{\imath} + 2\hat{\jmath} - 3\hat{k}$, and verify the relation, $l^2 + m^2 + n^2 = 1$.

Solution

Scalar component of $\vec{r}$ in x-direction is, $x = 1$.
Scalar component of $\vec{r}$ in y-direction is, $y = 2$.
Scalar component of $\vec{r}$ in z-direction is, $z = -3$.

$$\therefore |\vec{r}| = \sqrt{1^2 + 2^2 + (-3)^2} = \sqrt{14}$$

Direction cosines are:

$$l = \frac{x}{|\vec{r}|} = \frac{1}{\sqrt{14}} \;, \qquad m = \frac{y}{|\vec{r}|} = \frac{2}{\sqrt{14}} \;, \qquad n = \frac{z}{|\vec{r}|} = \frac{-3}{\sqrt{14}}$$

We write DCs are $\dfrac{1}{\sqrt{14}}, \dfrac{2}{\sqrt{14}}, \dfrac{-3}{\sqrt{14}}$.

$$\text{Now } l^2 + m^2 + n^2 = \left(\frac{1}{\sqrt{14}}\right)^2 + \left(\frac{2}{\sqrt{14}}\right)^2 + \left(\frac{-3}{\sqrt{14}}\right)^2 = 1$$

5.3 Direction Ratios (DRs)

The numbers proportional to the direction cosines of a vector, are called its direction ratios.

- In short, we can write Direction Ratios as DRs.
- They are usually denoted by **a, b, c**.
- If **l, m, n** are DCs , and **a, b, c** are DRs of a vector, then

$$\frac{l}{a} = \frac{m}{b} = \frac{n}{c}$$

- Also from the above relation, we can find that

$$l = \frac{a}{\sqrt{a^2+b^2+c^2}}, \; m = \frac{b}{\sqrt{a^2+b^2+c^2}} , n = \frac{c}{\sqrt{a^2+b^2+c^2}}$$

- As stated earlier that for vector $\vec{r} = x\,\hat{\imath} + y\,\hat{\jmath} + z\,\hat{k}$,

$$l = \frac{x}{|\vec{r}|} \;, \quad m = \frac{y}{|\vec{r}|} \quad \text{and } n = \frac{z}{|\vec{r}|}$$

$\Rightarrow l : m : n = x : y : z$

$\therefore$ Its DRs are x, y, z (because ratio of DCs are Drs)

It means the scalar components of a vector are DRs of the vector.

i.e., if vector is $\vec{r} = x\,\hat{i} + y\,\hat{j} + z\,\hat{k}$, then its DRs are x, y, z

- DCs of a vector are **unique**, but DRs are **not unique**.

<u>**Example**</u>

If direction angles of a vector are 30°, 60°, 90°, then find its DCs and DRs.

Solution

Here, we have $\alpha = 30°$, $\beta = 60°$, $\gamma = 90°$

DCs are given by $\cos \alpha$, $\cos \beta$, $\cos \gamma$

$\therefore$ DCs are $\cos 30°$, $\cos 60°$, $\cos 90°$

i.e., $\quad \dfrac{\sqrt{3}}{2}, \dfrac{1}{2}, 0$

DRs are numbers proportional to DCs.

i.e., DRs can be found as $\dfrac{\sqrt{3}}{2} : \dfrac{1}{2} : 0$

$\therefore$ DRs are $\sqrt{3}, 1, 0$

$\longrightarrow$ $\because$ There are many numbers which have same ratios, there are infinite DRs. Other DRs can be $2\sqrt{3}, 2, 0$; $3\sqrt{3}, 3, 0$, etc., which can be obtained by multiplying the DCs by any positive real number.

<u>**Example**</u>

Write the direction ratios of the vector $\vec{r} = \hat{i} + 2\hat{j} - 3\hat{k}$. Hence find its DCs.

Solution

Direction ratios of a vector are its scalar components.

$\therefore$ DRs of given vector are 1, 2, –3.

$\longrightarrow$ Numbers proportional to above DRs are also DRs of given vector.

e.g., 2, 4, –6 or 3, 6, –9 are also its DRs.

Now DCs are given by

$$l = \frac{a}{\sqrt{a^2+b^2+c^2}}, \quad m = \frac{b}{\sqrt{a^2+b^2+c^2}}, \quad n = \frac{c}{\sqrt{a^2+b^2+c^2}}$$

$$l = \frac{1}{\sqrt{1^2+2^2+(-3)^2}}, \quad m = \frac{2}{\sqrt{1^2+2^2+(-3)^2}}, \quad n = \frac{-3}{\sqrt{1^2+2^2+(-3)^2}}$$

$\therefore$ DCs are $\dfrac{1}{\sqrt{14}}, \dfrac{2}{\sqrt{14}}, \dfrac{-3}{\sqrt{14}}$

6   Vector joining two points

$$Required\ vector = \begin{pmatrix} Position\ vector \\ of\ terminal\ point \end{pmatrix} - \begin{pmatrix} Position\ vector \\ of\ initial\ point \end{pmatrix}$$

- **Given:** coordinates of two points $A(x_1, y_1, z_1)$ and $B(x_2, y_2, z_2)$

  Position vector of A is $\overrightarrow{OA} = \overrightarrow{r_1} = x_1\hat{\imath} + y_1\hat{\jmath} + z_1\hat{k}$

  Position vector of B is $\overrightarrow{OB} = \overrightarrow{r_2} = x_2\hat{\imath} + y_2\hat{\jmath} + z_2\hat{k}$

  - $\overrightarrow{AB}$ = (Position vector of B) − (Position vector of A)

    $\Rightarrow \overrightarrow{AB} = (x_2 - x_1)\hat{\imath} + (y_2 - y_1)\hat{\jmath} + (z_2 - z_1)\hat{k}$

  - $\overrightarrow{BA}$ = (Position vector of A) − (Position vector of B)

    $\Rightarrow \overrightarrow{BA} = (x_1 - x_2)\hat{\imath} + (y_1 - y_2)\hat{\jmath} + (z_1 - z_2)\hat{k}$

Explanation

Consider two points $A(x_1, y_1, z_1)$ and $B(x_2, y_2, z_2)$ as shown in the figure below.

By triangle law of vector addition, we see that $\overrightarrow{OA} + \overrightarrow{AB} = \overrightarrow{OB}$

$$\Rightarrow \overrightarrow{AB} = \overrightarrow{OB} - \overrightarrow{OA} = \overrightarrow{r_2} - \overrightarrow{r_1}$$

$$= \begin{pmatrix} Position\ vector \\ of\ terminal\ point \end{pmatrix} - \begin{pmatrix} Position\ vector \\ of\ initial\ point \end{pmatrix}$$

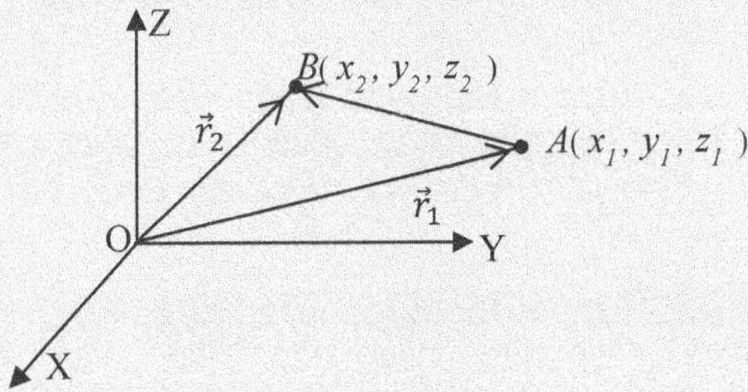

Similarly, by triangle law of vector addition we can also find that

$$\overrightarrow{OB} + \overrightarrow{BA} = \overrightarrow{OA}$$

$$\Rightarrow \overrightarrow{BA} = \overrightarrow{OA} - \overrightarrow{OB} = \overrightarrow{r_1} - \overrightarrow{r_2}$$

$$= \begin{pmatrix} Position\ vector \\ of\ terminal\ point \end{pmatrix} - \begin{pmatrix} Position\ vector \\ of\ initial\ point \end{pmatrix}$$

(i) Since,

$$\overrightarrow{AB} = (x_2 - x_1)\hat{\imath} + (y_2 - y_1)\hat{\jmath} + (z_2 - z_1)\hat{k}\ ,\ \text{we have}$$

- The scalar components of $\overrightarrow{AB}$: $(x_2 - x_1), (y_2 - y_1), (z_2 - z_1)$

- The vector components of $\overrightarrow{AB}$: $(x_2 - x_1)\hat{\imath}, (y_2 - y_1)\hat{\jmath}, (z_2 - z_1)\hat{k}$

- $\left|\overrightarrow{AB}\right| = \sqrt{(x_2 - x_1)^2 + (y_2 - y_1)^2 + (z_2 - z_1)^2}$

---

*Asterisk (*) marked article (if any) is **not** in CBSE 2025-26 syllabus.*

DRs and DCs of $\overrightarrow{AB}$

It is discussed earlier that the scalar components of position vector of a point are its DRs (*in art 5.3*). This is applicable for a vector joining two points also.

- Scalar components of a vector are its DRs.

  $\therefore$ DRs of $\overrightarrow{AB}$ are $(x_2 - x_1), (y_2 - y_1), (z_2 - z_1)$

- DCs of $\overrightarrow{AB}$ i.e., *l, m, n* are found as

$$l = \cos\alpha = \frac{x_2 - x_1}{|\overrightarrow{AB}|}$$

$$m = \cos\beta = \frac{y_2 - y_1}{|\overrightarrow{AB}|}$$

$$n = \cos\gamma = \frac{z_2 - z_1}{|\overrightarrow{AB}|}$$

where $\begin{cases} \alpha = \text{angle made by } \overrightarrow{AB} \text{ with } +\text{ve x-axis} \\ \beta = \text{angle made by } \overrightarrow{AB} \text{ with } +\text{ve y-axis} \\ \gamma = \text{angle made by } \overrightarrow{AB} \text{ with } +\text{ve z-axis} \end{cases}$

(ii) Similarly,

$$\overrightarrow{BA} = (x_1 - x_2)\,\hat{\imath} + (y_1 - y_2)\,\hat{\jmath} + (z_1 - z_2)\,\hat{k}$$

- The scalar components of $\overrightarrow{BA}$: $(x_1 - x_2), (y_1 - y_2), (z_1 - z_2)$
- The vector components of $\overrightarrow{BA}$: $(x_1 - x_2)\hat{\imath}, (y_1 - y_2)\hat{\jmath}, (z_1 - z_2)\hat{k}$
- $|\overrightarrow{BA}| = \sqrt{(x_1 - x_2)^2 + (y_1 - y_2)^2 + (z_1 - z_2)^2}$

DRs and DCs of $\overrightarrow{BA}$

- Scalar components of a vector are its DRs

  $\therefore$ DRs of $\overrightarrow{BA}$ are $(x_1 - x_2), (y_1 - y_2), (z_1 - z_2)$

- DCs of $\overrightarrow{BA}$ i.e., *l, m, n* are found as

$$l = \cos\alpha = \frac{x_1 - x_2}{|\overrightarrow{AB}|}$$

$$m = \cos\beta = \frac{y_1 - y_2}{|\overrightarrow{AB}|}$$

$$n = \cos\gamma = \frac{z_1 - z_2}{|\overrightarrow{AB}|}$$

where $\begin{cases} \alpha = \text{angle made by } \overrightarrow{BA} \text{ with } +\text{ve x-axis} \\ \beta = \text{angle made by } \overrightarrow{BA} \text{ with } +\text{ve y-axis} \\ \gamma = \text{angle made by } \overrightarrow{BA} \text{ with } +\text{ve z-axis} \end{cases}$

(iii) From the above points (i) and (ii) we conclude that

- $\overrightarrow{AB} = -\overrightarrow{BA}$ i.e., $\overrightarrow{AB}$ and $\overrightarrow{BA}$ have same magnitudes, but they have opposite direction.
- $\overrightarrow{AB} \neq \overrightarrow{BA}$ but $|\overrightarrow{AB}| = |\overrightarrow{BA}|$

<u>**Example**</u>

If coordinates of two points A & B are $(1,2,3)$ and $(3,-2,4)$, find the vector $\overrightarrow{AB}$ and $\overrightarrow{BA}$. Also find their DRs and DCs.

Solution

Rectangular components of position vector of a point are its coordinates.

$\therefore$ Position vector of A is $\overrightarrow{OA} = \hat{\imath} + 2\hat{\jmath} + 3\hat{k}$.

And position vector of B is $\overrightarrow{OB} = 3\hat{\imath} - 2\hat{\jmath} + 4\hat{k}$.

Now $\overrightarrow{AB} = \overrightarrow{OB} - \overrightarrow{OA}$ and $\overrightarrow{BA} = \overrightarrow{OA} - \overrightarrow{OB}$

$\therefore$ $\overrightarrow{AB} = 2\hat{\imath} - 4\hat{\jmath} + \hat{k}$ and $\overrightarrow{BA} = -2\hat{\imath} + 4\hat{\jmath} - \hat{k}$

We know that DRs of a vector are its scalar components.

$\therefore$ DRs of $\overrightarrow{AB}$ are $2, -4, 1$

And DRs of $\overrightarrow{BA}$ are $-2, 4, -1$

DCs can be found from DRs by using

$$l = \frac{a}{\sqrt{a^2+b^2+c^2}} \ , \quad m = \frac{b}{\sqrt{a^2+b^2+c^2}} \ , \quad n = \frac{c}{\sqrt{a^2+b^2+c^2}}$$

For $\overrightarrow{AB}$, we get

$$l = \frac{2}{\sqrt{2^2+(-4)^2+1^2}} \ , \quad m = \frac{-4}{\sqrt{2^2+(-4)^2+1^2}} \ , \quad n = \frac{1}{\sqrt{2^2+(-4)^2+1^2}}$$

$\therefore$ DCs of $\overrightarrow{AB}$ are $\dfrac{2}{\sqrt{21}}, \dfrac{-4}{\sqrt{21}}, \dfrac{1}{\sqrt{21}}$

For $\overrightarrow{BA}$, we get

$$l = \frac{-2}{\sqrt{(-2)^2+4^2+(-1)^2}} \ , \quad m = \frac{4}{\sqrt{(-2)^2+4^2+(-1)^2}} \ , \quad n = \frac{-1}{\sqrt{(-2)^2+4^2+(-1)^2}}$$

$\therefore$ DCs of $\overrightarrow{AB}$ are $\dfrac{-2}{\sqrt{21}}, \dfrac{4}{\sqrt{21}}, \dfrac{-1}{\sqrt{21}}$

7   Treating vectors in rectangular components

7.1   Unit Vector in component form

- For $\vec{a} = x\hat{\imath} + y\hat{\jmath} + z\hat{k}$

  unit vector in the direction of $\vec{a}$ is found as

$$\hat{a} = \frac{\vec{a}}{|\vec{a}|} \qquad \text{i.e.,} \qquad \hat{a} = \frac{x\hat{\imath} + y\hat{\jmath} + z\hat{k}}{\sqrt{x^2+y^2+z^2}}$$

- Scalar components of a unit vector are its DCs.

i.e., if l, m, n are DCs of $\vec{a}$

then $\hat{a} = l\,\hat{\imath} + m\,\hat{\jmath} + n\,\hat{k}$

Example

Write the unit vector in the direction of $\vec{a} = 4\,\hat{\imath} - 3\,\hat{\jmath} + 5\,\hat{k}$.
Write the scalar components of this unit vector. Hence, write DCs of $\vec{a}$.

Solution

$\vec{a} = 4\,\hat{\imath} - 3\,\hat{\jmath} + 5\,\hat{k}$

$|\vec{a}| = \sqrt{4^2 + (-3)^2 + 5^2} = \sqrt{50} = 5\sqrt{2}$

Now $\hat{a} = \dfrac{\vec{a}}{|\vec{a}|}$

$\therefore$ Required unit vector is:

$$\hat{a} = \frac{4\,\hat{\imath} - 3\,\hat{\jmath} + 5\,\hat{k}}{5\sqrt{2}}$$

$$\Rightarrow \quad \hat{a} = \frac{4}{5\sqrt{2}}\,\hat{\imath} - \frac{3}{5\sqrt{2}}\,\hat{\jmath} + \frac{1}{\sqrt{2}}\,\hat{k}$$

Its scalar components are $\dfrac{4}{5\sqrt{2}}, \dfrac{-3}{5\sqrt{2}}, \dfrac{1}{\sqrt{2}}$

We know that scalar components of a unit vector are DCs of the vector.

$\therefore$ DCs of $\vec{a}$ are $\dfrac{4}{5\sqrt{2}}, \dfrac{-3}{5\sqrt{2}}, \dfrac{1}{\sqrt{2}}$.

7.2 Sum and Difference of vectors in component forms

For $\vec{a} = a_1\,\hat{\imath} + a_2\,\hat{\jmath} + a_3\,\hat{k}$ and $\vec{b} = b_1\,\hat{\imath} + b_2\,\hat{\jmath} + b_3\,\hat{k}$

- $\vec{a} + \vec{b} = (a_1 + b_1)\hat{\imath} + (a_2 + b_2)\hat{\jmath} + (a_3 + b_3)\hat{k}$
- $\vec{a} - \vec{b} = (a_1 - b_1)\hat{\imath} + (a_2 - b_2)\hat{\jmath} + (a_3 - b_3)\hat{k}$

Example

Two vectors are $\vec{a} = 4\,\hat{\imath} - 3\,\hat{\jmath} + 5\,\hat{k}$ and $\vec{b} = \hat{\imath} - 3\,\hat{\jmath} + 2\,\hat{k}$.
Find $\vec{a} + \vec{b}$ and $\vec{a} - \vec{b}$.

Solution

$$\vec{a} + \vec{b} = \left(4\,\hat{\imath} - 3\,\hat{\jmath} + 5\,\hat{k}\right) + \left(\hat{\imath} - 3\,\hat{\jmath} + 2\,\hat{k}\right)$$

$$\Rightarrow \quad \vec{a} + \vec{b} = 5\,\hat{\imath} - 6\,\hat{\jmath} + 7\,\hat{k}$$

And $\quad \vec{a} - \vec{b} = \left(4\,\hat{\imath} - 3\,\hat{\jmath} + 5\,\hat{k}\right) - \left(\hat{\imath} - 3\,\hat{\jmath} + 2\,\hat{k}\right)$

$$\Rightarrow \quad \vec{a} - \vec{b} = 3\,\hat{\imath} + 3\,\hat{k}$$

7.3 Multiplication of vector in component form by a scalar

If $\vec{a} = a_1\,\hat{\imath} + a_2\,\hat{\jmath} + a_3\,\hat{k}$ and λ is a scalar, then

- $\lambda\,\vec{a} = \lambda(a_1\,\hat{\imath} + a_2\,\hat{\jmath} + a_3\,\hat{k}) = \lambda a_1\hat{\imath} + a_2\hat{\jmath} + \lambda a_3\hat{k}$

Example

If $\vec{a} = 4\hat{\imath} - 3\hat{\jmath} + 5\hat{k}$, then find $-\frac{1}{3}\vec{a}$.

Solution

$$-\frac{1}{3}\vec{a} = -\frac{1}{3}\left(4\hat{\imath} - 3\hat{\jmath} + 5\hat{k}\right) = -\frac{4}{3}\hat{\imath} + \hat{\jmath} - \frac{5}{3}\hat{k}$$

7.4 Collinearity of vectors

We now know that

(i) If $\vec{a} = \lambda\vec{b}$ for some scalar λ, then $\vec{a}$ & $\vec{b}$ are collinear vectors.

(ii) If $\vec{a}$ & $\vec{b}$ are collinear vectors, then $\vec{a} = \lambda\vec{b}$ for some scalar λ .

In component form we conclude the following:

Two vectors are collinear if and only if their corresponding components are in proportion.

- For $\vec{a} = a_1\hat{\imath} + a_2\hat{\jmath} + a_3\hat{k}$ and $\vec{b} = b_1\hat{\imath} + b_2\hat{\jmath} + b_3\hat{k}$

  (i) If $\dfrac{a_1}{b_1} = \dfrac{a_2}{b_2} = \dfrac{a_3}{b_3}$

  then $\vec{a}$ & $\vec{b}$ are collinear vectors.

  (ii) If $\vec{a}$ & $\vec{b}$ are collinear vectors,

  then $\dfrac{a_1}{b_1} = \dfrac{a_2}{b_2} = \dfrac{a_3}{b_3}$

<u>Example</u>

Check whether the vectors $\vec{a} = -2\hat{\imath} + 6\hat{\jmath} - 4\hat{k}$ and $\vec{b} = \hat{\imath} - 3\hat{\jmath} + 2\hat{k}$ are collinear or not. If they are collinear, then write them in the form $\vec{a} = \lambda\vec{b}$, and find whether they are in same direction or opposite to each other.

Solution

Here, the components of $\vec{a}$ are

$$a_1 = -2, \quad a_2 = 6, \, a_3 = -4$$

and the components of $\vec{b}$ are

$$b_1 = 1, \quad b_2 = -3, \quad b_3 = 2$$

Now, $\dfrac{a_1}{b_1} = \dfrac{-2}{1} = -2 ,$

$\dfrac{a_2}{b_2} = \dfrac{6}{-3} = -2 ,$

$\dfrac{a_3}{b_3} = \dfrac{-4}{2} = -2$

$\therefore \dfrac{a_1}{b_1} = \dfrac{a_2}{b_2} = \dfrac{a_3}{b_3}$

$\therefore \qquad \vec{a}$ and $\vec{b}$ are collinear vectors.

and $\quad \vec{a} = -2\,\vec{b}$

Here, negative sign shows that $\vec{a}$ and $\vec{b}$ are in opposite direction.

7.5 Equality of two vectors

Two vectors are equal if and only if their corresponding components are equal.

- For $\vec{a} = a_1\,\hat{\imath} + a_2\,\hat{\jmath} + a_3\,\hat{k}$ and $\quad \vec{b} = b_1\,\hat{\imath} + b_2\,\hat{\jmath} + b_3\,\hat{k}$

  (i) If $\quad a_1 = b_1\,,\quad a_2 = b_2\ \&\ a_3 = b_3$

  then $\quad \vec{a} = \vec{b}$

  (ii) If $\quad \vec{a} = \vec{b}$

  then $\quad a_1 = b_1\,,\quad a_2 = b_2\ \&\ a_3 = b_3$

Example

If the vectors $\vec{a} = -x\,\hat{\imath} + y\hat{\jmath} - z\,\hat{k}$ and $\vec{b} = \hat{\imath} - 3\hat{\jmath} + 2\,\hat{k}$ are equal, then find the values x, y, and z.

Solution

We know that if two vectors are equal, then their corresponding components are equal.

$\therefore \qquad -x = 1\,, \qquad y = -3\,, \qquad -z = 2$

$\Rightarrow \qquad x = -1\,, \qquad y = -3\,, \qquad z = -2$

8 Section Formula

8.1 Internal Division

If point P divides AB internally in the ratio $m : n$

i.e., PA : PB $= m : n$ in the figure and

$\vec{a}$ = position vector of point A

$\vec{b}$ = position vector of point B

$\vec{r}$ = position vector of point P

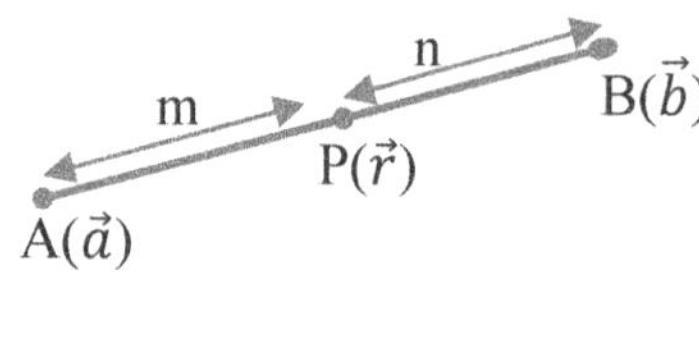

then $\quad \vec{r} = \dfrac{m\,\vec{b} + n\,\vec{a}}{m + n}$

- Observe that $\vec{b}$ is multiplied by m and $\vec{a}$ is multiplied by n. It means position vector of 1st point, A is multiplied by 2nd term, n of the ratio $m : n$ and vice-versa.

Example

Find the position vector of the point, which divides the line segment joining the 2 points with position vectors, $\vec{a}$ and $\vec{b}$, internally in the ratio $2 : 3$, where $\vec{a} = -2\hat{\imath} + 3\hat{\jmath} - 4\hat{k}$ and $\vec{b} = \hat{\imath} + \hat{\jmath} + \hat{k}$.

Solution

Using section formula for internal division, $\vec{r} = \dfrac{m\,\vec{b} + n\,\vec{a}}{m + n}$, the required position vector of the point is:

$$\vec{r} = \frac{2\,\vec{b} + 3\,\vec{a}}{2 + 3} = \frac{2(\hat{\imath} + \hat{\jmath} + \hat{k}) + 3(-2\hat{\imath} + 3\hat{\jmath} - 4\hat{k})}{5} = \frac{-4\hat{\imath} + 11\hat{\jmath} - 10\hat{k}}{5}$$

8.2 External Division

If point P divides AB externally in the ratio $m : n$

i.e., $\text{PA} : \text{PB} = m : n$ in

the figure and

$\vec{a}$ = position vector of point A

$\vec{b}$ = position vector of point B

$\vec{r}$ = position vector of point P

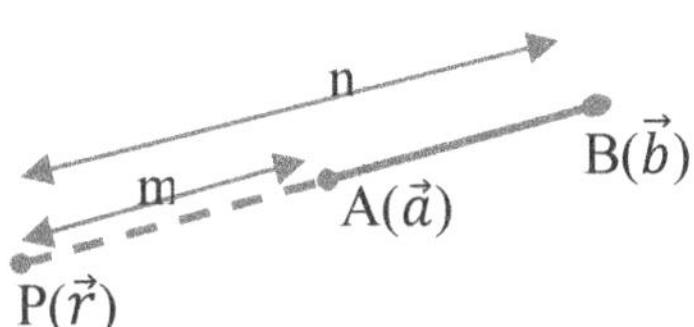

then $\quad \vec{r} = \dfrac{m\,\vec{b} - n\,\vec{a}}{m - n}$

Example

Find the position vector of the point, which divides the line segment joining the 2 points with position vectors, $\vec{a}$ and $\vec{b}$ externally in the ratio $1 : 2$, where $\vec{a} = -2\hat{\imath} + 3\hat{\jmath} - 4\hat{k}$ and $\vec{b} = \hat{\imath} + \hat{\jmath} + \hat{k}$.

Solution

Using section formula for internal division, $\vec{r} = \dfrac{m\,\vec{b} - n\,\vec{a}}{m - n}$, the required position vector of the point is:

$$\vec{r} = \frac{\vec{b} - 2\,\vec{a}}{1 - 2} = \frac{(\hat{\imath} + \hat{\jmath} + \hat{k}) - 2(-2\hat{\imath} + 3\hat{\jmath} - 4\hat{k})}{-1} = -5\hat{\imath} + 5\hat{\jmath} - 9\hat{k}$$

8.3 Mid-Point formula

If point P is mid-point of AB and

$\vec{a}$ = position vector of point A

$\vec{b}$ = position vector of point B

$\vec{r}$ = position vector of point P

then $\quad \vec{r} = \dfrac{\vec{a} + \vec{b}}{2}$

Example

Find the position vector of the mid-point of the line segment joining the 2 points, $\vec{a} = -2\hat{\imath} + 3\hat{\jmath} - 4\hat{k}$ and $\vec{b} = \hat{\imath} + \hat{\jmath} + \hat{k}$.

Solution

Using mid-point formula, $\vec{r} = \dfrac{\vec{a} + \vec{b}}{2}$, the required position vector of the mid-point is

$$\vec{r} \;=\; \frac{-2\hat{\imath} + 3\hat{\jmath} - 4\hat{k} + \hat{\imath} + \hat{\jmath} + \hat{k}}{2} = \frac{-\hat{\imath} + 4\hat{\jmath} - 3\hat{k}}{2}$$

9 Product of two vectors

Two types of products are: (i) scalar product and (ii) vector product

- In scalar product, the result of product is a scalar quantity.
- In vector product, the result of product is a vector quantity.

9.1 Scalar Product of two vectors (Dot Product)

- Scalar product is represented by a dot(.) between the two vectors.

  $\therefore$ it is also called as **dot product**.

9.1.1 Definition

$$\vec{a} \cdot \vec{b} = |\vec{a}|\,|\vec{b}|\ cos\ \theta$$

where θ is angle between $\vec{a}$ and $\vec{b}$

- Angle between two vectors exists from $0°$ to $180°$.

  i.e., $0 \le \theta \le \pi$ or $0° \le \theta \le 180°$

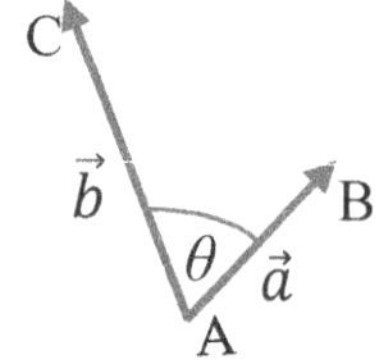

<u>Example</u>

Magnitudes of two vectors, $\vec{a}$ & $\vec{b}$, are 3 & 4 respectively. The angle between them is $30°$. Find their scalar product.

Solution

Here, $\quad |\vec{a}| = 3\,,\qquad |\vec{b}| = 4\,,\qquad \theta = 30°$

$$\therefore \vec{a}\cdot\vec{b} = |\vec{a}|\,|\vec{b}|\ cos\ \theta = (3)(4)\,cos30° = 12\left(\tfrac{\sqrt{3}}{2}\right) = 6\sqrt{3}$$

9.1.2 Observations from Definition

(i) For $0° \le \theta < 90°$, $\quad \vec{a}\cdot\vec{b} > 0$

  ($\vec{a}\cdot\vec{b}$ is positive for acute angles & $0°$ because $cos\theta$ is positive for these angles)

(ii) For $90° < \theta \le 180°$, $\vec{a}\cdot\vec{b} < 0$

  ($\vec{a}\cdot\vec{b}$ is negative for obtuse angles & $180°$ because $cos\theta$ is negative for these angles)

(iii) If $\vec{a} \perp \vec{b}$ then $\vec{a}\cdot\vec{b} = 0$

  ($\vec{a}\cdot\vec{b} = 0$ for $\theta = 90°$ because $cos90° = 0$)

(iv) If $\vec{a}$ and $\vec{b}$ are in same direction (i.e., for $\theta = 0°$), then

$$\vec{a}\cdot\vec{b} = |\vec{a}|\,|\vec{b}|$$

(v) If $\vec{a}$ and $\vec{b}$ are in opposite direction (i.e., for $\theta = 180°$), then $\vec{a}\cdot\vec{b} = -|\vec{a}|\,|\vec{b}|$

(vi) If $\vec{a} \cdot \vec{b} = 0$, then $\vec{a} \perp \vec{b}$ (provided $\vec{a} \neq \vec{0}$ & $\vec{b} \neq \vec{0}$)

9.1.3 Properties of Scalar Product

(i) **Commutative:** $\vec{a} \cdot \vec{b} = \vec{b} \cdot \vec{a}$

(Dot product is Commutative)

(ii) **Distributive:** $\vec{a} \cdot (\vec{b} \pm \vec{c}) = \vec{a} \cdot \vec{b} \pm \vec{a} \cdot \vec{c}$

(Dot product is Distributive over +, –)

9.1.4 Other Important Observations

(i) $\vec{a} \cdot \vec{a} = |\vec{a}|^2$

(Since angle between $\vec{a}$ & $\vec{a}$ is $0°$ and $cos0° = 1$

therefore, $\vec{a} \cdot \vec{a} = |\vec{a}||\vec{a}|cos0° = |\vec{a}|^2$)

(ii) $\hat{\imath} \cdot \hat{\imath} = 1$ $\qquad$ $\hat{\jmath} \cdot \hat{\jmath} = 1$ $\qquad$ $\hat{k} \cdot \hat{k} = 1$

(Since magnitude of $\hat{\imath}$ is 1 therefore, $\hat{\imath} \cdot \hat{\imath} = |\hat{\imath}|^2 = 1$.

Similarly, $\hat{\jmath} \cdot \hat{\jmath} = 1$ and $\hat{k} \cdot \hat{k} = 1$)

(iii) $\hat{\imath} \cdot \hat{\jmath} = 0$ $\qquad$ $\hat{\jmath} \cdot \hat{k} = 0$ $\qquad$ $\hat{k} \cdot \hat{\imath} = 0$

(Since $\hat{\imath} \perp \hat{\jmath}$ therefore, $\hat{\imath} \cdot \hat{\jmath} = |\hat{\imath}||\hat{\jmath}|cos90° = 0$.

Similarly, $\hat{\jmath} \cdot \hat{k} = 0$ and $\hat{k} \cdot \hat{\imath} = 0$)

9.1.5 Scalar product in terms of rectangular components

If $\vec{a} = a_1\,\hat{\imath} + a_2\,\hat{\jmath} + a_3\,\hat{k}$ and $\vec{b} = b_1\,\hat{\imath} + b_2\,\hat{\jmath} + b_3\,\hat{k}$,

then $\qquad \vec{a} \cdot \vec{b} = a_1 b_1 + a_2 b_2 + a_3 b_3$

<u>Explanation</u>

If $\vec{a} = a_1\,\hat{\imath} + a_2\,\hat{\jmath} + a_3\,\hat{k}$ and $\vec{b} = b_1\,\hat{\imath} + b_2\,\hat{\jmath} + b_3\,\hat{k}$,

then $\vec{a} \cdot \vec{b} = (a_1\,\hat{\imath} + a_2\,\hat{\jmath} + a_3\,\hat{k}) \cdot (b_1\,\hat{\imath} + b_2\,\hat{\jmath} + b_3\,\hat{k})$

$\qquad = a_1 b_1\hat{\imath} \cdot \hat{\imath} + a_1 b_2\hat{\imath} \cdot \hat{\jmath} + a_1 b_3\hat{\imath} \cdot \hat{k}$

$\qquad\quad + a_2 b_1\hat{\jmath} \cdot \hat{\imath} + a_2 b_2\hat{\jmath} \cdot \hat{\jmath} + a_2 b_3\hat{\jmath} \cdot \hat{k}$

$\qquad\quad + a_3 b_1\hat{k} \cdot \hat{\imath} + a_3 b_2\hat{k} \cdot \hat{\jmath} + a_3 b_3\hat{k} \cdot \hat{k}$

$\qquad = a_1 b_1 + a_2 b_2 + a_3 b_3$

(since $\hat{\imath} \cdot \hat{\imath} = 1,\ \hat{\jmath} \cdot \hat{\jmath} = 1,\ \hat{k} \cdot \hat{k} = 1$

$\hat{\imath} \cdot \hat{\jmath} = 0,\ \hat{\jmath} \cdot \hat{k} = 0,\ \hat{k} \cdot \hat{\imath} = 0$)

<u>Example</u>

Find the scalar product of vectors $\vec{a} = \hat{\imath} - \hat{\jmath} + 2\hat{k}$ and $\vec{b} = -2\hat{\imath} + 3\hat{\jmath} - 4\hat{k}$.

Solution

$\vec{a} \cdot \vec{b} = (\hat{\imath} - \hat{\jmath} + 2\hat{k}) \cdot (-2\hat{\imath} + 3\hat{\jmath} - 4\hat{k})$

$\qquad = (1)(-2) + (-1)(3) + (2)(-4) = -13$

$$[\text{Using } \vec{a} \cdot \vec{b} = (a_1\hat{\imath} + a_2\hat{\jmath} + a_3\hat{k}) \cdot (b_1\hat{\imath} + b_2\hat{\jmath} + b_3\hat{k})$$
$$= a_1 b_1 + a_2 b_2 + a_3 b_3]$$

9.1.6 Angle between 2 Vectors

$$cos\,\theta = \frac{\vec{a} \cdot \vec{b}}{|\vec{a}|\,|\vec{b}|} \qquad (\theta = \text{angle between } \vec{a} \,\&\, \vec{b})$$

Example

Find the angle between following vectors:

$\vec{a} = \hat{\imath} - \hat{\jmath} + 2\hat{k}$ and $\vec{b} = 2\hat{\imath} + \hat{\jmath} + \hat{k}$.

Solution

$\vec{a} = \hat{\imath} - \hat{\jmath} + 2\hat{k}$ and $\vec{b} = 2\hat{\imath} + \hat{\jmath} + \hat{k}$

$|\vec{a}| = \sqrt{(1)^2 + (-1)^2 + (2)^2} = \sqrt{6}$

$|\vec{b}| = \sqrt{(2)^2 + (1)^2 + (1)^2} = \sqrt{6}$

$\vec{a} \cdot \vec{b} = (\hat{\imath} - \hat{\jmath} + 2\hat{k}) \cdot (2\hat{\imath} + \hat{\jmath} + \hat{k})$

$\qquad = (1)(2) + (-1)(1) + (2)(1) = 3$

$\therefore$ Angle, θ between $\vec{a}$ and $\vec{b}$ is found by $cos\,\theta = \dfrac{\vec{a} \cdot \vec{b}}{|\vec{a}|\,|\vec{b}|}$

$\Rightarrow \quad cos\,\theta = \dfrac{3}{\sqrt{6}\,\sqrt{6}} = \dfrac{1}{2}$

$\Rightarrow \quad \theta = 60°$

9.2 Projection of $\vec{a}$ on $\vec{b}$

9.2.1 Vector Projection

*If perpendiculars are drawn from initial and terminal points of $\vec{a}$ on a line along $\vec{b}$, then the vector from the foot of perpendicular from the initial point to the foot of perpendicular from the terminal point of $\vec{a}$ is called as **vector projection** of $\vec{a}$ on $\vec{b}$.*

Vector Projection of $\vec{a}$ on $\vec{b}$ $= \dfrac{\vec{a} \cdot \vec{b}}{|\vec{b}|}\,\hat{b}$

Explanation

In the following figure, foots of perpendiculars from initial point and from terminal point of $\vec{a}$ on $\vec{b}$ are P and Q respectively.

$\therefore$ Projection of $\vec{a}$ on $\vec{b} = \vec{p} = \overrightarrow{PQ}$

And $\left|\overrightarrow{PQ}\right| = |\vec{a}|\,cos\theta$

$\Rightarrow \vec{p} = \overrightarrow{PQ} = \left|\overrightarrow{PQ}\right|\hat{b} = |\vec{a}|\,cos\theta\,\hat{b}$ .... (i)

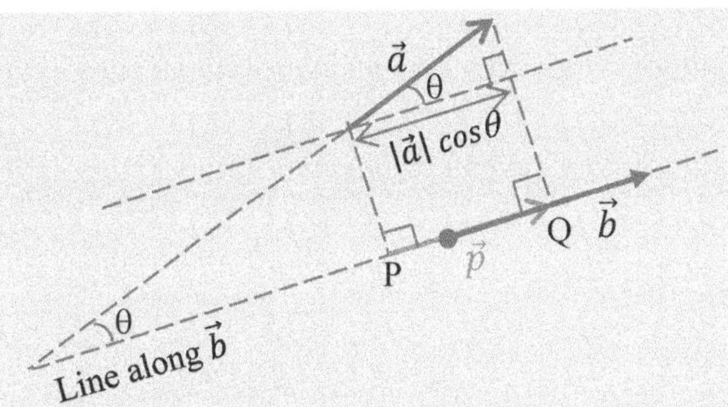

Now $\vec{a} \cdot \vec{b} = |\vec{a}|\,|\vec{b}|\,cos\theta \;\Rightarrow\; |\vec{a}|\,cos\theta = \dfrac{\vec{a}\cdot\vec{b}}{|\vec{b}|}$ .... (ii)

From eqn. (i) and (ii), we have

$$\vec{p} = \dfrac{\vec{a}\cdot\vec{b}}{|\vec{b}|}\,\hat{b}$$

Example

Find Vector Projection of $\vec{a} = \hat{\imath} - \hat{\jmath} + 2\hat{k}$ on $\vec{b} = -2\hat{\imath} + 3\hat{\jmath} - 4\hat{k}$.

Solution

$\vec{a}\cdot\vec{b} = (\hat{\imath} - \hat{\jmath} + 2\hat{k})\cdot(-2\hat{\imath} + 3\hat{\jmath} - 4\hat{k})$

$\qquad = (1)(-2) + (-1)(3) + (2)(-4) = -13$

$|\vec{b}| = \sqrt{(1)^2 + (-1)^2 + (2)^2} = \sqrt{6}$

$\therefore \qquad \hat{b} = \dfrac{\vec{b}}{|\vec{b}|} = \dfrac{-2\hat{\imath} + 3\hat{\jmath} - 4\hat{k}}{\sqrt{6}}$

Now vector projection of $\vec{a}$ on $\vec{b}$ is given by $\vec{p} = \dfrac{\vec{a}\cdot\vec{b}}{|\vec{b}|}\,\hat{b}$

$\therefore \qquad \vec{p} = \dfrac{-13}{\sqrt{6}}\left(\dfrac{-2\hat{\imath} + 3\hat{\jmath} - 4\hat{k}}{\sqrt{6}}\right) = \dfrac{-13}{6}\left(-2\hat{\imath} + 3\hat{\jmath} - 4\hat{k}\right)$

9.2.2 Scalar Projection

*If perpendiculars are drawn from initial and terminal points of $\vec{a}$ on a line along $\vec{b}$, then the length between the feet of these perpendiculars (with negative sign if vector projection is opposite to $\vec{b}$ and positive if it is in the direction of $\vec{b}$) is called as **scalar projection** of $\vec{a}$ on $\vec{b}$ or simply projection of $\vec{a}$ on $\vec{b}$.*

Projection of $\vec{a}$ **on** $\vec{b}$ $= \dfrac{\vec{a}\cdot\vec{b}}{|\vec{b}|}$

<u>**Explanation**</u>

In the following figure, foots of perpendiculars from initial point and from terminal point of $\vec{a}$ on $\vec{b}$ are P and Q respectively.

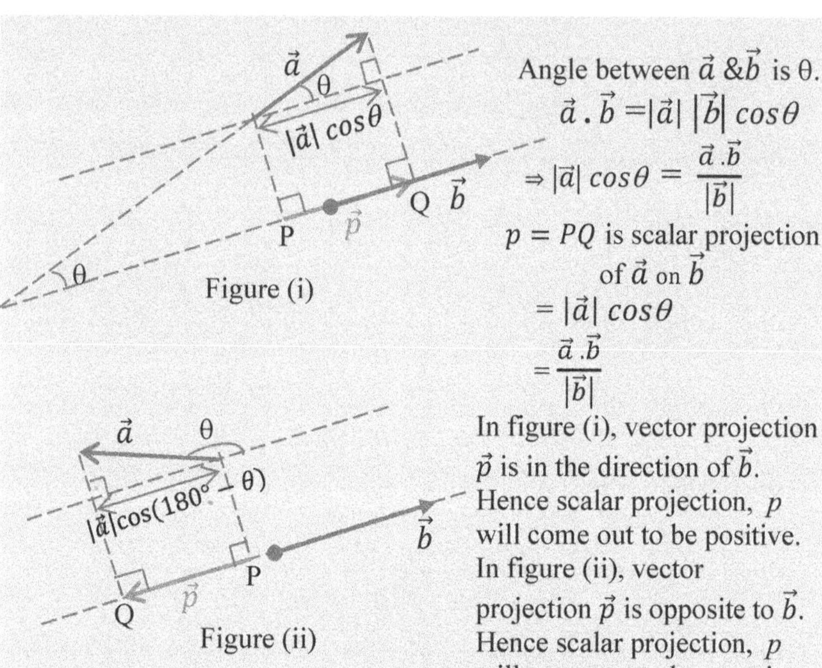

$\therefore$ Projection of $\vec{a}$ on $\vec{b} = \vec{p} = \overrightarrow{PQ}$

<u>**Example**</u>

Find Scalar Projection of $\vec{a} = \hat{\imath} - \hat{\jmath} + 2\hat{k}$ on $\vec{b} = -2\hat{\imath} + 3\hat{\jmath} - 4\hat{k}$.

Solution

$\vec{a}.\vec{b} = (\hat{\imath} - \hat{\jmath} + 2\hat{k}).(-2\hat{\imath} + 3\hat{\jmath} - 4\hat{k})$

$\qquad = (1)(-2) + (-1)(3) + (2)(-4) = -13$

$|\vec{b}| = \sqrt{(1)^2 + (-1)^2 + (2)^2} = \sqrt{6}$

Now scalar projection of $\vec{a}$ on $\vec{b}$ is $= \dfrac{\vec{a}.\vec{b}}{|\vec{b}|}$

$\therefore \qquad$ **Projection of $\vec{a}$ on $\vec{b}$** $= \dfrac{-13}{\sqrt{6}}$

9.3   Vector Product of two vectors (Cross Product)

- Vector product is represented by a cross ($\times$) between the two vectors.

  $\therefore$ it is also called as **cross product**.

9.3.1 Definition

$$\vec{a} \times \vec{b} = |\vec{a}|\,|\vec{b}|\,sin\theta\,\hat{n} \quad \text{where } 0 \le \theta \le \pi$$

$\hat{n}$ = unit vector perpendicular to both $\vec{a}$ & $\vec{b}$.
Its direction is given by Right Hand Thumb Rule

9.3.2 Right Hand Thumb rule (RHT rule)

If we curl the fingers of our right hand from vector $\vec{a}$ to $\vec{b}$ through smaller angle, then our thumb will open in the direction $\vec{a} \times \vec{b}$ i.e., in the direction of $\hat{n}$.

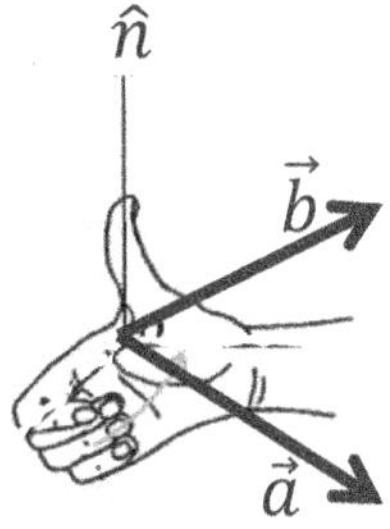

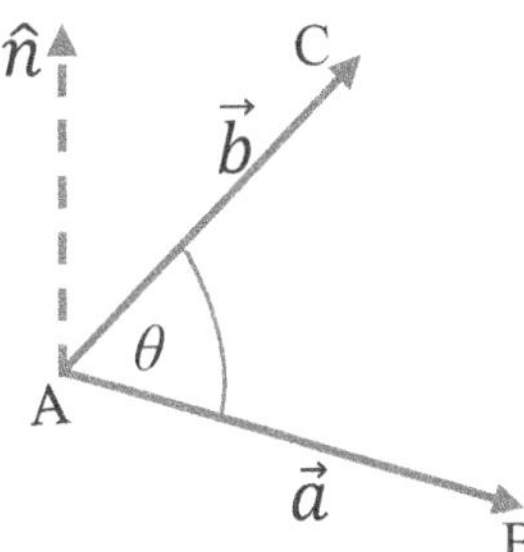

- According to this rule, we find that the direction of $(\vec{b} \times \vec{a})$ is opposite to the direction of $(\vec{a} \times \vec{b})$.

9.3.3 Observations from definition and RHT rule

(i) $\vec{a} \times \vec{b}$ vector is perpendicular to both $\vec{a}$ & $\vec{b}$.

(ii) $|\vec{a} \times \vec{b}| = |\vec{a}|\,|\vec{b}|\,sin\theta$

Also $|\vec{b} \times \vec{a}| = |\vec{b}|\,|\vec{a}|\,sin\theta$

(iii) $|\vec{a} \times \vec{b}| = |\vec{b} \times \vec{a}|$

(iv) $\vec{a} \times \vec{b} = -\,\vec{b} \times \vec{a}$

It means $(\vec{a} \times \vec{b})$ & $(\vec{b} \times \vec{a})$ are opposite in direction but equal in magnitude.

(v) If $\vec{a}$ and $\vec{b}$ are collinear i.e., they are in same direction or in opposite direction, then $\theta = 0°$ or $180°$, and

$$\vec{a} \times \vec{b} = \vec{0} \qquad [\text{It is because } sin0° = sin180° = 0\,]$$

(vi) If $\vec{a} \perp \vec{b}$, then $|\vec{a} \times \vec{b}| = |\vec{a}|\,|\vec{b}|$ (i.e., for $\theta = 90°$)

(vii) If $\vec{a} \times \vec{b} = \vec{0}$, then $\vec{a}$ and $\vec{b}$ are collinear.

$$(\text{provided } \vec{a} \ne \vec{0}\ \&\ \vec{b} \ne \vec{0})$$

9.3.4 Properties of Vector Product

(i) **Non-Commutative:** $\vec{a} \times \vec{b} \neq \vec{b} \times \vec{a}$ for **non**-collinear

$\vec{a}$ & $\vec{b}$ (Cross product is **not** Commutative)

(ii) **Distributive:** $\vec{a} \times (\vec{b} \pm \vec{c}) = \vec{a} \times \vec{b} \pm \vec{a} \times \vec{c}$

(Cross product is Distributive over $+, -$)

9.3.5 Other Important Observations

(i) $\vec{a} \times \vec{a} = \vec{0}$

(Since angle between $\vec{a}$ & $\vec{a}$ is $0°$, and $sin\,0° = 0$

therefore, $\vec{a} \times \vec{a} = |\vec{a}||\vec{a}|sin0°\,\hat{n} = \vec{0}$)

(ii) $\hat{\imath} \times \hat{\imath} = \vec{0}$ $\qquad \hat{\jmath} \times \hat{\jmath} = \vec{0}$ $\qquad \hat{k} \times \hat{k} = \vec{0}$

(iii) $\hat{\imath} \times \hat{\jmath} = \hat{k}$ $\qquad \hat{\jmath} \times \hat{k} = \hat{\imath}$ $\qquad \hat{k} \times \hat{\imath} = \hat{\jmath}$

$\hat{\jmath} \times \hat{\imath} = -\hat{k}$ $\qquad \hat{k} \times \hat{\jmath} = -\hat{\imath}$ $\qquad \hat{\imath} \times \hat{k} = -\hat{\jmath}$

<u>Explanation</u>

According to right hand thumb rule,

$\hat{\imath} \times \hat{\jmath}$ will be in the direction of $\hat{k}$ (i.e., in the direction of positive z-axis),

$\hat{\jmath} \times \hat{k}$ will be in the direction of $\hat{\imath}$ (i.e., in the direction of positive x-axis),

$\hat{k} \times \hat{\imath}$ will be in the direction of $\hat{\jmath}$ (i.e., in the direction of positive y-axis),

Since $|\hat{\imath}| = |\hat{\jmath}| = |\hat{k}| = 1$, and $\hat{\imath} \perp \hat{\jmath},\ \hat{\jmath} \perp \hat{k},\ \hat{k} \perp \hat{\imath}$

therefore, $\qquad \hat{\imath} \times \hat{\jmath} = |\hat{\imath}||\hat{\jmath}|sin90°\,\hat{k} = \hat{k}.$

$\hat{\jmath} \times \hat{k} = |\hat{\jmath}||\hat{k}|sin90°\,\hat{\imath} = \hat{\imath}.$

$\hat{k} \times \hat{\imath} = |\hat{k}||\hat{\imath}|sin90°\,\hat{\jmath} = \hat{\jmath}.$

Also accordingly,

$\hat{\jmath} \times \hat{\imath}$ will be in the direction of $-\hat{k}$ (i.e., in the direction of negative z-axis),

$\hat{k} \times \hat{\jmath}$ will be in the direction of $-\hat{\imath}$ (i.e., in the direction of negative x-axis),

$\hat{\imath} \times \hat{k}$ will be in the direction of $-\hat{\jmath}$ (i.e., in the direction of negative y-axis),

Since $|\hat{\imath}| = |\hat{\jmath}| = |\hat{k}| = 1$, and $\hat{\imath} \perp \hat{\jmath},\ \hat{\jmath} \perp \hat{k},\ \hat{k} \perp \hat{\imath}$

therefore, $\qquad \hat{\jmath} \times \hat{\imath} = |\hat{\jmath}||\hat{\imath}|sin90°\,(-\hat{k}) = -\hat{k}.$

$\hat{k} \times \hat{\jmath} = |\hat{k}||\hat{\jmath}|sin90°\,(-\hat{\imath}) = -\hat{\imath}.$

$\hat{\imath} \times \hat{k} = |\hat{\imath}||\hat{k}|sin90°\,(-\hat{\jmath}) = -\hat{\jmath}.$

9.3.6 Vector product in terms of rectangular components

If $\vec{a} = a_1\,\hat{\imath} + a_2\,\hat{\jmath} + a_3\,\hat{k}$ and $\vec{b} = b_1\,\hat{\imath} + b_2\,\hat{\jmath} + b_3\,\hat{k}$,

$$\text{then} \quad \vec{a} \times \vec{b} = \begin{vmatrix} \hat{\imath} & \hat{\jmath} & \hat{k} \\ a_1 & a_2 & a_3 \\ b_1 & b_2 & b_3 \end{vmatrix}$$

<u>Explanation</u>

If $\vec{a} = a_1\,\hat{\imath} + a_2\,\hat{\jmath} + a_3\,\hat{k}$ and $\vec{b} = b_1\,\hat{\imath} + b_2\,\hat{\jmath} + b_3\,\hat{k}$,

$$\begin{aligned}
\vec{a} \times \vec{b} &= (a_1\,\hat{\imath} + a_2\,\hat{\jmath} + a_3\,\hat{k}) \times (b_1\,\hat{\imath} + b_2\,\hat{\jmath} + b_3\,\hat{k}) \\
&= a_1 b_1 \hat{\imath} \times \hat{\imath} + a_1 b_2 \hat{\imath} \times \hat{\jmath} + a_1 b_3 \hat{\imath} \times \hat{k} \\
&\quad + a_2 b_1 \hat{\jmath} \times \hat{\imath} + a_2 b_2 \hat{\jmath} \times \hat{\jmath} + a_2 b_3 \hat{\jmath} \times \hat{k} \\
&\quad + a_3 b_1 \hat{k} \times \hat{\imath} + a_3 b_2 \hat{k} \times \hat{\jmath} + a_3 b_3 \hat{k} \times \hat{k}
\end{aligned}$$

$$\begin{aligned}
[\text{use } &\hat{\imath} \times \hat{\imath} = \vec{0},\ \hat{\jmath} \times \hat{\jmath} = \vec{0},\ \hat{k} \times \hat{k} = \vec{0}, \\
&\hat{\imath} \times \hat{\jmath} = \hat{k},\ \hat{\jmath} \times \hat{k} = \hat{\imath},\ \hat{k} \times \hat{\imath} = \hat{\jmath} \\
&\hat{\jmath} \times \hat{\imath} = -\hat{k},\ \hat{k} \times \hat{\jmath} = -\hat{\imath},\ \hat{\imath} \times \hat{k} = -\hat{\jmath}\,]
\end{aligned}$$

$$= (a_2 b_3 - a_3 b_2)\,\hat{\imath} + (a_3 b_1 - a_1 b_3)\,\hat{\jmath} + (a_1 b_2 - a_2 b_1)\,\hat{k}$$

This is same as the determinant $\begin{vmatrix} \hat{\imath} & \hat{\jmath} & \hat{k} \\ a_1 & a_2 & a_3 \\ b_1 & b_2 & b_3 \end{vmatrix}$

<u>Example</u>

Find the vector product of vectors $\vec{a} = \hat{\imath} - \hat{\jmath} + 2\hat{k}$ and $\vec{b} = -2\hat{\imath} + 3\hat{\jmath} - 4\hat{k}$.

Solution

Using determinant method, we can find $\vec{a} \times \vec{b}$ as follows:

$$\vec{a} \times \vec{b} = \begin{vmatrix} \hat{\imath} & \hat{\jmath} & \hat{k} \\ a_1 & a_2 & a_3 \\ b_1 & b_2 & b_3 \end{vmatrix}$$

(Where a_1, a_2, a_3 are components of vector $\vec{a}$, and b_1, b_2, b_3 are components of vector $\vec{b}$)

$$\begin{aligned}
\therefore \ \vec{a} \times \vec{b} &= \begin{vmatrix} \hat{\imath} & \hat{\jmath} & \hat{k} \\ 1 & -1 & 2 \\ -2 & 3 & -4 \end{vmatrix} \\
&= [(-1)(-4) - (3)(2)]\,\hat{\imath} - [(1)(-4) - (-2)(2)]\,\hat{\jmath} \\
&\quad + [(1)(3) - (-2)(-1)]\,\hat{k} \\
&= -2\hat{\imath} + \hat{k}
\end{aligned}$$

9.4 Area of Triangle

- If $\vec{a}$ & $\vec{b}$ represent 2 sides of a triangle, then

  Area of triangle $= \frac{1}{2}\left|\vec{a}\times\vec{b}\right|$

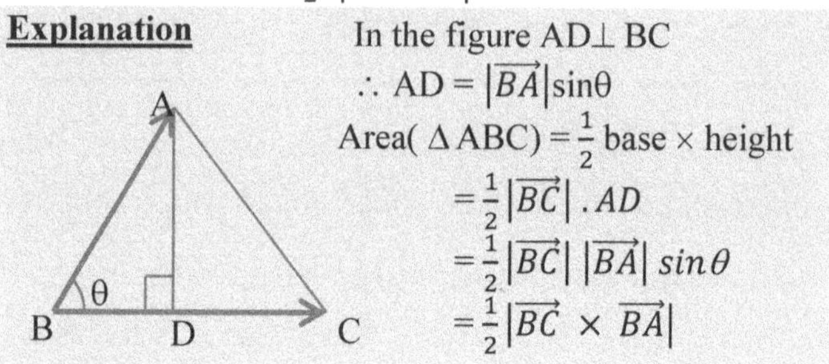

Explanation

In the figure $AD \perp BC$

$\therefore AD = \left|\vec{BA}\right|\sin\theta$

$\text{Area}(\triangle ABC) = \frac{1}{2}\,\text{base}\times\text{height}$

$= \frac{1}{2}\left|\vec{BC}\right|.AD$

$= \frac{1}{2}\left|\vec{BC}\right|\left|\vec{BA}\right|\sin\theta$

$= \frac{1}{2}\left|\vec{BC}\times\vec{BA}\right|$

- In component form:

- If $\vec{a} = a_1\,\hat{\imath} + a_2\,\hat{\jmath} + a_3\,\hat{k}$ and $\vec{b} = b_1\,\hat{\imath} + b_2\,\hat{\jmath} + b_3\,\hat{k}$, then **Area** $= \frac{1}{2}\left|\vec{a}\times\vec{b}\right|$

$$= \frac{1}{2}\left|\begin{vmatrix} \hat{\imath} & \hat{\jmath} & \hat{k} \\ a_1 & a_2 & a_3 \\ b_1 & b_2 & b_3 \end{vmatrix}\right|$$

Example

Find the area of triangle whose two sides are represented by the vectors:

$$\vec{a} = \hat{\imath} - \hat{\jmath} + 2\hat{k} \quad \text{and} \quad \vec{b} = -2\hat{\imath} + 3\hat{\jmath} - 4\hat{k}.$$

Solution

We can find the area of triangle by using the formula:

Area $= \frac{1}{2}\left|\vec{a}\times\vec{b}\right|$

$$= \frac{1}{2}\left|\begin{vmatrix} \hat{\imath} & \hat{\jmath} & \hat{k} \\ a_1 & a_2 & a_3 \\ b_1 & b_2 & b_3 \end{vmatrix}\right|$$

(where a_1, a_2, a_3 are components of vector $\vec{a}$, and b_1, b_2, b_3 are components of vector $\vec{b}$)

$$\therefore \text{Area of triangle} = \frac{1}{2}\left|\begin{vmatrix} \hat{\imath} & \hat{\jmath} & \hat{k} \\ 1 & -1 & 2 \\ -2 & 3 & -4 \end{vmatrix}\right|$$

$$= \frac{1}{2}\left| \left[(-1)(-4) - (3)(2)\right]\hat{\imath} - \left[(1)(-4) - (-2)(2)\right]\hat{\jmath} \right.$$
$$\left. + \left[(1)(3) - (-2)(-1)\right]\hat{k}\right|$$

$$= \frac{1}{2}\left|-2\hat{\imath} + \hat{k}\right|$$

$$= \frac{1}{2}\sqrt{(-2)^2 + (1)^2} = \frac{\sqrt{5}}{2}\ \text{sq.units}$$

9.5 Area of Parallelogram

- If $\vec{a}$ & $\vec{b}$ represent 2 adjacent sides of a parallelogram, then **Area of parallelogram** $= \left| \vec{a} \times \vec{b} \right|$

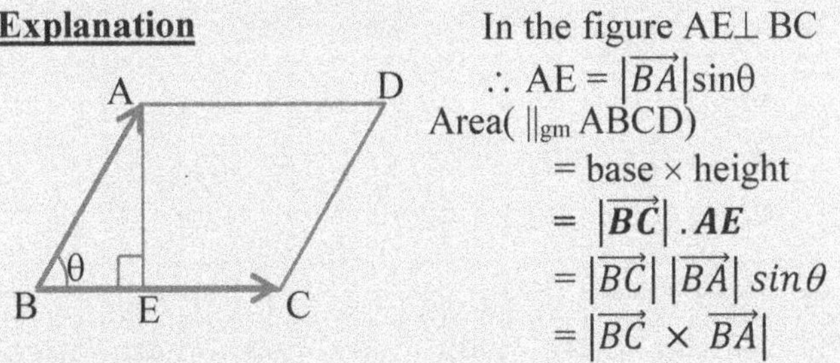

In the figure AE⊥ BC

$\therefore$ AE $= \left| \overrightarrow{BA} \right| \sin\theta$

Area($\|_{gm}$ ABCD)

$=$ base $\times$ height

$= \left| \overrightarrow{BC} \right| . AE$

$= \left| \overrightarrow{BC} \right| \left| \overrightarrow{BA} \right| \sin\theta$

$= \left| \overrightarrow{BC} \times \overrightarrow{BA} \right|$

- In component form:
- If $\vec{a} = a_1\,\hat{\imath} + a_2\,\hat{\jmath} + a_3\,\hat{k}$ and $\vec{b} = b_1\,\hat{\imath} + b_2\,\hat{\jmath} + b_3\,\hat{k}$, then **Area** $= \left| \vec{a} \times \vec{b} \right|$

$$= \left| \left| \begin{matrix} \hat{\imath} & \hat{\jmath} & \hat{k} \\ a_1 & a_2 & a_3 \\ b_1 & b_2 & b_3 \end{matrix} \right| \right|$$

Example

Find the area of parallelogram whose two adjacent sides are represented by the vectors:

$$\vec{a} = \hat{\imath} - \hat{\jmath} + 2\hat{k} \text{ and } \vec{b} = -2\hat{\imath} + 3\hat{\jmath} - 4\hat{k}.$$

Solution

We can find the area of parallelogram by using the formula:

Area $= \left| \vec{a} \times \vec{b} \right|$

$$= \left| \left| \begin{matrix} \hat{\imath} & \hat{\jmath} & \hat{k} \\ a_1 & a_2 & a_3 \\ b_1 & b_2 & b_3 \end{matrix} \right| \right|$$

(where a_1, a_2, a_3 are components of vector $\vec{a}$, and b_1, b_2, b_3 are components of vector $\vec{b}$)

$$\therefore \text{ Area of triangle} = \left| \left| \begin{matrix} \hat{\imath} & \hat{\jmath} & \hat{k} \\ 1 & -1 & 2 \\ -2 & 3 & -4 \end{matrix} \right| \right|$$

$$= \left| [(-1)(-4) - (3)(2)]\,\hat{\imath} - [(1)(-4) - (-2)(2)]\,\hat{\jmath} + [(1)(3) - (-2)(-1)]\,\hat{k} \right|$$

$$= \left| -2\hat{\imath} + \hat{k} \right|$$

$$= \sqrt{(-2)^2 + (1)^2} = \sqrt{5} \text{ sq.units}$$

---

10 *Scalar Triple Product

Dot product of a vector, with the cross product of other two vectors, is a scalar. Product of three vectors in such a manner is called **scalar triple product of vectors**.

10.1 *Definition

- If $\vec{a}$, $\vec{b}$ & $\vec{c}$ are 3 vectors, then their scalar triple product is $= \vec{a} \cdot (\vec{b} \times \vec{c})$

- It is denoted as $[\vec{a}\ \vec{b}\ \vec{c}]$

  Thus $[\vec{a}\ \vec{b}\ \vec{c}] = \vec{a} \cdot (\vec{b} \times \vec{c})$

10.2 *Scalar triple product in terms of components

- We can find $\vec{a} \cdot (\vec{b} \times \vec{c})$ (or $[\vec{a}\ \vec{b}\ \vec{c}]$) by using determinant as

$$\vec{a} \cdot (\vec{b} \times \vec{c}) = [\vec{a}\ \vec{b}\ \vec{c}] = \begin{vmatrix} a_1 & a_2 & a_3 \\ b_1 & b_2 & b_3 \\ c_1 & c_2 & c_3 \end{vmatrix}$$

Here a_1, a_2, a_3 are components of vector $\vec{a}$; b_1, b_2, b_3 are components of vector $\vec{b}$, and c_1, c_2, c_3 are components of vector $\vec{c}$.

<u>Explanation</u>

If $\quad \vec{a} = a_1\,\hat{\imath} + a_2\,\hat{\jmath} + a_3\,\hat{k}$

$\qquad \vec{b} = b_1\,\hat{\imath} + b_2\,\hat{\jmath} + b_3\,\hat{k}$

and $\vec{c} = c_1\,\hat{\imath} + c_2\,\hat{\jmath} + c_3\,\hat{k}$,

then we can obtain $\vec{b} \times \vec{c}$ as explained in vector product, and after that we can obtain its scalar product with $\vec{a}$ to find $\vec{a} \cdot (\vec{b} \times \vec{c})$.

We will find that it is same as the determinant

$$\begin{vmatrix} a_1 & a_2 & a_3 \\ b_1 & b_2 & b_3 \\ c_1 & c_2 & c_3 \end{vmatrix}$$

<u>Example</u>

If $\vec{a} = -2\hat{\imath} + 3\hat{\jmath} - 4\hat{k}$, $\vec{b} = \hat{\imath} - \hat{\jmath} + 2\hat{k}$ and $\vec{c} = 2\hat{\imath} + \hat{\jmath} - \hat{k}$, then find $\vec{a} \cdot (\vec{b} \times \vec{c})$.

Solution

By determinant method, we can find $\vec{a} \cdot (\vec{b} \times \vec{c})$ as follows:

$$\vec{a} \cdot (\vec{b} \times \vec{c}) = \begin{vmatrix} a_1 & a_2 & a_3 \\ b_1 & b_2 & b_3 \\ c_1 & c_2 & c_3 \end{vmatrix}$$

(here a_1, a_2, a_3 are components of vector $\vec{a}$; b_1, b_2, b_3 are components of vector $\vec{b}$, and c_1, c_2, c_3 are components of vector $\vec{c}$)

$$\therefore \ \vec{a}.(\vec{b} \times \vec{c}) = \begin{vmatrix} -2 & 3 & -4 \\ 1 & -1 & 2 \\ 2 & 1 & -1 \end{vmatrix}$$

$$= -2[(-1)(-1) - (1)(2)] - 3[(1)(-1) - (2)(2)]$$
$$-4[(1)(1) - (2)(-1)]$$

$$= 2 + 15 - 12$$
$$= 5$$

10.3 *Properties of scalar triple product

Following properties can easily be observed from the definition of scalar triple product:

(i) In scalar triple product of 3 given vectors, positions of dot and cross do not matter till the cyclic order in the product remains same.

$$\vec{a}.(\vec{b} \times \vec{c}) = (\vec{a} \times \vec{b}).\vec{c} = [\vec{a}\,\vec{b}\,\vec{c}]$$

$$\vec{b}.(\vec{c} \times \vec{a}) = (\vec{b} \times \vec{c}).\vec{a} = [\vec{b}\,\vec{c}\,\vec{a}]$$

$$\vec{c}.(\vec{a} \times \vec{b}) = (\vec{c} \times \vec{a}).\vec{b} = [\vec{c}\,\vec{a}\,\vec{b}]$$

Also $[\vec{a}\,\vec{b}\,\vec{c}] = [\vec{b}\,\vec{c}\,\vec{a}] = [\vec{c}\,\vec{a}\,\vec{b}]$

(ii) If the cyclic order is changed, then the value of scalar triple product changes its sign.

$$[\vec{a}\,\vec{b}\,\vec{c}] = -[\vec{a}\,\vec{c}\,\vec{b}]$$
$$= -[\vec{c}\,\vec{b}\,\vec{a}]$$
$$= -[\vec{b}\,\vec{a}\,\vec{c}]$$

(iii) If any two vectors in scalar triple products are equal, then its value becomes zero.

$$[\vec{a}\,\vec{a}\,\vec{b}] = 0, \qquad [\vec{a}\,\vec{b}\,\vec{b}] = 0, \qquad [\vec{a}\,\vec{b}\,\vec{a}] = 0$$

Or $[\vec{a}\,\vec{b}\,\vec{c}] = 0$, if $\vec{a} = \vec{b}$ or $\vec{b} = \vec{c}$ or $\vec{a} = \vec{c}$

(iv) If any two vectors in scalar triple product are parallel (or collinear), then its value is zero.

$$[\vec{a}\,\vec{b}\,\vec{c}] = 0 \quad \text{if } \vec{a} \ \& \ \vec{b} \ \text{are parallel (or collinear)}$$

$$[\vec{a}\,\vec{b}\,\vec{c}] = 0 \quad \text{if } \vec{b} \ \& \ \vec{c} \ \text{are parallel (or collinear)}$$

$$[\vec{a}\,\vec{b}\,\vec{c}] = 0 \quad \text{if } \vec{a} \ \& \ \vec{c} \ \text{are parallel (or collinear)}$$

10.4 *Volume of Parallelopiped

- If $\vec{a}$, $\vec{b}$ & $\vec{c}$ represent 3 adjacent edges of a Parallelopiped, then

$$\textbf{Volume} = \vec{a}\cdot(\vec{b}\times\vec{c}) = \left[\vec{a}\ \vec{b}\ \vec{c}\right]$$

Explanation

In the figure, $\|_{gm}$ ABCD is bottom-base & EFGH is top-base .
ABEF is front face and DCGH is back face.

$\vec{a}$, $\vec{b}$ & $\vec{c}$ are vectors along adjacent edges AE, AB & AD respectively.

using formula of area of parallelogram, we get the following:

Area of base ABCD $= \left|\vec{b}\times\vec{c}\right|$

EM is height of parallelepiped and is perpendicular to face ABCD.

$\vec{b}\times\vec{c}$ is also $\perp$ to ABCD i.e., plane of $\vec{b}$ & $\vec{c}$.

(by definition of cross product)

$\therefore$ EM will be $\|$ to $\vec{b}\times\vec{c}$ and

EM = AP = projection of $\vec{a}$ on $\vec{b}\times\vec{c}$

$$= \frac{\vec{a}\cdot(\vec{b}\times\vec{c})}{\left|\vec{b}\times\vec{c}\right|}$$

Volume
=(area of base)x (height)
=(area of ABCD)xEM
$= \vec{a}\cdot(\vec{b}\times\vec{c})$
$= \left[\vec{a}\ \vec{b}\ \vec{c}\right]$

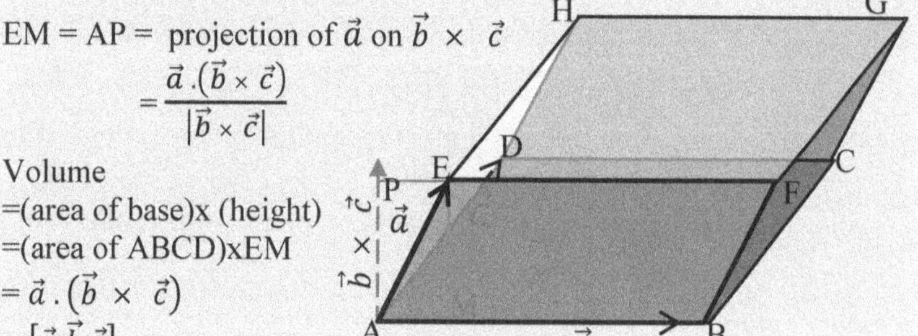

- **In component form:**

If $\qquad \vec{a} = a_1\,\hat{i} + a_2\,\hat{j} + a_3\,\hat{k}$

$\qquad\qquad \vec{b} = b_1\,\hat{i} + b_2\,\hat{j} + b_3\,\hat{k}$

and $\qquad \vec{c} = c_1\,\hat{i} + c_2\,\hat{j} + c_3\,\hat{k}$

then $\qquad$ **Volume** $= \left[\vec{a}\ \vec{b}\ \vec{c}\right] = \vec{a}\cdot(\vec{b}\times\vec{c})$

$$= \begin{vmatrix} a_1 & a_2 & a_3 \\ b_1 & b_2 & b_3 \\ c_1 & c_2 & c_3 \end{vmatrix}$$

(Volume can't be $-$ve , so take its absolute value)

Example

Find the volume of parallelopiped whose three adjacent sides are represented by the vectors:

$\vec{a} = -2\hat{\imath} + 3\hat{\jmath} - 4\hat{k}$, $\vec{b} = \hat{\imath} - \hat{\jmath} + 2\hat{k}$ and $\vec{c} = 2\hat{\imath} + \hat{\jmath} - \hat{k}$.

Solution

We can find volume of parallelopiped by using the formula:

$$\text{Volume} = \left[\vec{a}\ \vec{b}\ \vec{c}\right] = \vec{a} \cdot \left(\vec{b} \times \vec{c}\right)$$

$$= \begin{vmatrix} a_1 & a_2 & a_3 \\ b_1 & b_2 & b_3 \\ c_1 & c_2 & c_3 \end{vmatrix}$$

(where a_1, a_2, a_3 are components of vector $\vec{a}$; b_1, b_2, b_3 are components of vector $\vec{b}$, and c_1, c_2, c_3 are components of vector $\vec{c}$)

$$\therefore \ \text{Volume} = \begin{vmatrix} -2 & 3 & -4 \\ 1 & -1 & 2 \\ 2 & 1 & -1 \end{vmatrix}$$

$$= -2[(-1)(-1) - (1)(2)] - 3[(1)(-1) - (2)(2)]$$
$$-4[(1)(1) - (2)(-1)]$$

$$= 2 + 15 - 12$$

$$= 5 \text{ cu.units}$$

10.5 *Coplanarity of 3 vectors

Three vectors are coplanar if and only if their scalar triple product is zero.

- If 3 vectors are coplanar, then their scalar triple product is equal to zero.

Explanation

Let three vectors are $\vec{a}$, $\vec{b}$ & $\vec{c}$.

$\vec{b} \times \vec{c}$ is perpendicular to $\vec{b}$ & $\vec{c}$.

If $\vec{a}$, $\vec{b}$ & $\vec{c}$ are coplanar, then $\vec{b} \times \vec{c}$ is perpendicular to $\vec{a}$ also.

It means dot product of $\vec{a}$ & $\vec{b} \times \vec{c}$ is zero.

$$\therefore \vec{a} \cdot \left(\vec{b} \times \vec{c}\right) = 0$$

(*It is explained for non collinear and non-zero vectors. However, if any of them are collinear vectors or zero vectors, then also $\vec{a} \cdot \left(\vec{b} \times \vec{c}\right) = 0$ for them to be coplanar*)

- If $\vec{a} = a_1\,\hat{\imath} + a_2\,\hat{\jmath} + a_3\,\hat{k}$, $\vec{b} = b_1\,\hat{\imath} + b_2\,\hat{\jmath} + b_3\,\hat{k}$ and $\vec{c} = c_1\,\hat{\imath} + c_2\,\hat{\jmath} + c_3\,\hat{k}$,

  then **for their coplanarity,** $\left[\vec{a}\ \vec{b}\ \vec{c}\right] = 0$

  i.e., $$\begin{vmatrix} a_1 & a_2 & a_3 \\ b_1 & b_2 & b_3 \\ c_1 & c_2 & c_3 \end{vmatrix} = 0$$

Example

Find λ if the vectors $\hat{\imath} - \hat{\jmath} + \hat{k}$, $3\hat{\imath} + \hat{\jmath} - 4\hat{k}$ and $\hat{\imath} + \lambda\hat{\jmath} - 3\hat{k}$ are coplanar.

Solution

---

*Asterisk (*) marked article (if any) is **not** in CBSE 2025-26 syllabus.*

Let $\vec{a} = \hat{\imath} - \hat{\jmath} + \hat{k}$, $\vec{b} = 3\hat{\imath} + \hat{\jmath} - 4\hat{k}$ and $\vec{c} = \hat{\imath} + \lambda\hat{\jmath} - 3\hat{k}$

3 vectors $\vec{a}$, $\vec{b}$, $\vec{c}$ are coplanar if their scalar triple product = 0

i.e., $[\vec{a}\,\vec{b}\,\vec{c}] = 0$

$$\Rightarrow \begin{vmatrix} a_1 & a_2 & a_3 \\ b_1 & b_2 & b_3 \\ c_1 & c_2 & c_3 \end{vmatrix} = 0$$

(where a_1, a_2, a_3 are components of vector $\vec{a}$; b_1, b_2, b_3 are components of vector $\vec{b}$; and c_1, c_2, c_3 are components of vector $\vec{c}$

$$\therefore \quad \begin{vmatrix} 1 & -1 & 1 \\ 3 & 1 & -4 \\ 1 & \lambda & -3 \end{vmatrix} = 0$$

$1[(1)(-3) - (\lambda)(-4)] + 1[(3)(-3) - (1)(-4)] + 1[(3)(\lambda) - (1)(1)] = 0$

$\Rightarrow -3 + 4\lambda - 5 + 3\lambda - 1 = 0$

$\Rightarrow 7\lambda - 9 = 0 \qquad \Rightarrow \lambda = \dfrac{9}{7}$

10.6 *Coplanarity of 4 points

Four points A, B, C and D are coplanar if $\overrightarrow{AB}$, $\overrightarrow{AC}$ and $\overrightarrow{AD}$ are coplanar.

i.e., scalar triple product of $\overrightarrow{AB}$, $\overrightarrow{AC}$ and $\overrightarrow{AD}$ is zero.

- If $\overrightarrow{AB} \cdot (\overrightarrow{AC} \times \overrightarrow{AD}) = 0$, then points A, B, C & D are coplanar.

Example

Find x such that four points A $(3, 2, 1)$ B $(4, x, 5)$, C $(4, 2, -2)$ and D $(6, 5, -1)$ are coplanar.

Solution

Here, $\overrightarrow{AB} = (4 - 3)\hat{\imath} + (x - 2)\hat{\jmath} + (5 - 1)\hat{k} = \hat{\imath} + (x - 2)\hat{\jmath} + 4\hat{k}$

$\overrightarrow{AC} = (4 - 3)\hat{\imath} + (2 - 2)\hat{\jmath} + (-2 - 1)\hat{k} = \hat{\imath} - 3\hat{k}$

and $\overrightarrow{AD} = (6 - 3)\hat{\imath} + (5 - 2)\hat{\jmath} + (-1 - 1)\hat{k} = 3\hat{\imath} + 3\hat{\jmath} - 2\hat{k}$

Four points A, B, C and D are coplanar if $\overrightarrow{AB}$, $\overrightarrow{AC}$ and $\overrightarrow{AD}$ are coplanar.

i.e., scalar triple product of $\overrightarrow{AB}$, $\overrightarrow{AC}$ and $\overrightarrow{AD}$ is zero.

$\therefore \quad \overrightarrow{AB} \cdot (\overrightarrow{AC} \times \overrightarrow{AD}) = 0$

$$\Rightarrow \begin{vmatrix} 1 & x - 2 & 4 \\ 1 & 0 & -3 \\ 3 & 3 & -2 \end{vmatrix} = 0$$

$\Rightarrow 1[(0)(-2) - (3)(-3)] - (x - 2)[(1)(-2) - (3)(-3)]$
$+ 4[(1)(3) - (3)(0)] = 0$

$\Rightarrow 9 - 7(x - 2) + 12 = 0$

$\Rightarrow -7x + 35 = 0 \qquad \Rightarrow x = 5$

Chapter-12   Three – Dimensional Geometry

1   Direction Cosines and Direction Ratios of a Line

Concepts of direction cosines and direction ratios of a line are similar to that of a vector. (*see* 'Position Vector of a point' in the previous chapter – Vector Algebra)

So, we state as follows:

- If α, β and γ are the angles made by a line with positive direction of X-axis, Y-axis, and Z-axis respectively, then its *Direction Cosines* (DCs) are $\cos\alpha, \cos\beta, \cos\gamma$.
  They are denoted by l, m, n respectively.

- The numbers proportional to DCs are called *Direction Ratios* (DRs).
  It means if l, m, n are DCs , and a, b, c are DRs of a line, then

  $$l : m : n \quad :: \quad a : b : c$$

  Or $\qquad \dfrac{l}{a} = \dfrac{m}{b} = \dfrac{n}{c}$

- $l^2 + m^2 + n^2 = 1$

- In short, we write direction cosines as DCs and direction ratios as DRs.

<u>Example</u>

A line makes angles $60°$, $120°$, $45°$ with positive direction of x, y & z – axes respectively. Find its direction cosines and direction ratios.

Solution

Here, we have $\alpha = 30°$, $\beta = 120°$, $\gamma = 45°$

DCs are given by $\cos\alpha$, $\cos\beta$, $\cos\gamma$

$\therefore$ DCs are $\cos 60°, \cos 120°, \cos 45°$

i.e., $\qquad \dfrac{1}{2}, -\dfrac{1}{2}, \dfrac{1}{\sqrt{2}}$

DRs are numbers proportional to DCs.

i.e., DRs can be found as $\dfrac{1}{2} : -\dfrac{1}{2} : \dfrac{1}{\sqrt{2}}$

$\therefore$ DRs are $1, -1, \sqrt{2}$ (multiplying throughout by 2)

$\rightarrow$ $\because$ There are many numbers which have same ratios,

---

∴ there are infinite DRs which can be obtained by multiplying the DCs by any positive real number.

e.g., DRs can be $2, -2, 2\sqrt{2}$ (multiplying DCs by 4)

or   DRs can be $\sqrt{2}, -\sqrt{2}, 2$ (multiplying DCs by $2\sqrt{2}$)

2 Line and Directed Line

(i) **Line :** A line on which we can move in any of the two directions from a point on it. (*See* the next figure below)

- So , if $\boldsymbol{\alpha}, \boldsymbol{\beta}$ and $\boldsymbol{\gamma}$ are the angle made by a line with positive direction of X-axis, Y-axis, and Z-axis, respectively, from one side, then

  180° − α, 180° − β and **180° − γ** are the angle made by it with positive direction of X-axis, Y-axis, and Z-axis from other side. (*See* the next figure below)

  ∴ it can have 2 sets of DCs.

  i.e., *cos α, cos β, cos γ*

  and $cos(180° - \alpha)$, $cos(180° - \beta)$, $cos(180° - \gamma)$

  or   *cos α, cos β, cos γ* and $- cos\ \alpha, - cos\ \beta, - cos\ \gamma$

In the following figure, if we are at point A, then we can move in any of the two directions: from A to B or from A to C on the line *t* .

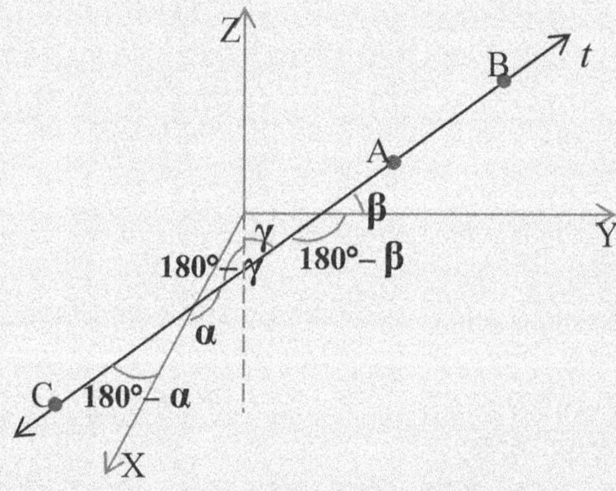

On moving from A to B, if line *t* is making angles α, β, γ with positive directions of X , Y and Z-axes respectively,

then it will make angles 180°− α , 180°− β , 180°− γ with positive directions of X , Y and Z-axes respectively if we move from A to C (as shown in above figure).

- If l, m, n are DCs , and a, b, c are DRs of a line, then by using $\dfrac{l}{a} = \dfrac{m}{b} = \dfrac{n}{c} = \lambda$, we can find following relations between DCs from DRs.

$$l = \pm \frac{a}{\sqrt{a^2+b^2+c^2}}, \quad m = \pm \frac{b}{\sqrt{a^2+b^2+c^2}}, \quad n = \pm \frac{c}{\sqrt{a^2+b^2+c^2}}$$

- $l^2 + m^2 + n^2 = 1$

Example

A line makes angles 60°, 120°, 45° with positive direction of x, y, and z – axes respectively. What are the possible two sets of its direction cosines?

Solution

If a line makes angles 60°, 120°, 45° with positive direction of x, y, and z – axes on moving in one direction on it, then it will make angles 120°, 60°, 135° with positive direction of x, y, and z – axes on moving in opposite direction on it.

∴ Its DCs can be $cos\ 60°$, $cos\ 120°$, $cos\ 45°$

$$\text{or} \quad cos\ 120°, cos\ 60°, cos\ 135°$$

i.e., DCs can be $\dfrac{1}{2}, -\dfrac{1}{2}, \dfrac{1}{\sqrt{2}}$ or $-\dfrac{1}{2}, \dfrac{1}{2}, -\dfrac{1}{\sqrt{2}}$

(ii) **Directed Line**: A line on which we move only in one direction from a point on it. (*See* the next figure below)

- So, it has only one set of DCs.

    i.e., $cos\ \alpha, \ cos\ \beta, \ cos\ \gamma$

In the following figure, if we are at any point A, then we move in only one direction: from A to B on the line t . We don't move towards C.

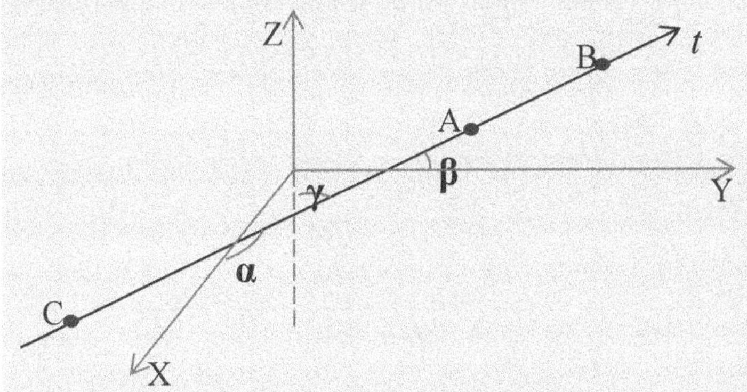

On moving from A to B, line t is making angles α , β , γ with positive directions of X , Y and Z-axes respectively.

∴ Its DCs are $cos\ \alpha, \ cos\ \beta, \ cos\ \gamma$.

- If l, m, n are DCs, and a, b, c are DRs of a directed line,
  then $l = \dfrac{a}{\sqrt{a^2+b^2+c^2}}$, $m = \dfrac{b}{\sqrt{a^2+b^2+c^2}}$, $n = \dfrac{c}{\sqrt{a^2+b^2+c^2}}$
- $l^2 + m^2 + n^2 = 1$

3 DCs and DRs of X, Y and Z-axis

- **DCs and DRs of X-axis are 1,0,0**
- **DCs and DRs of Y-axis are 0,1,0**
- **DCs and DRs of Z-axis are 0,0,1**

<u>Explanation</u>

Angle made by X-axis with positive directions of X, Y and Z-axis are $0°$, $90°$ and $90°$ respectively. So, DCs are $\cos 0°$, $\cos 90°$, $\cos 90°$ or 1,0,0.

Here, number proportional to these DCs are also 1,0,0. So, DRs are also 1,0,0.

Similarly, we can give DCs and DRs of Y and Z-axes.

4 DCs and DRs of line through two points

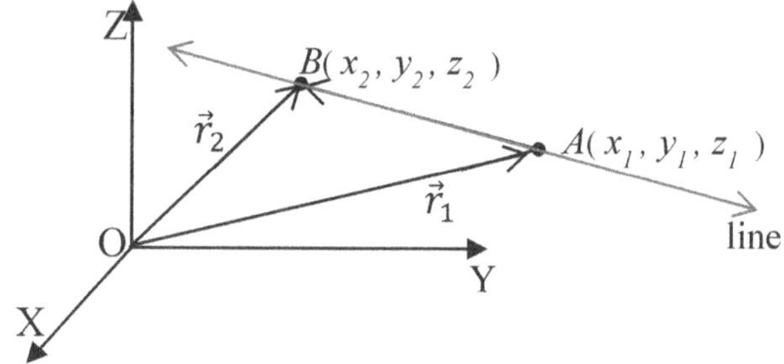

If a line passes through two given points $A(x_1, y_1, z_1)$ and $B(x_2, y_2, z_2)$, then its direction cosines and direction ratios will be same as that of the vector joining these two points.
(*see* 'Vector joining 2 points' in the previous chapter – Vector Algebra)

So, we state as follows:

- DRs of line AB are: $x_2 - x_1$, $y_2 - y_1$, $z_2 - z_1$

- DCs are:

$$l = \frac{x_2 - x_1}{\sqrt{(x_2 - x_1)^2 + (y_2 - y_1)^2 + (z_2 - z_1)^2}}$$

$$m = \frac{y_2 - y_1}{\sqrt{(x_2 - x_1)^2 + (y_2 - y_1)^2 + (z_2 - z_1)^2}}$$

$$n = \frac{z_2 - z_1}{\sqrt{(x_2 - x_1)^2 + (y_2 - y_1)^2 + (z_2 - z_1)^2}}$$

<u>**Example**</u>

Find the direction ratios and direction cosines of a line passing through the two points A & B whose coordinates are $(1,2,3)$ and $(3,-2,4)$ respectively.

Solution

DRs of line passing through two points are given by:

$$x_2 - x_1 \,,\, y_2 - y_1 \,,\, z_2 - z_1$$

$\therefore$ DRs of line AB are $3-1, -2-2, 4-3$ i.e., $2, -4, 1$

DCs can be found from DRs by using

$$l = \frac{a}{\sqrt{a^2+b^2+c^2}} \,,\quad m = \frac{b}{\sqrt{a^2+b^2+c^2}} \,,\quad n = \frac{c}{\sqrt{a^2+b^2+c^2}}$$

where a, b, c denote DRs, and l, m, n denote DCs of line.

[we are considering a directed line. $\therefore$ Only one set of DCs]

$$\Rightarrow l = \frac{2}{\sqrt{2^2+(-4)^2+1^2}} \,,\quad m = \frac{-4}{\sqrt{2^2+(-4)^2+1^2}} \,,\quad n = \frac{1}{\sqrt{2^2+(-4)^2+1^2}}$$

$\therefore$ DCs of line AB are $\dfrac{2}{\sqrt{21}}, \dfrac{-4}{\sqrt{21}}, \dfrac{1}{\sqrt{21}}$

5   Equation of Line

Just like the coordinates of general point are taken as (x, y, z) in cartesian equations, $\vec{r}$ is taken as the position vector of general point in vector equations.

- $\vec{r} = x\,\hat{\imath} + y\,\hat{\jmath} + z\,\hat{k}$ is position vector of the general point in vector equations.

5.1   Point – Direction form

1) <u>**Vector Equation:**</u>

Given : (i) $\vec{a}$ = Position Vector of a point on the line.

(ii) $\vec{b}$ = a vector parallel to the given line

Required Equation: $\boldsymbol{\vec{r} = \vec{a} + \lambda\vec{b}}$

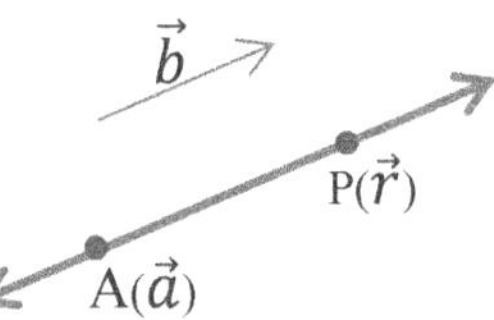

<u>**Explanation**</u>

Let $\vec{a}$ be the position vector of given point A on the line and $\vec{b}$ be parallel vector as shown in figure above.

If $\vec{r} = x\,\hat{\imath} + y\,\hat{\jmath} + z\,\hat{k}$ is position vector of any general point P on the given line, then $\overrightarrow{AP} = \vec{r} - \vec{a}$.

Since $\overrightarrow{AP} \parallel \vec{b}$, therefore $\overrightarrow{AP} = \lambda\vec{b}$.

       (*see* 'Collinear Vectors' in chapter - Vector Algebra)

i.e., $\vec{r} - \vec{a} = \lambda\vec{b} \Rightarrow \vec{r} = \vec{a} + \lambda\vec{b}$ which is the required eqn.

<u>**Example**</u>

Find the vector equation of a line which is parallel to the vector $-\hat{\imath} + \hat{\jmath} + 2\hat{k}$ and passes through a point whose position vector is $2\hat{\imath} - \hat{\jmath} + \hat{k}$.

Solution

Here, we have vector parallel to the line, $\vec{b} = -\hat{\imath} + \hat{\jmath} + 2\hat{k}$

and position vector of a point on the line, $\vec{a} = 2\hat{\imath} - \hat{\jmath} + \hat{k}$

Now equation of a line is given by $\vec{r} = \vec{a} + \lambda\vec{b}$

$\therefore$ Equation of the required line is:

$$\vec{r} = 2\hat{\imath} - \hat{\jmath} + \hat{k} + \lambda\left(-\hat{\imath} + \hat{\jmath} + 2\hat{k}\right)$$

- If we are given vector equation of a line, we can compare it with $\vec{r} = \vec{a} + \lambda\vec{b}$ to obtain parallel vector, $\vec{b}$ and position vector, $\vec{a}$ of a point on the line.

<u>Example</u>

If the equation of a line is $\vec{r} = \hat{\imath} - 2\hat{\jmath} + 3\hat{k} + \lambda(\hat{\imath} + \hat{\jmath} + \hat{k})$, find a vector parallel to it and the position vector of a point lying on it.

Solution

We know that if equation of a line is $\vec{r} = \vec{a} + \lambda\vec{b}$, then $\vec{a}$ is position vector of a point on it, and $\vec{b}$ is its parallel vector.

$\therefore$ In the given equation, we have parallel vector, $\vec{b} = \hat{\imath} + \hat{\jmath} + \hat{k}$

and position vector of a point on the line is, $\vec{a} = \hat{\imath} - 2\hat{\jmath} + 3\hat{k}$

2) **<u>Cartesian Equation:</u>**

Given : (i) Coordinates of a point (x_1, y_1, z_1) on line

(ii) DRs : a, b, c of line

Required Equation :

$$\frac{x - x_1}{a} = \frac{y - y_1}{b} = \frac{z - z_1}{c}$$

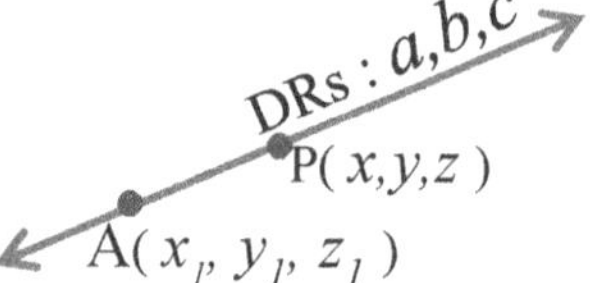

<u>Explanation</u>

Let (x_1, y_1, z_1) be the coordinates of given point A on the line, and a, b, c are DRs of the line.

If (x, y, z) are coordinates of any general point P on the line, then DRs of AP are $x - x_1$, $y - y_1$, $z - z_1$.

DRs of AP should be in proportion to the given DRs of line because AP is along the given line.

$\therefore \quad \dfrac{x - x_1}{a} = \dfrac{y - y_1}{b} = \dfrac{z - z_1}{c}$ This is the required equation.

<u>Example</u>

Find the cartesian equation of a line whose DRs are $-1, 1, 2$ and passing through a point whose coordinates are $(2, -1, 1)$.

Solution

Here, we have DRs of the line, a, b, c as $-1, 1, 2$,

and coordinates of a point on the line, (x_1, y_1, z_1) as $(2, -1, 1)$

Now equation of a line is given by $\dfrac{x-x_1}{a} = \dfrac{y-y_1}{b} = \dfrac{z-z_1}{c}$

$\therefore$ Equation of the required line is $\dfrac{x-2}{-1} = \dfrac{y+1}{1} = \dfrac{z-1}{2}$

- If we are given cartesian equation of a line, we can compare it with $\dfrac{x-x_1}{a} = \dfrac{y-y_1}{b} = \dfrac{z-z_1}{c}$ to obtain DRs, a,b,c of the line and the coordinates (x_1, y_1, z_1) of a point on the line.

<u>Example</u>

If the equation of a line is $\dfrac{x-1}{2} = \dfrac{y+2}{3} = \dfrac{z-3}{-2}$, find its DRs and the coordinates of a point lying on it.

Solution

We know that if equation of a line is $\dfrac{x-x_1}{a} = \dfrac{y-y_1}{b} = \dfrac{z-z_1}{c}$,

then (x_1, y_1, z_1) are coordinates of a point on it and a, b, c are its DRs.

$\therefore$ From the given equation, DRs of line are $2, 3, -2$.

And coordinates of a point on the line are $(1, -2, 3)$.

- If we know DRs a,b,c of the line, then we can write parallel vector of the line as $a\hat{\imath} + b\hat{\jmath} + c\hat{k}$.

- If know a parallel vector of the line as $\vec{b} = b_1\hat{\imath} + b_2\hat{\jmath} + b_3\hat{k}$, then its components b_1, b_2, b_3 can be taken as DRs of the line.

- If we know the coordinates (x_1, y_1, z_1) of a point on the line , then we can write its position vector as $x_1\hat{\imath} + y_1\hat{\jmath} + z_1\hat{k}$

- If we know the position vector of a point on the line as $\vec{a} = x_1\hat{\imath} + y_1\hat{\jmath} + z_1\hat{k}$, then we can write its coordinates (x_1, y_1, z_1) .

Hence, we can convert cartesian equation into vector equation and vector equation into cartesian equation easily.

<u>Example</u>

(i) If DRs of a line are $2, 3, -2$, then write a vector which is parallel to this line.

(ii) If the coordinates of a point lying on a line are $(1, 2, 3)$, then write the position vector of this point.

Solution

(i) Vector parallel to the line is $2\hat{\imath} + 3\hat{\jmath} - 2\hat{k}$

(ii) position vector of the point is $\hat{\imath} + 2\hat{\jmath} + 3\hat{k}$

Example

1) If a line is parallel to the vector $-\hat{\imath} + \hat{\jmath} + 2\hat{k}$, then write DRs of line.

2) If the position vector of a point lying on a line is $2\hat{\imath} - \hat{\jmath} + \hat{k}$, write the coordinates of this point.

Solution

1) Components of a vector are its DRs.

$\therefore$ DRs of given parallel vector are $-1, 1, 2$

Now DRs of parallel vector are also DRs of the line.

$\therefore$ DRs of the line are $-1, 1, 2$

2) If a vector represents a point in cartesian system, then its components represent coordinates of that point.

$\therefore$ Coordinates of the point are $(2, -1, 1)$.

5.2 Two Point form

1) <u>**Vector Equation:**</u>

Given : Position Vectors $\vec{a}_1$ & $\vec{a}_2$ of 2 points on the line

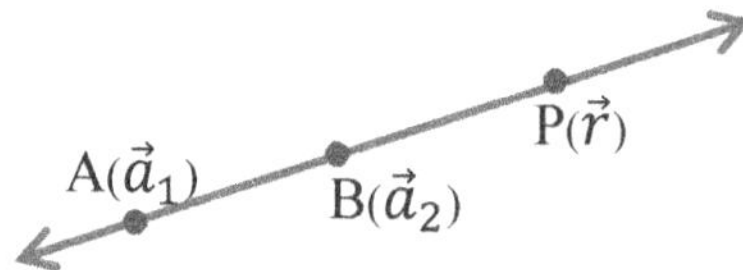

Required Equation : $\quad \vec{r} = \vec{a}_1 + \lambda\,(\vec{a}_2 - \vec{a}_1)$

Explanation

Let $\vec{a}_1$ & $\vec{a}_2$ be the position vectors of given points A & B on the line (*see* figure above).

If $\vec{r} = x\,\hat{\imath} + y\,\hat{\jmath} + z\,\hat{k}$ is position vector of any general point P on the line, then $\overrightarrow{AP} = \vec{r} - \vec{a}_1$ and $\overrightarrow{AB} = \vec{a}_2 - \vec{a}_1$.

[*see* 'Vector joining two points' in chapter – Vector Algebra]

Since $\overrightarrow{AP}$ and $\overrightarrow{AB}$ are collinear, $\therefore \overrightarrow{AP} = \lambda\,\overrightarrow{AB}$.

(*see* 'Collinear Vectors' in chapter - Vector Algebra)

i.e., $\vec{r} - \vec{a}_1 = \lambda\,(\vec{a}_2 - \vec{a}_1)$

$\Rightarrow \vec{r} = \vec{a}_1 + \lambda\,(\vec{a}_2 - \vec{a}_1)$ This is the required equation.

Example

Find the vector equation of a line which passes the two points whose position vectors are $\hat{\imath} + 2\hat{\jmath} + 3\hat{k}$ and $2\hat{\imath} - \hat{\jmath} + \hat{k}$.

Solution

Here, we have position vectors of two points on the line as,

$$\vec{a}_1 = \hat{\imath} + 2\hat{\jmath} + 3\hat{k} \text{ and } \vec{a}_2 = 2\hat{\imath} - \hat{\jmath} + \hat{k}$$

Equation of a line is given by $\vec{r} = \vec{a}_1 + \lambda(\vec{a}_2 - \vec{a}_1)$

$\therefore$ Equation of the required line is

$$\vec{r} = \hat{\imath} + 2\hat{\jmath} + 3\hat{k} + \lambda\left[2\hat{\imath} - \hat{\jmath} + \hat{k} - (\hat{\imath} + 2\hat{\jmath} + 3\hat{k})\right]$$

Or $\quad \vec{r} = \hat{\imath} + 2\hat{\jmath} + 3\hat{k} + \lambda(\hat{\imath} - 3\hat{\jmath} - 2\hat{k})$

2) Cartesian Equation:

Given: Coordinates of 2 points $(x_1, y_1, z_1) \& (x_2, y_2, z_2)$ on the line

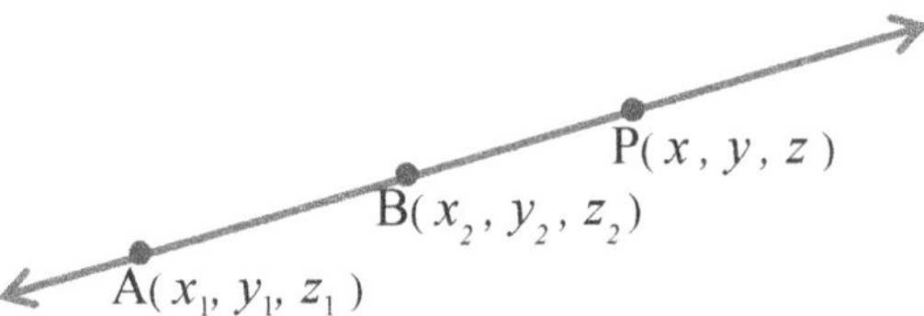

Required Equation : $\quad \dfrac{x - x_1}{x_2 - x_1} = \dfrac{y - y_1}{y_2 - y_1} = \dfrac{z - z_1}{z_2 - z_1}$

Explanation

Let (x_1, y_1, z_1) and (x_2, y_2, z_2) be the coordinates of given points A & B on the line.

If (x, y, z) are coordinates of any general point P on the line, then DRs of AP are $x - x_1,\ y - y_1,\ z - z_1$, while DRs of AB are $x_2 - x_1,\ y_2 - y_1,\ z_2 - z_1$.

   [*see* 'DCs and DRs of line through two points' in this chapter]

Since lines AP and AB coincide,

$\therefore$ DRs of AP should be in proportion to the DRs of AB.

i.e., $\dfrac{x - x_1}{x_2 - x_1} = \dfrac{y - y_1}{y_2 - y_1} = \dfrac{z - z_1}{z_2 - z_1}$ This is the required eqn.

Example

Find the cartesian equation of a line which passes the two points A(1, 2, 3) and B(2, $-$ 1, 1).

Solution

Here, coordinates of two points on the line, (x_1, y_1, z_1) and (x_2, y_2, z_2) are (1, 2, 3) and (2, -1, 1)

Equation of a line is given by $\dfrac{x - x_1}{x_2 - x_1} = \dfrac{y - y_1}{y_2 - y_1} = \dfrac{z - z_1}{z_2 - z_1}$

$\therefore$ Equation of the required line is $\dfrac{x-1}{2-1} = \dfrac{y-2}{-1-2} = \dfrac{z-3}{1-3}$

Or $\quad \dfrac{x-1}{1} = \dfrac{y-2}{-3} = \dfrac{z-3}{-2}$

Asterisk (*) marked article (if any) is **not** *in CBSE 2025-26 syllabus.*

6 Angle between two Lines

1) __Vector Form__:

Given : Vector equations of 2 lines
$$\vec{r} = \vec{a}_1 + \lambda_1 \vec{b}_1 \ \text{ and}$$
$$\vec{r} = \vec{a}_2 + \lambda_2 \vec{b}_2$$

From these equations, we find their parallel vectors as $\vec{b}_1$ & $\vec{b}_2$ respectively.

If θ = acute angle between the lines, then

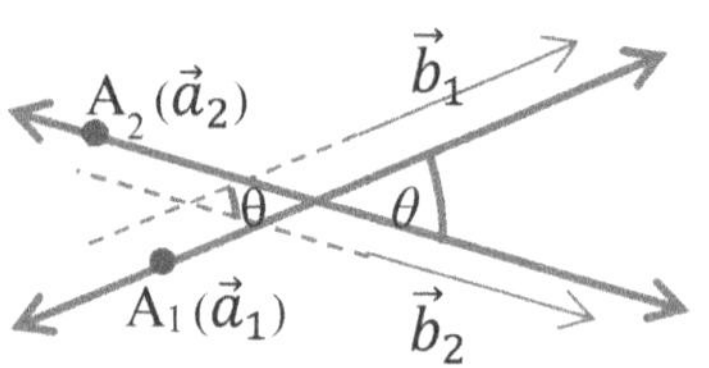

$$\boldsymbol{cos\ \theta} = \left| \frac{\vec{b}_1 \cdot \vec{b}_2}{|\vec{b}_1||\vec{b}_2|} \right|$$

__Explanation__

From the given equations of lines, we can obtain their parallel vectors $\vec{b}_1$ & $\vec{b}_2$.

Angle, θ between two lines will be the same as the angle between their parallel vectors (as shown in the above figure). And angle between two vectors can be found by their scalar product:

$$\vec{b}_1 \cdot \vec{b}_2 = |\vec{b}_1| \cdot |\vec{b}_2| \cos\theta$$

(*see* 'Angle between two vectors' in chapter - Vector Algebra)

For acute angle θ, the scalar product should be positive.

$$\therefore \ \cos \theta = \left| \frac{\vec{b}_1 \cdot \vec{b}_2}{|\vec{b}_1||\vec{b}_2|} \right|$$

__Example__

Find the angle between the pair of lines given by
$$\vec{r} = 3\hat{\imath} + 2\hat{\jmath} - 4\hat{k} + \lambda(\hat{\imath} + 2\hat{\jmath} + 2\hat{k})$$
And $\vec{r} = 5\hat{\imath} - 2\hat{\jmath} + \mu(3\hat{\imath} + 2\hat{\jmath} + 6\hat{k})$

__Solution__

We know that if equation of a line is $\vec{r} = \vec{a} + \lambda\vec{b}$, then $\vec{a}$ is position vector of a point on it, and $\vec{b}$ is its parallel vector.

Here, Parallel vectors of two lines, respectively, are
$$\vec{b}_1 = \hat{\imath} + 2\hat{\jmath} + 2\hat{k} \ \text{ and } \ \vec{b}_2 = 3\hat{\imath} + 2\hat{\jmath} + 6\hat{k}$$

If θ is acute angle between the lines, then
$$\cos \theta = \left| \frac{\vec{b}_1 \cdot \vec{b}_2}{|\vec{b}_1||\vec{b}_2|} \right|$$

$$\Rightarrow \quad \cos \theta = \left| \frac{(\hat{\imath}+2\hat{\jmath}+2\hat{k}).(3\hat{\imath}+2\hat{\jmath}+6\hat{k})}{|\hat{\imath}+2\hat{\jmath}+2\hat{k}|\,|3\hat{\imath}+2\hat{\jmath}+6\hat{k}|} \right|$$

---

*Asterisk (*) marked article (if any) is **not** in CBSE 2025-26 syllabus.*

$$\Rightarrow \quad \cos\theta = \left|\frac{3+4+12}{\sqrt{1^2+2^2+2^2}\;\sqrt{3^2+2^2+6^2}}\right| = \frac{19}{21}$$

$$\Rightarrow \quad \theta = \cos^{-1}\frac{19}{21}$$

2) Cartesian Form:

Given: Cartesian equations of 2 lines
$$\frac{x-x_1}{a_1} = \frac{y-y_1}{b_1} = \frac{z-z_1}{c_1}$$

and
$$\frac{x-x_2}{a_2} = \frac{y-y_2}{b_2} = \frac{z-z_2}{c_2}$$

From these equations, we find their DRs as a_1, b_1, c_1 & a_2, b_2, c_2 respectively.

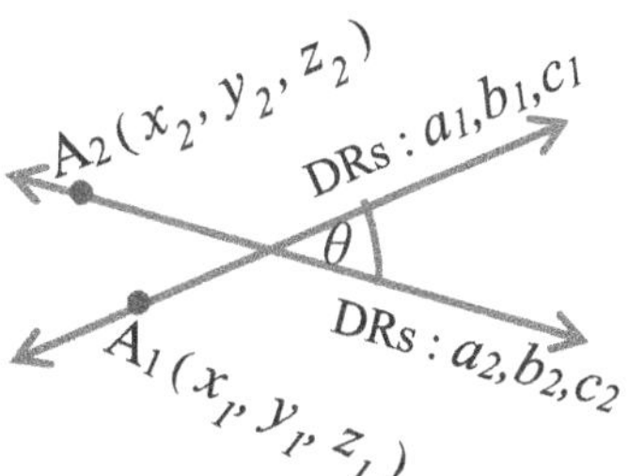

If $\theta =$ acute angle between the lines, then

$$\boldsymbol{\cos\theta} = \left|\frac{a_1a_2+b_1b_2+c_1c_2}{\sqrt{a_1{}^2+b_1{}^2+c_1{}^2}\;\sqrt{a_2{}^2+b_2{}^2+c_2{}^2}}\right|$$

Explanation

From the given equations of lines, we can obtain their DRs as a_1, b_1, c_1 & a_2, b_2, c_2 respectively.

We recall that from DRs, their parallel vectors can be written as $a_1\hat{i}+b_1\hat{j}+c_1\hat{k}$ and $a_2\hat{i}+b_2\hat{j}+c_2\hat{k}$ respectively.

Now, angle between two lines will be the same as the angle between their parallel vectors, and angle between two vectors can be found by their scalar product as discussed above (in the vector form).

Also, for acute angle θ, the scalar product should be positive.

$$\therefore \cos\theta = \frac{\left|(a_1\hat{i}+b_1\hat{j}+c_1\hat{k})\cdot(a_2\hat{i}+b_2\hat{j}+c_2\hat{k})\right|}{\left|a_1\hat{i}+b_1\hat{j}+c_1\hat{k}\right|\left|a_2\hat{i}+b_2\hat{j}+c_2\hat{k}\right|}$$

(As discussed above for vector form)

$$\Rightarrow \cos\theta = \frac{\left|a_1a_2+b_1b_2+c_1c_2\right|}{\sqrt{a_1^2+b_1^2+c_1^2}\;\sqrt{a_2^2+b_2^2+c_2^2}}$$

Example

Find the angle between the pair of lines:
$$\frac{x-2}{2} = \frac{y-1}{5} = \frac{z+3}{-3} \quad \text{and} \quad \frac{x+2}{-1} = \frac{y-4}{8} = \frac{z-5}{4}$$

Solution

We know that if equation of a line is $\dfrac{x-x_1}{a} = \dfrac{y-y_1}{b} = \dfrac{z-z_1}{c}$, then a, b, c are its DRs.

$\therefore$ Here, DRs of the given lines, respectively, are 2, 5, –3 and –1, 8, 4.

i.e., $a_1 = 2$, $b_1 = 5$, $c_1 = -3$ and $a_2 = -1$, $b_2 = 8$, $c_2 = 4$

If θ is acute angle between the lines, then

$$\cos\theta = \dfrac{|a_1\,a_2 + b_1\,b_2 + c_1\,c_2|}{\sqrt{a_1^2 + b_1^2 + c_1^2}\ \sqrt{a_2^2 + b_2^2 + c_2^2}}$$

$$\Rightarrow \cos\theta = \dfrac{|(2)(-1) + (5)(8) + (-3)(4)|}{\sqrt{2^2 + 5^2 + (-3)^2}\ \sqrt{(-1)^2 + 8^2 + 4^2}} = \left|\dfrac{26}{\sqrt{38}\,\sqrt{81}}\right| = \dfrac{26}{9\sqrt{38}}$$

$$\Rightarrow \theta = \cos^{-1}\left(\dfrac{26}{9\sqrt{38}}\right)$$

- Also, $\cos\theta = |\,l_1 l_2 + m_1 m_2 + n_1 n_2\,|$

  Where l_1, m_1, n_1 & l_2, m_2, n_2 are DCs of two given lines.

<u>Explanation</u>

If we know DRs a_1, b_1, c_1 & a_2, b_2, c_2 of two lines, respectively, then we can obtain their DCs l_1, m_1, n_1 & l_2, m_2, n_2 respectively (*see* 'Line and Directed Line' in this chapter). So,

$$l_1 = \dfrac{a_1}{\sqrt{a_1^2 + b_1^2 + c_1^2}}, \ m_1 = \dfrac{b_1}{\sqrt{a_1^2 + b_1^2 + c_1^2}}, \ n_1 = \dfrac{c_1}{\sqrt{a_1^2 + b_1^2 + c_1^2}}$$

And

$$l_2 = \dfrac{a_2}{\sqrt{a_2^2 + b_2^2 + c_2^2}}, \ m_2 = \dfrac{b_2}{\sqrt{a_2^2 + b_2^2 + c_2^2}}, \ n_2 = \dfrac{c_2}{\sqrt{a_2^2 + b_2^2 + c_2^2}}$$

Using these relations between DRs and DCs we can convert expression for acute angle θ between two lines in terms of DCs, which was given earlier in term of DRs as follows:

$$\cos\theta = \left|\dfrac{a_1\,a_2 + b_1\,b_2 + c_1\,c_2}{\sqrt{a_1^2 + b_1^2 + c_1^2}\ \sqrt{a_2^2 + b_2^2 + c_2^2}}\right|$$

$$\Rightarrow \cos\theta = |\,l_1 l_2 + m_1 m_2 + n_1 n_2\,|$$

<u>Example</u>

Direction cosines of 2 lines are $\dfrac{3}{5\sqrt{2}}$, $\dfrac{1}{\sqrt{2}}$, $\dfrac{4}{5\sqrt{2}}$ and $\dfrac{1}{\sqrt{6}}$, $\dfrac{1}{\sqrt{6}}$, $\dfrac{2}{\sqrt{6}}$ respectively. Find the angle between them.

Solution

Here, DCs of the given lines, respectively, are:

$$\dfrac{3}{5\sqrt{2}}, \ \dfrac{1}{\sqrt{2}}, \ \dfrac{4}{5\sqrt{2}} \ \text{ and } \ \dfrac{1}{\sqrt{6}}, \ \dfrac{1}{\sqrt{6}}, \ \dfrac{2}{\sqrt{6}}.$$

---

i.e., $l_1 = \dfrac{3}{5\sqrt{2}}$, $m_1 = \dfrac{1}{\sqrt{2}}$, $n_1 = \dfrac{4}{5\sqrt{2}}$ and $l_2 = \dfrac{1}{\sqrt{6}}$, $m_2 = \dfrac{1}{\sqrt{6}}$, $n_2 = \dfrac{2}{\sqrt{6}}$

If θ is acute angle between the lines, then

$$\cos\theta = |\, l_1 l_2 + m_1 m_2 + n_1 n_2 \,|$$

$$\Rightarrow \cos\theta = \left| \left(\dfrac{3}{5\sqrt{2}}\right)\left(\dfrac{1}{\sqrt{6}}\right) + \left(\dfrac{1}{\sqrt{2}}\right)\left(\dfrac{1}{\sqrt{6}}\right) + \left(\dfrac{4}{5\sqrt{2}}\right)\left(\dfrac{2}{\sqrt{6}}\right) \right|$$

$$\Rightarrow \cos\theta = \left| \left(\dfrac{3}{5\sqrt{12}}\right) + \left(\dfrac{1}{\sqrt{12}}\right) + \left(\dfrac{8}{5\sqrt{12}}\right) \right| = \left| \dfrac{16}{5\sqrt{12}} \right| = \dfrac{16}{5\times 2\sqrt{3}} = \dfrac{8}{5\sqrt{3}}$$

$$\Rightarrow \theta = \cos^{-1}\left(\dfrac{8}{5\sqrt{3}}\right)$$

- And in terms of $\sin\theta$

$$\sin\theta$$
$$= \sqrt{(l_1 m_2 - l_2 m_1)^2 + (m_1 n_2 - m_2 n_1)^2 + (n_1 l_2 - m_2 l_1)^2}$$

It can be obtained by using $\sin\theta = \sqrt{1 - \cos^2\theta}$ and putting

$$\cos\theta = |l_1 l_2 + m_1 m_2 + n_1 n_2|$$

7 Conditions for Parallel and Perpendicular Lines

If a_1, b_1, c_1 & a_2, b_2, c_2 are DRs , and l_1, m_1, n_1 & l_2, m_2, n_2 are DCs of two given lines, respectively, then

(i) **For Parallel Lines:** $\dfrac{a_1}{a_2} = \dfrac{b_1}{b_2} = \dfrac{c_1}{c_2}$ OR $\dfrac{l_1}{l_2} = \dfrac{m_1}{m_2} = \dfrac{n_1}{n_2}$

(ii) **For perpendicular lines:** $\quad a_1 a_2 + b_1 b_2 + c_1 c_2 = 0$

$$\text{OR} \quad l_1 l_2 + m_1 m_2 + n_1 n_2 = 0$$

Explanation

Angle between parallel lines is $0°$ or $180°$.

$\therefore$ Condition for parallel lines can be easily obtained by putting, $\theta = 0°$ or $180°$ in the relation mentioned earlier for angle between two lines in terms of $\sin\theta$.

(*see* 'Angle between two lines' in this chapter)

Angle between perpendicular lines is $90°$.

$\therefore$ Conditions for perpendicular lines can be easily obtained by putting $\theta = 90°$ in the relation mentioned earlier for angle between lines in terms of $\cos\theta$.

Example

DCs of two lines are $\dfrac{12}{13}$, $\dfrac{-3}{13}$, $\dfrac{-4}{13}$ and $\dfrac{3}{13}$, $\dfrac{-4}{13}$, $\dfrac{12}{13}$. Show that they are perpendicular to each other.

Solution

Here, DCs of the given lines, respectively, are:

$\dfrac{12}{13}$, $\dfrac{-3}{13}$, $\dfrac{-4}{13}$ and $\dfrac{3}{13}$, $\dfrac{-4}{13}$, $\dfrac{12}{13}$.

i.e., $l_1 = \dfrac{12}{13}$, $m_1 = \dfrac{-3}{13}$, $n_1 = \dfrac{-4}{13}$ and $l_2 = \dfrac{3}{13}$, $m_2 = \dfrac{-4}{13}$, $n_2 = \dfrac{12}{13}$

---

*Asterisk (*) marked article (if any) is **not** in CBSE 2025-26 syllabus.*

For lines to be perpendicular, we should have
$$l_1 l_2 + m_1 m_2 + n_1 n_2 = 0$$
Now $l_1 l_2 + m_1 m_2 + n_1 n_2 = \left(\frac{12}{13}\right)\left(\frac{3}{13}\right) + \left(\frac{-3}{13}\right)\left(\frac{-4}{13}\right) + \left(\frac{-4}{13}\right)\left(\frac{12}{13}\right)$
$$\Rightarrow l_1 l_2 + m_1 m_2 + n_1 n_2 = 0$$
$\therefore$ Given lines are perpendicular.

Example

Equations of two lines are $\dfrac{x-2}{7} = \dfrac{y-1}{-5} = \dfrac{z+3}{1}$ and $\dfrac{x+2}{1} = \dfrac{y-4}{2} = \dfrac{z-5}{3}$.
Show that they are perpendicular to each other.

Solution

We know that if equation of a line is $\dfrac{x-x_1}{a} = \dfrac{y-y_1}{b} = \dfrac{z-z_1}{c}$, then
a, b, c are its DRs.

$\therefore$ From the given equations, DRs of lines, respectively, are:
$$7, -5, 1 \text{ and } 1, 2, 3.$$
i.e., $a_1 = 7,\ b_1 = -5,\ c_1 = 1$ and $a_2 = 1,\ b_2 = 2,\ c_2 = 3$

For lines to be perpendicular, we should have
$$a_1 a_2 + b_1 b_2 + c_1 c_2 = 0$$
Now $a_1 a_2 + b_1 b_2 + c_1 c_2 = (7)(1) + (-5)(2) + (1)(3)$
$$\Rightarrow \quad a_1 a_2 + b_1 b_2 + c_1 c_2 = 0$$
$\therefore$ Given lines are perpendicular.

Example

DRs of two lines are $12, -6, -4$ and $-6, 3, 2$ respectively.
Show that they are parallel to each other.

Solution

Here, DCs of the given lines, respectively, are:
$$12, -6, -4 \text{ and } -6, 3, 2.$$
i.e., $a_1 = 12,\ b_1 = -6,\ c_1 = -4$ and $a_2 = -6,\ b_2 = 3,\ c_2 = 2$

For lines to be parallel, we should have
$$\frac{a_1}{a_2} = \frac{b_1}{b_2} = \frac{c_1}{c_2}$$
Now $\dfrac{a_1}{a_2} = \dfrac{12}{-6} = -2,\quad \dfrac{b_1}{b_2} = \dfrac{-6}{3} = -2$ and $\dfrac{c_1}{c_2} = \dfrac{-4}{2} = -2$

$\therefore \quad \dfrac{a_1}{a_2} = \dfrac{b_1}{b_2} = \dfrac{c_1}{c_2}$

$\therefore$ Given lines are parallel.

8   Shortest Distance between Two Skew Lines

Two lines in space which are neither intersecting nor parallel (or coincident) are called skew lines.

- Skew lines are always non coplanar.

- Shortest distance between them is along the line which is perpendicular to both lines.

1) **<u>Vector Form:</u>**

Given : Vector equations of 2 lines

$$\vec{r} = \vec{a}_1 + \lambda_1 \vec{b}_1 \quad \text{and} \quad \vec{r} = \vec{a}_2 + \lambda_2 \vec{b}_2$$

From these equations, we find their parallel vectors as $\vec{b}_1$ & $\vec{b}_2$ respectively and position vectors $\vec{a}_1$ & $\vec{a}_2$ of points on these lines, respectively.

$$\textbf{Shortest Distance} = \frac{\left|(\vec{a}_2 - \vec{a}_1) \cdot (\vec{b}_1 \times \vec{b}_2)\right|}{\left|\vec{b}_1 \times \vec{b}_2\right|}$$

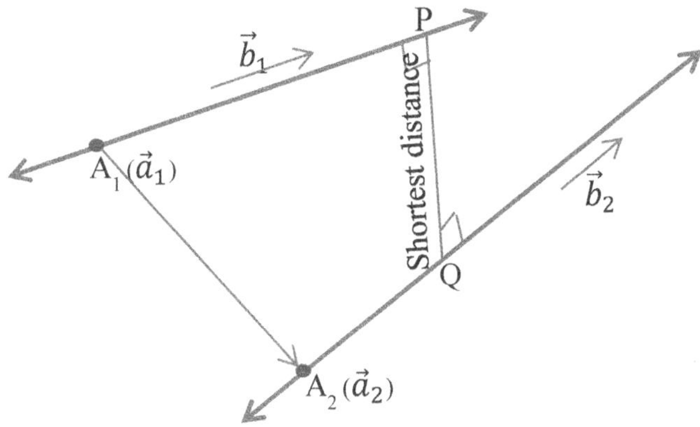

<u>Explanation</u>

From the given equations of lines, we can obtain their parallel vectors $\vec{b}_1$ & $\vec{b}_2$

and position vectors of points, A_1 as $(\vec{a}_1)$ & A_2 as $(\vec{a}_2)$ lying on them respectively (as shown in above figure).

Vector $\vec{b}_1 \times \vec{b}_2$ will be perpendicular to both the lines

(*see* 'Vector Product of two vectors' in chapter – Vector Algebra)

and shortest distance PQ will be along this vector.

Now projection, of a vector from any point on one given line to any point on the other given line, will be equal to PQ.

$\therefore$ Projection of vector $\overrightarrow{A_1 A_2}$ on $\vec{b}_1 \times \vec{b}_2$ will be equal to PQ.

And $\overrightarrow{A_1 A_2} = \vec{a}_2 - \vec{a}_1$

So, shortest distance $PQ = \dfrac{\left|(\vec{a}_2 - \vec{a}_1) \cdot (\vec{b}_1 \times \vec{b}_2)\right|}{\left|\vec{b}_1 \times \vec{b}_2\right|}$

(*see* 'Projection of $\vec{a}$ on $\vec{b}$' in chapter – Vector Algebra)

<u>**Example**</u>

Find the shortest distance between lines whose vector equations are:

$$\vec{r} = \hat{\imath} + 2\hat{\jmath} + 3\hat{k} + \lambda(\hat{\imath} - 3\hat{\jmath} + 2\hat{k})$$

And $\quad \vec{r} = 4\hat{\imath} + 5\hat{\jmath} + 6\hat{k} + \mu(2\hat{\imath} + 3\hat{\jmath} + \hat{k})$

Solution

We know that if equation of a line is $\vec{r} = \vec{a} + \lambda\vec{b}$, then $\vec{a}$ is position vector of a point on it, and $\vec{b}$ is its parallel vector.

$\therefore$ From the given equation, we have parallel vectors of lines, respectively, as

$$\vec{b_1} = \hat{\imath} - 3\hat{\jmath} + 2\hat{k} \qquad \text{and} \qquad \vec{b_2} = 2\hat{\imath} + 3\hat{\jmath} + \hat{k}$$

And position vector of points on the lines, respectively, are

$$\vec{a_1} = \hat{\imath} + 2\hat{\jmath} + 3\hat{k} \qquad \text{and} \qquad \vec{a_2} = 4\hat{\imath} + 5\hat{\jmath} + 6\hat{k}$$

Shortest distance between line is given by $\dfrac{|(\vec{a_2} - \vec{a_1}) \cdot (\vec{b_1} \times \vec{b_2})|}{|\vec{b_1} \times \vec{b_2}|}$

Now $\vec{a_2} - \vec{a_1} = \left(4\hat{\imath} + 5\hat{\jmath} + 6\hat{k}\right) - \left(\hat{\imath} + 2\hat{\jmath} + 3\hat{k}\right) = 3\hat{\imath} + 3\hat{\jmath} + 3\hat{k}$

And $\vec{b_1} \times \vec{b_2} = \begin{vmatrix} \hat{\imath} & \hat{\jmath} & \hat{k} \\ 1 & -3 & 2 \\ 2 & 3 & 1 \end{vmatrix}$

$= \hat{\imath}(-3 - 6) - \hat{\jmath}(1 - 4) + \hat{k}(3 + 6) \ldots$ [expanding along first row]

$= -9\hat{\imath} + 3\hat{\jmath} + 9\hat{k}$

$\Rightarrow |\vec{b_1} \times \vec{b_2}| = \sqrt{(-9)^2 + (3)^2 + (9)^2} = \sqrt{171} = 3\sqrt{19}$

$\therefore$ Shortest distance $= \dfrac{|(\vec{a_2} - \vec{a_1}) \cdot (\vec{b_1} \times \vec{b_2})|}{|\vec{b_1} \times \vec{b_2}|}$

$\qquad = \dfrac{|(3\hat{\imath} + 3\hat{\jmath} + 3\hat{k}) \cdot (-9\hat{\imath} + 3\hat{\jmath} + 9\hat{k})|}{3\sqrt{19}}$

$\qquad = \dfrac{|-27 + 9 + 27|}{3\sqrt{19}} = \dfrac{3}{\sqrt{19}} = \dfrac{3\sqrt{19}}{19}$

2) <u>**Cartesian Form**</u>:

Given :   Cartesian equations of 2 lines,

$$\frac{x - x_1}{a_1} = \frac{y - y_1}{b_1} = \frac{z - z_1}{c_1} \quad \text{and} \quad \frac{x - x_2}{a_2} = \frac{y - y_2}{b_2} = \frac{z - z_2}{c_2}$$

From these equations, we find their DRs as $a_1,\ b_1,\ c_1$ & $a_2,\ b_2,\ c_2$ respectively.

Also, we can find coordinates $(x_1,\ y_1,\ z_1)$ & $(x_2,\ y_2,\ z_2)$ of points lying on these lines, respectively.

Shortest Distance $=$

$$\frac{\left| \begin{vmatrix} x_2 - x_1 & y_2 - y_1 & z_2 - z_1 \\ a_1 & b_1 & c_1 \\ a_2 & b_2 & c_2 \end{vmatrix} \right|}{\sqrt{(a_1 b_2 - a_2 b_1)^2 + (b_1 c_2 - b_2 c_1)^2 + (c_1 a_2 - c_2 a_1)^2}}$$

---

*Asterisk (*) marked article (if any) is **not** in CBSE 2025-26 syllabus.*

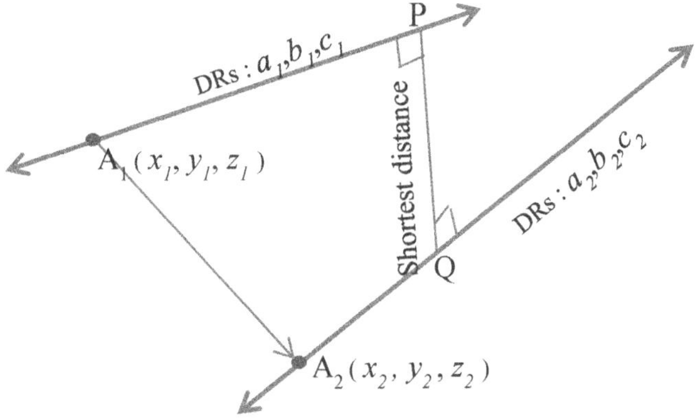

<u>Explanation</u>

From the given equations of lines, we can obtain their DRs as a_1, b_1, c_1 & a_2, b_2, c_2 respectively.

We recall that from DRs, their parallel vectors $\vec{b}_1$ & $\vec{b}_2$ can be written as

$a_1\hat{\imath} + b_1\hat{\jmath} + c_1\hat{k}$ and $a_2\hat{\imath} + b_2\hat{\jmath} + c_2\hat{k}$ respectively.

Also, we can obtain coordinates of points A_1 as (x_1, y_1, z_1) and A_2 as (x_2, y_2, z_2) lying on the lines respectively from their equations (shown in above figure).

From these coordinates we can write their position vectors:

$\vec{a}_1 = x_1\hat{\imath} + y_1\hat{\jmath} + z_1\hat{k}$ & $\vec{a}_2 = x_2\hat{\imath} + y_2\hat{\jmath} + z_2\hat{k}$.

Now, as explained earlier (in the vector form) , shortest distance is

$$PQ = \frac{\left|(\vec{a}_2 - \vec{a}_1).\,(\vec{b}_1 \times \vec{b}_2)\right|}{\left|\vec{b}_1 \times \vec{b}_2\right|}$$

If we find scalar triple product of vectors in the numerator and magnitude of $\vec{b}_1 \times \vec{b}_2$ in the denominator, we can obtain the cartesian form of this expression as:

$$PQ = \frac{\left|\begin{vmatrix} x_2-x_1 & y_2-y_1 & z_2-z_1 \\ a_1 & b_1 & c_1 \\ a_2 & b_2 & c_2 \end{vmatrix}\right|}{\sqrt{(a_1b_2-a_2b_1)^2+(b_1c_2-b_2c_1)^2+(c_1a_2-c_2a_1)^2}}$$

<u>Example</u>

Find the shortest distance between the lines:

$$\frac{x+1}{7} = \frac{y+1}{-6} = \frac{z+1}{1} \quad \text{and} \quad \frac{x-3}{1} = \frac{y-5}{-2} = \frac{z-7}{1}.$$

Solution

We know that if equation of a line is $\dfrac{x-x_1}{a} = \dfrac{y-y_1}{b} = \dfrac{z-z_1}{c}$, then a, b, c are its DRs and (x_1, y_1, z_1) are coordinates of a point on it.

---

*Asterisk (*) marked article (if any) is **not** in CBSE 2025-26 syllabus.*

$\therefore$ From the given equations, DRs of lines, respectively, are:
  7, –6, 1 and 1, –2, 1 .

i.e., $a_1 = 7$, $b_1 = -6$, $c_1 = 1$ and $a_2 = 1$, $b_2 = -2$, $c_2 = 1$ and coordinates of points on them, respectively, are:
  (–1, –1, –1) and (3, 5, 7).

i.e., $x_1 = -1$, $y_1 = -1$, $z_1 = -1$ and $x_2 = 3$, $y_2 = 5$, $z_2 = 7$

Shortest distance between line is given by

$$= \frac{\left| \begin{array}{ccc} x_2-x_1 & y_2-y_1 & z_2-z_1 \\ a_1 & b_1 & c_1 \\ a_2 & b_2 & c_2 \end{array} \right|}{\sqrt{(a_1 b_2 - a_2 b_1)^2 + (b_1 c_2 - b_2 c_1)^2 + (c_1 a_2 - c_2 a_1)^2}}$$

$$= \frac{\left| \begin{array}{ccc} 3+1 & 5+1 & 7+1 \\ 7 & -6 & 1 \\ 1 & -2 & 1 \end{array} \right|}{\sqrt{[(7)(-2)-(1)(-6)]^2 + [(-6)(1)-(-2)(1)]^2 + [(1)(1)-(1)(7)]^2}}$$

$$= \frac{116}{\sqrt{116}} = \sqrt{116} = 2\sqrt{29}$$

9 Distance between Two Parallel Lines

Vector Form:

Given : Vector equations of 2 lines

$$\vec{r} = \vec{a}_1 + \lambda_1 \vec{b} \quad \text{and} \quad \vec{r} = \vec{a}_2 + \lambda_2 \vec{b}$$

From these equations, we find their parallel vector as $\vec{b}$ and position vectors $\vec{a}_1$ & $\vec{a}_2$ of points on these lines respectively.

$$\textbf{Required Distance} = \frac{\left|(\vec{a}_2 - \vec{a}_1) \times \vec{b}\right|}{|\vec{b}|}$$

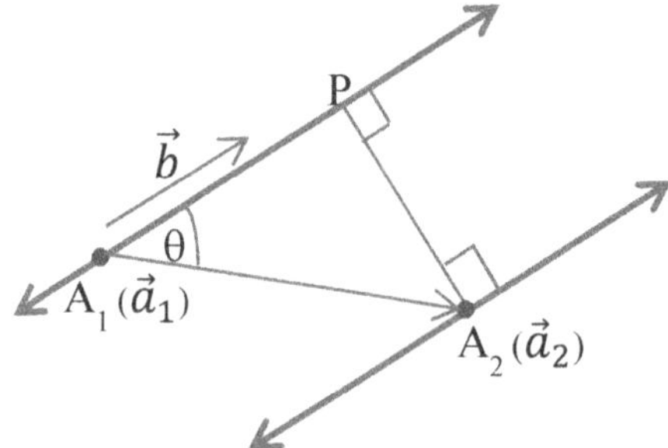

Explanation

From the given equations of lines, we can obtain their parallel vectors, and observe that they are same, or their components are in proportion. By this observation, we can say that lines are parallel.

We can take any of these vector as $\vec{b}$.

Also, we can obtain position vectors of points, A_1 as ($\vec{a}_1$) & A_2 as ($\vec{a}_2$) lying on them respectively.

---

*Asterisk (*) marked article (if any) is **not** in CBSE 2025-26 syllabus.*

Shortest distance will be along the perpendicular from any point on a line to the other line. So, A_2P will be the required distance as shown in the figure above.

$$A_2P = A_1A_2 \, \sin\theta = \left|\overrightarrow{A_1A_2}\right| \sin\theta$$

Now, $\left|\overrightarrow{A_1A_2} \times \vec{b}\right| = \left|\overrightarrow{A_1A_2}\right| \left|\vec{b}\right| \sin\theta$

$$\Rightarrow \left|\overrightarrow{A_1A_2}\right| \sin\theta = \frac{\left|\overrightarrow{A_1A_2} \times \vec{b}\right|}{\left|\vec{b}\right|}$$

$$\therefore \quad A_2P = \left|\overrightarrow{A_1A_2}\right| \sin\theta$$
$$= \frac{\left|\overrightarrow{A_1A_2} \times \vec{b}\right|}{\left|\vec{b}\right|}$$
$$= \frac{\left|(\vec{a}_2 - \vec{a}_1) \times \vec{b}\right|}{\left|\vec{b}\right|}$$

Example

Find the distance between the lines whose vector equations are

$$\vec{r} = \hat{\imath} + 2\hat{\jmath} - 4\hat{k} + \lambda(2\hat{\imath} + 3\hat{\jmath} + 6\hat{k})$$

And $\vec{r} = 3\hat{\imath} + 3\hat{\jmath} - 5\hat{k} + \mu(2\hat{\imath} + 3\hat{\jmath} + 6\hat{k})$

Solution

We know that if equation of a line is $\vec{r} = \vec{a} + \lambda\vec{b}$, then $\vec{a}$ is position vector of a point on it, and $\vec{b}$ is its parallel vector.

$\therefore$ From the given equations, position vector of points on the line, respectively, are:

$$\vec{a_1} = \hat{\imath} + 2\hat{\jmath} - 4\hat{k} \quad \text{and} \quad \vec{a_2} = 3\hat{\imath} + 3\hat{\jmath} - 5\hat{k}$$

And we have parallel vectors, respectively, as:

$$\vec{b_1} = 2\hat{\imath} + 3\hat{\jmath} + 6\hat{k} \quad \text{and} \quad \vec{b_2} = 2\hat{\imath} + 3\hat{\jmath} + 6\hat{k}$$

If parallel vectors are same or their components are in proportion, then lines are parallel.

$\therefore$ Given lines are parallel, and their parallel vector is:

$$\vec{b} = 2\hat{\imath} + 3\hat{\jmath} + 6\hat{k}$$

Now the distance between parallel lines is $= \dfrac{\left|(\vec{a}_2 - \vec{a}_1) \times \vec{b}\right|}{\left|\vec{b}\right|}$

Here, $\vec{a}_2 - \vec{a}_1 = (3\hat{\imath} + 3\hat{\jmath} - 5\hat{k}) - (\hat{\imath} + 2\hat{\jmath} - 4\hat{k}) = 2\hat{\imath} + \hat{\jmath} - \hat{k}$

And $(\vec{a}_2 - \vec{a}_1) \times \vec{b} = \begin{vmatrix} \hat{\imath} & \hat{\jmath} & \hat{k} \\ 2 & 1 & -1 \\ 2 & 3 & 6 \end{vmatrix}$

$$= \hat{\imath}(6 + 3) - \hat{\jmath}(12 + 2) + \hat{k}(6 - 2)$$

. . . .[expanding along first row]

$$= 9\hat{\imath} - 14\hat{\jmath} + 4\hat{k}$$

$$\Rightarrow \quad |(\vec{a}_2 - \vec{a}_1) \times \vec{b}| = \sqrt{(9)^2 + (-14)^2 + (4)^2} = \sqrt{293}$$

$$\text{Also } |\vec{b}| = \sqrt{(2)^2 + (3)^2 + (6)^2} = \sqrt{49} = 7$$

$$\therefore \text{ The distance between the given lines is} = \frac{|(\vec{a}_2 - \vec{a}_1) \times \vec{b}|}{|\vec{b}|}$$

$$= \frac{\sqrt{293}}{7}$$

10   *Equation of Plane

10.1   *Normal form

1) **Vector Equation:**

Given: (i)   d = perpendicular distance of plane from origin

(ii) $\hat{n}$ = unit normal vector to plane

Required Equation : $\vec{r} \cdot \hat{n} = \mathbf{d}$

General form: $\vec{r} \cdot \vec{n} = $ D

where $\vec{n}$ = normal vector to the plane

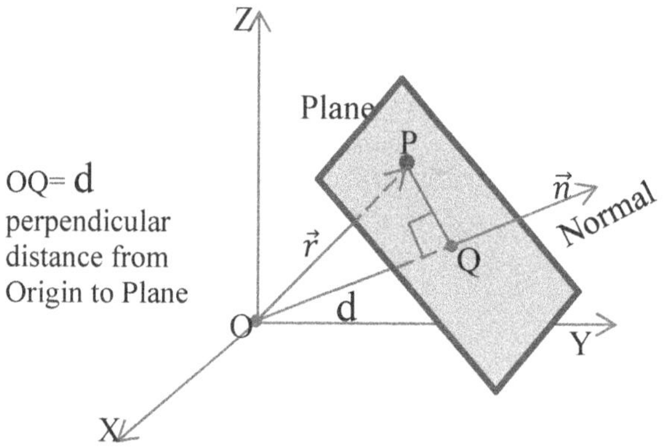

Explanation

Let OQ = 'd' be perpendicular distance of plane from origin, and $\vec{n}$ be its normal vector as shown in the figure.

If $\vec{r} = x\,\hat{\imath} + y\,\hat{\jmath} + z\,\hat{k}$ is position vector of any general point, P on the plane, then the projection of $\overrightarrow{OP}$ on normal vector $\vec{n}$ will be equal to OQ.

$$OQ = \frac{\vec{r} \cdot \vec{n}}{|\vec{n}|}$$

(*see* 'Projection of $\vec{a}$ on $\vec{b}$ ' in chapter – Vector Algebra)

$$\Rightarrow d = \vec{r} \cdot \hat{n} \qquad \text{where } \hat{n} = \frac{\vec{n}}{|\vec{n}|} \text{ is unit normal vector}$$

It is the required equation.

If we simplify this equation, then it can be written as

$\vec{r} . \vec{n} = D,$ where $D = d \, |\vec{n}|$

In fact, any equation of plane can be written in this form. That's why we call it as **general form** of vector equation of a plane.

<u>**Example**</u>

Find the vector equation of a plane which is at a distance of 7 units from the origin, and normal vector to the plane is $3\,\hat{\imath} + 5\,\hat{\jmath} - 6\hat{k}$. Express it in general form.

Solution

Normal vector to the plane is, $\vec{n} = 3\,\hat{\imath} + 5\,\hat{\jmath} - 6\hat{k}$

$$\text{and } |\vec{n}| = \sqrt{(3)^2 + (5)^2 + (-6)^2} = \sqrt{70}$$

$\therefore$ Unit normal vector is, $\hat{n} = \dfrac{3\,\hat{\imath} + 5\,\hat{\jmath} - 6\hat{k}}{\sqrt{70}}$

Perpendicular distance of plane from origin is $d = 7$ ...(given)

Equation of plane, in normal form, is given by $\vec{r} . \hat{n} = d$

$\therefore$ Required equation of plane, in **normal form**, is

$$\vec{r} . \left(\frac{3\,\hat{\imath} + 5\,\hat{\jmath} - 6\hat{k}}{\sqrt{70}} \right) = 7$$

In **general form**, we can write it as $\vec{r} . (3\,\hat{\imath} + 5\,\hat{\jmath} - 6\hat{k}) = 7\sqrt{70}$

- If we are given vector equation of a plane in normal form, we can compare it with $\vec{r} . \hat{n} = d$, and hence obtain its unit normal vector, $\hat{n}$ and perpendicular distance, d of plane from origin.
- If we are given vector equation of a plane in general form, we can compare it with $\vec{r} . \vec{n} = D$, and obtain its normal vector, $\vec{n}$.

<u>**Example**</u>

Vector equation of a plane is $\vec{r} . \left(\hat{\imath} + \hat{\jmath} - \hat{k} \right) = 2$. Find the perpendicular distance of the plane from the origin, and also find its unit normal vector.

Solution

We know that vector equation of a plane, in general form is given by $\vec{r} . \vec{n} = D$, where $\vec{n}$ is vector normal to the plane.

$\therefore$ From the given equation, $\vec{r} . \left(\hat{\imath} + \hat{\jmath} - \hat{k} \right) = 2$,

we find that normal vector is, $\vec{n} = \hat{\imath} + \hat{\jmath} - \hat{k}$

and $|\vec{n}| = \sqrt{(1)^2 + (1)^2 + (-1)^2} = \sqrt{3}$

$\Rightarrow$ **unit normal vector** is, $\hat{n} = \dfrac{\hat{\imath} + \hat{\jmath} - \hat{k}}{\sqrt{3}}$

In vector equation, in normal form (i.e., $\vec{r} . \hat{n} = d$), d is perpendicular distance of the plane from the origin.

To convert the given equation into normal form (i.e., $\vec{r} . \hat{n} = d$), divide the equation by $|\vec{n}|$. On dividing, we get

$$\vec{r} \cdot \left(\frac{\hat{\imath} + \hat{\jmath} - \hat{k}}{\sqrt{3}} \right) = \frac{2}{\sqrt{3}}$$

$\therefore$ Perpendicular distance of the plane from the origin is $\ d = \dfrac{2}{\sqrt{3}}$

2) **<u>Cartesian Equation</u>:**

Given: (i) d = perpendicular distance of plane from origin

(ii) DCs: l, m, n of normal to plane

Required Equation : $\quad \boldsymbol{l\,x + m\,y + n\,z \;=\; d}$

<u>General form</u>: $A\,x + B\,y + C\,z + D = 0$

where A , B , C are DRs of normal to plane

<u>Explanation</u>

Let d be the perpendicular distance of plane from origin, and l, m, n are DCs of normal to the plane.

From DCs l, m, n of normal to the plane, we can write its unit normal vector as $\ \hat{N} = l\,\hat{\imath} + m\,\hat{\jmath} + n\,\hat{k}$

$(\because$ the components of a unit vector are it DCs)

If (x, y, z) are coordinates of any general point, P on the plane, then its position vector is $\ \vec{r} = x\,\hat{\imath} + y\,\hat{\jmath} + z\,\hat{k}$.

$\therefore$ Vector equation of plane, as explained in vector form, will be

$$\vec{r} \cdot \hat{N} = d$$

$$\Rightarrow \left(x\,\hat{\imath} + y\,\hat{\jmath} + z\,\hat{k} \right) \cdot \left(l\,\hat{\imath} + m\,\hat{\jmath} + n\,\hat{k} \right) = d$$

$$\Rightarrow l\,x + m\,y + n\,z \;=\; d$$

It is the required equation.

Since, l, m, n are DCs which always exist in fractions so, we can simplify the equation to eliminate denominator, and write it as $A\,x + B\,y + C\,z + D = 0$

Here, A, B, C will be DRs of normal to plane.

In fact, any equation of plane can be written in this form. That's why we call it as **general form** of cartesian equation of a plane.

<u>Example</u>

Find the cartesian equation of a plane which is at a distance of 7 units from the origin, and DRs of its normal are 3, 5, −6 . Express it in general form.

Solution

DRs of normal to the plane are, 3, 5, −6 .

i.e., $\quad A = 3, \ B = 5, \ C = -6$

$\Rightarrow \quad \sqrt{A^2 + B^2 + C^2} = \sqrt{(3)^2 + (5)^2 + (-6)^2} = \sqrt{70}$

$\therefore$ Its DCs are $\dfrac{3}{\sqrt{70}}, \dfrac{5}{\sqrt{70}}, \dfrac{-6}{\sqrt{70}}$.

i.e., $\quad l = \dfrac{3}{\sqrt{70}}, \ m = \dfrac{5}{\sqrt{70}}, \ n = \dfrac{-6}{\sqrt{70}}$.

(*see* 'Line and Directed Line' in this chapter to find DCs from DRs)

Perpendicular distance of plane from origin is $d = 7$ ....(given)

Equation of plane, in normal form, is given by

$l\,x + m\,y + n\,z = d$

$\therefore$ Required equation of plane, in **normal form**, is

$$\frac{3}{\sqrt{70}}\,x + \frac{5}{\sqrt{70}}\,y + \frac{-6}{\sqrt{70}}\,z = 7$$

In **general form**, we can write it as $3\,x + 5\,y - 6\,z = 7\sqrt{70}$

- If we are given cartesian equation of a plane in normal form, we can compare it with $l\,x + m\,y + n\,z = d$, and obtain DCs of normal to the plane as $l, m, n,$ and perpendicular distance of plane from origin, d.

- If we are given cartesian equation of a plane in general form, we can compare it with $A\,x + B\,y + C\,z + D = 0$, and obtain DRs of normal to the plane as A, B, C.

- If we know DCs l, m, n of normal to the plane, then we can write its unit normal vector as $l\hat{\imath} + m\hat{\jmath} + n\hat{k}$.

- If we know DRs, A, B, C of normal to the plane, then we can write its normal vector as $A\hat{\imath} + B\hat{\jmath} + C\hat{k}$.

- If we know unit normal vector to the plane, $\hat{N} = l\hat{\imath} + m\hat{\jmath} + n\hat{k}$, then its components, l, m, n are DCs of normal to the plane.

- If we know normal vector to the plane, $\vec{N} = A\hat{\imath} + B\hat{\jmath} + C\hat{k}$, then its components, A, B, C can be taken as DRs of normal to the plane..

Using above points, we can convert a cartesian equation into vector and a vector equation into cartesian equation easily.

<u>**Example**</u>

Cartesian equation of a plane is $2\,x + 3\,y + 4\,z - 12 = 0$. Find the perpendicular distance of the plane from the origin, and also find DRs and DCs of its normal.

Solution

We know that cartesian equation of a plane, in general form, is given by $A\,x + B\,y + C\,z + D = 0$,

where A, B, C are DRs of normal to plane.

$\therefore$ From the given equation, $2\,x + 3\,y + 4\,z - 12 = 0$,

we find that **DRs of normal** to plane are $2, 3, 4$.

i.e., $\quad$ A = 2, B = 3, C = 4

$\Rightarrow \quad \sqrt{A^2 + B^2 + C^2} = \sqrt{(2)^2 + (3)^2 + (4)^2} = \sqrt{29}$

$\therefore$ Its **DCs are** $\dfrac{2}{\sqrt{29}}, \dfrac{3}{\sqrt{29}}, \dfrac{4}{\sqrt{29}}$.

---

*Asterisk (*) marked article (if any) is **not** in CBSE 2025-26 syllabus.*

To convert the given equation into normal form (i.e., into the form $l\,x + m\,y + n\,z = d$), divide the equation by $\sqrt{29}$.
On dividing, we get

$$\frac{2}{\sqrt{29}}\,x + \frac{3}{\sqrt{29}}\,y + \frac{4}{\sqrt{29}}\,z = \frac{12}{\sqrt{29}}$$

$\therefore$ Perpendicular distance of the plane from the origin is $d = \dfrac{12}{\sqrt{29}}$

Example

Cartesian equation of a plane is $2\,x + 3\,y + 4\,z - 12 = 0$.
Convert it into vector form.

Solution

Given equation is cartesian equation of a plane in general form
i.e., $A\,x + B\,y + C\,z + D = 0$,
where A , B , C **are DRs of normal to plane.**
$\therefore$ DRs of normal to given plane are 2, 3, 4.
Using DRs of normal, we can write normal vector as
$\quad \vec{n} = 2\hat{\imath} + 3\hat{\jmath} + 4\hat{k}$
A general point on plane is given by $\vec{r} = x\hat{\imath} + y\hat{\jmath} + z\hat{k}$
And $\vec{r} \cdot \vec{n} = 2x + 3y + 4z$
$\therefore$ We can write $\vec{r} \cdot \vec{n}$ in place of $2x + 3y + 4z$ in the given equation to obtain vector equation as
$\quad \vec{r} \cdot \left(2\hat{\imath} + 3\hat{\jmath} + 4\hat{k}\right) = 12$

Example

Vector equation of a plane is $\vec{r} \cdot \left(\hat{\imath} + \hat{\jmath} - \hat{k}\right) = 2$.
Convert it into cartesian form.

Solution

We can convert it into cartesian equation by replacing, $\vec{r}$ with $x\hat{\imath} + y\hat{\jmath} + z\hat{k}$, and then simplifying it as follows:
$\quad \left(x\hat{\imath} + y\hat{\jmath} + z\hat{k}\right) \cdot \left(\hat{\imath} + \hat{\jmath} - \hat{k}\right) = 2$
$\Rightarrow \quad x + y - z = 2$
$\quad$ This is the required equation of plane in cartesian form.

10.2 *Point & DRs form

1) **Vector Equation:**

Given: (i) $\vec{a}$ = Position Vector of a point on plane
$\quad\quad$ (ii) $\vec{n}$ = normal vector to plane
Required Equation : $\quad (\vec{r} - \vec{a}) \cdot \vec{n} = 0$

Explanation

Let $\vec{a}$ be position vector of given point M on the plane, and $\vec{n}$ be its normal vector (as shown in the figure below).
If $\vec{r} = x\hat{\imath} + y\hat{\jmath} + z\hat{k}$ is position vector of any general point, P on the plane, then $\overrightarrow{MP} = \vec{r} - \vec{a}$.

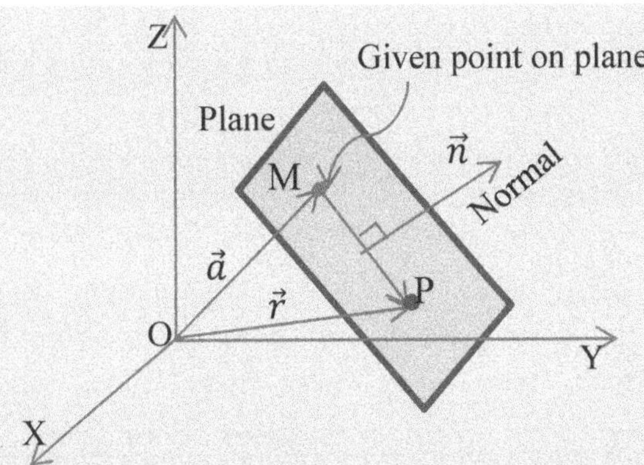

Since $\overrightarrow{MP}$ will lie on the plane so, it will be perpendicular to $\vec{n}$ as shown in the figure.

Since $\overrightarrow{MP} \perp \vec{n}$

$\therefore \overrightarrow{MP} \cdot \vec{n} = 0$

[see 'Scalar Product of two vectors' in chapter – Vector Algebra]

$\Rightarrow (\vec{r} - \vec{a}) \cdot \vec{n} = 0$ which is the required equation.

Example

Find the vector equation of a plane that passes through the point $(1, 0, -2)$, and the normal to the plane is $\hat{\imath} + \hat{\jmath} - \hat{k}$.

Solution

A point on the plane is $(1, 0, -2)$.

Its position vector is, $\vec{a} = \hat{\imath} - 2\hat{k}$

Vector normal to the plane is, $\vec{n} = \hat{\imath} + \hat{\jmath} - \hat{k}$

Vector equation of plane is given by $(\vec{r} - \vec{a}) \cdot \vec{n} = 0$

$\Rightarrow \quad [\vec{r} - (\hat{\imath} - 2\hat{k})] \cdot (\hat{\imath} + \hat{\jmath} - \hat{k}) = 0$

$\Rightarrow \quad \vec{r} \cdot (\hat{\imath} + \hat{\jmath} - \hat{k}) - (\hat{\imath} - 2\hat{k}) \cdot (\hat{\imath} + \hat{\jmath} - \hat{k}) = 0$

$\Rightarrow \quad \vec{r} \cdot (\hat{\imath} + \hat{\jmath} - \hat{k}) - (1 + 0 + 2) = 0$

[*see* 'Scalar product of vectors in terms of rectangular components' in Chapter- Vector Algebra]

$\Rightarrow \quad \vec{r} \cdot (\hat{\imath} + \hat{\jmath} - \hat{k}) = 3$

This is the required vector equation of plane.

2) **Cartesian Equation:**

Given: (i) Coordinates of a point (x_1, y_1, z_1) on plane

     (ii) DRs A, B, C of normal to plane

Required Equation:

$$A(x - x_1) + B(y - y_1) + C(z - z_1) = 0$$

<u>**Explanation**</u>

Let (x_1, y_1, z_1) be the coordinates of given point, M on the plane, and A, B, C are DRs of normal to the plane.

If (x, y, z) are coordinates of any general point, P on the plane, then DRs of MP are $x-x_1, y-y_1, z-z_1$.

Since MP will lie on the plane, so it will be perpendicular to normal to the plane as shown in the previous figure above. Applying condition for perpendicular between MP and the normal in terms of their DRs, we get

$$A(x-x_1) + B(y-y_1) + C(z-z_1) = 0$$

(*See* condition of 'Parallel and Perpendicular Lines' in this chapter)

which is the required equation.

<u>**Example**</u>

Find the cartesian equation of plane that passes through the point $(1, 0, -2)$, and the direction ratio of its normal are $1, 1, -2$.

Solution

A point on the plane is $(1, 0, -2)$.

i.e., $(x_1, y_1, z_1) = (1, 0, -2)$

DRs of normal to the plane are $1, 1, -2$.

i.e., $A = 1, \ B = 1, \ C = -2$

Cartesian equation of plane is given by :

$$A(x-x_1) + B(y-y_1) + C(z-z_1) = 0$$

$$\Rightarrow \quad 1(x-1) + 1(y-0) - 2(z+2) = 0$$

$$\Rightarrow \quad x + y - 2z = 5$$

This is the required cartesian equation of plane.

10.3 *Three Point form

1) <u>**Vector Equation:**</u>

Given: Position Vectors $\vec{a}_1, \vec{a}_2$ & $\vec{a}_3$ of 3 non-collinear points on plane

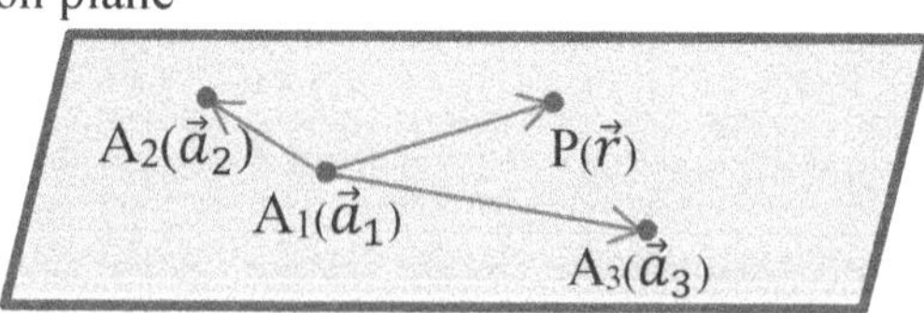

Required Equation: $(\vec{r} - \vec{a}_1) \cdot [(\vec{a}_2 - \vec{a}_1) \times (\vec{a}_3 - \vec{a}_1)] = 0$

<u>**Explanation**</u>

Let $\vec{a}_1, \vec{a}_2$ & $\vec{a}_3$ be the position vectors of 3 non-collinear points A_1, A_2 & A_3 on the plane (as shown in the figure above).

---

*Asterisk (*) marked article (if any) is **not** in CBSE 2025-26 syllabus.*

308

If $\vec{r} = x\,\hat{\imath} + y\,\hat{\jmath} + z\,\hat{k}$ is position vector of any general point, P on the plane, then 3 vectors starting from point, A_1 are :

$$\overrightarrow{A_1P} = \vec{r} - \vec{a}_1 , \quad \overrightarrow{A_1A_2} = \vec{a}_2 - \vec{a}_1 \quad \text{and} \quad \overrightarrow{A_1A_3} = \vec{a}_3 - \vec{a}_1 .$$

$\because$ These 3 vectors are coplanar, so their scalar triple product will be zero.

(*see* 'coplanarity of 3 vectors' in chapter – Vector Algebra)

i.e., $\quad \overrightarrow{A_1P} \cdot (\overrightarrow{A_1A_2} \times \overrightarrow{A_1A_3}) = 0$

$\Rightarrow \quad (\vec{r} - \vec{a}_1) \cdot [(\vec{a}_2 - \vec{a}_1) \times (\vec{a}_3 - \vec{a}_1)] = 0$

which is the required equation.

Example

Find the vector equation of a plane that passes through three points whose coordinates are $(1, 1, 0), (1, 2, 1), (-2, 2, -1)$.

Solution

3 points on plane are $(1, 1, 0), (1, 2, 1), (-2, 2, -1)$

Their position vectors, respectively, will be

$$\vec{a}_1 = \hat{\imath} + \hat{\jmath} , \quad \vec{a}_2 = \hat{\imath} + 2\hat{\jmath} + \hat{k} , \quad \vec{a}_3 = -2\hat{\imath} + 2\hat{\jmath} - \hat{k}$$

$$\therefore \quad \vec{a}_2 - \vec{a}_1 = \hat{\jmath} + \hat{k} \quad \text{and} \quad \vec{a}_3 - \vec{a}_1 = -3\hat{\imath} + \hat{\jmath} - \hat{k}$$

$$\Rightarrow (\vec{a}_2 - \vec{a}_1) \times (\vec{a}_3 - \vec{a}_1) = \begin{vmatrix} \hat{\imath} & \hat{\jmath} & \hat{k} \\ 0 & 1 & 1 \\ -3 & 1 & -1 \end{vmatrix} = -2\hat{\imath} - 3\hat{\jmath} + 3\hat{k}$$

Vector equation of plane is given by:

$(\vec{r} - \vec{a}_1) \cdot [(\vec{a}_2 - \vec{a}_1) \times (\vec{a}_3 - \vec{a}_1)] = 0$

$\therefore \quad [\vec{r} - (\hat{\imath} + \hat{\jmath})] \cdot (-2\hat{\imath} - 3\hat{\jmath} + 3\hat{k}) = 0$

$\Rightarrow \quad \vec{r} \cdot (-2\hat{\imath} - 3\hat{\jmath} + 3\hat{k}) - (\hat{\imath} + \hat{\jmath}) \cdot (-2\hat{\imath} - 3\hat{\jmath} + 3\hat{k}) = 0$

$\Rightarrow \quad \vec{r} \cdot (-2\hat{\imath} - 3\hat{\jmath} + 3\hat{k}) - (-2 - 3) = 0$

[*see* 'Scalar product of vectors in terms of rectangular components' in Chapter- Vector Algebra]

$\Rightarrow \quad \vec{r} \cdot (-2\hat{\imath} - 3\hat{\jmath} + 3\hat{k}) + 5 = 0$

This is the required vector equation of plane.

2) Cartesian Equation:

Given: Coordinates of 3 non-collinear points on plane

$$(x_1, y_1, z_1) , (x_2, y_2, z_2) \,\&\, (x_3, y_3, z_3)$$

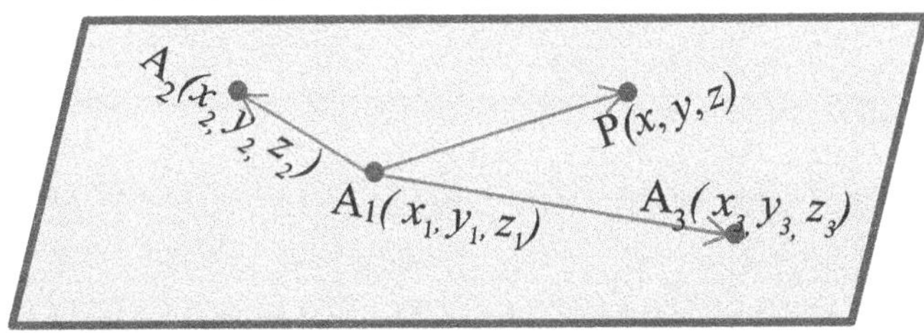

Required Equation :
$$\begin{vmatrix} x - x_1 & y - y_1 & z - z_1 \\ x_2 - x_1 & y_2 - y_1 & z_2 - z_1 \\ x_2 - x_1 & y_2 - y_1 & z_2 - z_1 \end{vmatrix} = 0$$

Explanation

Let (x_1, y_1, z_1) , (x_2, y_2, z_2) and (x_3, y_3, z_3) be the coordinates of 3 non-collinear points A_1 , A_2 & A_3 on the plane (as shown in the figure above).

If (x, y, z) are coordinates of any general point, P on the plane, then 3 vectors starting from point, A_1 are :

$$\overrightarrow{A_1P} = (x - x_1)\,\hat{\imath} + (y - y_1)\,\hat{\jmath} + (z - z_1)\,\hat{k}$$
$$\overrightarrow{A_1A_2} = (x_2 - x_1)\,\hat{\imath} + (y_2 - y_1)\,\hat{\jmath} + (z_2 - z_1)\,\hat{k}$$

And $\quad \overrightarrow{A_1A_3} = (x_3 - x_1)\,\hat{\imath} + (y_3 - y_1)\,\hat{\jmath} + (z_3 - z_1)\,\hat{k}$

Since these 3 vectors are coplanar, so their scalar triple product will be zero.

(*see* 'Coplanarity of 3 vectors' in chapter – Vector Algebra)

i.e., $\quad \overrightarrow{A_1P} \cdot (\overrightarrow{A_1A_2} \times \overrightarrow{A_1A_3}) = 0$

and in cartesian form it can be written as:

$$\begin{vmatrix} x - x_1 & y - y_1 & z - z_1 \\ x_2 - x_1 & y_2 - y_1 & z_2 - z_1 \\ x_2 - x_1 & y_2 - y_1 & z_2 - z_1 \end{vmatrix} = 0$$

which is the required equation.

Example

Find the cartesian equation of a plane that passes through three points whose coordinates are $(1, 1, 0), (1, 2, 1), (-2, 2, -1)$.

Solution

3 points on plane are $(1, 1, 0), (1, 2, 1), (-2, 2, -1)$

i.e., $\quad (x_1, y_1, z_1) = (1, 1, 0)$

$\quad\quad (x_2, y_2, z_2) = (1, 2, 1)$

$\quad\quad (x_3, y_3, z_3) = (-2, 2, -1)$

Cartesian equation of a plane passing through 3 non-collinear points is given by:

$$\begin{vmatrix} x - x_1 & y - y_1 & z - z_1 \\ x_2 - x_1 & y_2 - y_1 & z_2 - z_1 \\ x_2 - x_1 & y_2 - y_1 & z_2 - z_1 \end{vmatrix} = 0$$

$$\Rightarrow \begin{vmatrix} x - 1 & y - 1 & z \\ 1 - 1 & 2 - 1 & 1 - 0 \\ -2 - 1 & 2 - 1 & -1 - 0 \end{vmatrix} = 0$$

$$\Rightarrow \begin{vmatrix} x - 1 & y - 1 & z \\ 0 & 1 & 1 \\ -3 & 1 & -1 \end{vmatrix} = 0$$

$\Rightarrow \quad (x-1)(-1-1)-(y-1)(0+3)+z(0+3)=0$

$\Rightarrow \quad -2x-3y+3z+5=0$

This is the required cartesian equation of plane.

10.4 *Intercept form

Given: Intercepts a, b, c of plane on X, Y and Z – axes respectively.

Required Equation : $\quad \dfrac{x}{a}+\dfrac{y}{b}+\dfrac{z}{c}=1$

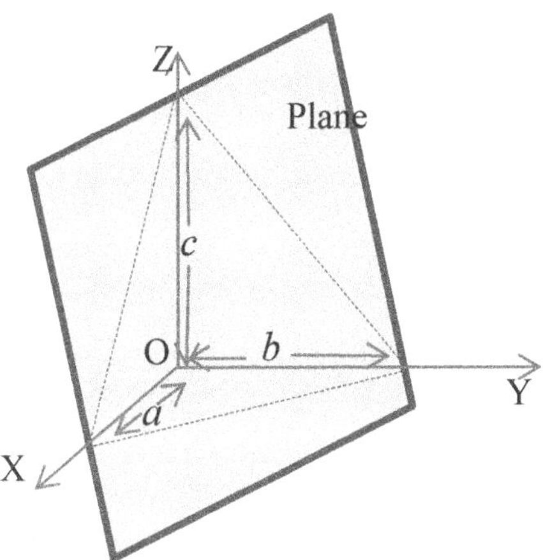

<u>**Explanation**</u>

If a, b, c be the intercepts of plane on X, Y and Z – axes respectively (as shown in the figure above),

then $(a,0,0), (0,b,0)$ and $(0,0,c)$ are the coordinates of 3 non-collinear points on the plane.

Now we can obtain the equation of plane containing 3 non-collinear points as follows:

$$\begin{vmatrix} x-a & y-0 & z-0 \\ 0-a & b-0 & 0-0 \\ 0-a & 0-0 & c-0 \end{vmatrix}=0$$

(*see* 'Three Point form' in 'Equation of Plane' in this chapter)

$$\Rightarrow \quad \begin{vmatrix} x-a & y & z \\ -a & b & 0 \\ -a & 0 & c \end{vmatrix}=0$$

Expanding along first row, we get

$(x-a)(bc-0)-y(-ac-0)+z(0+ab)=0$

$\Rightarrow \quad xbc-abc+yac+zab=0$

$\Rightarrow \quad xbc+yac+zab=abc$

Dividing whole equation by abc, we get

$$\frac{x}{a} + \frac{y}{b} + \frac{z}{c} = 1$$

This is the required equation.

Example

A plane makes intercepts of 6, 4, 3 on x, y, and z-axes respectively. Find its equation.

Solution

Here, intercepts of plane on x, y, and z-axes, respectively, are: 6, 4, 3.

i.e., $a = 6$, $b = 4$, $c = 3$

Now equation of plane in intercept form is $\frac{x}{a} + \frac{y}{b} + \frac{z}{c} = 1$

$$\Rightarrow \quad \frac{x}{6} + \frac{y}{4} + \frac{z}{3} = 1$$

$$\Rightarrow \quad 2x + 3y + 4z = 12$$

This is the required equation of plane.

11 *Equation of Plane passing through intersection of two planes

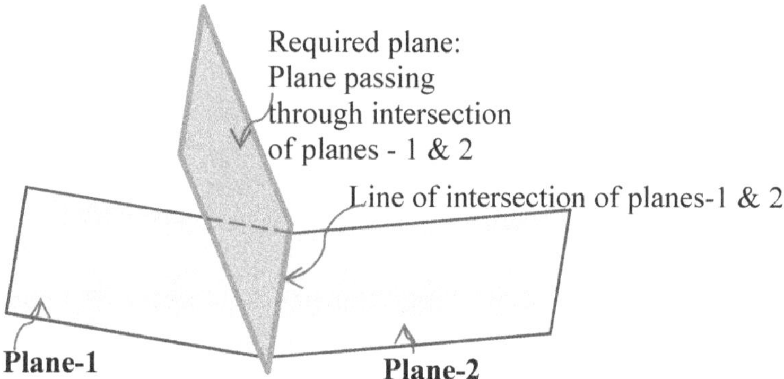

1) <u>**Vector Equation:**</u>

Given: Vector equations of 2 planes

$$\vec{r} \cdot \vec{n}_1 = D_1 \quad \text{and} \quad \vec{r} \cdot \vec{n}_1 = D_2$$

Required Equation of plane: $\vec{r} \cdot (\vec{n}_1 + \lambda \vec{n}_2) = \mathbf{D}_1 + \lambda \mathbf{D}_2$

- **This will be equation of family of planes** (representing all planes passing through line of intersection of given planes). To find the equation of a particular plane, we will be given some information related to that plane and using it, we will be able to find the equation of that plane (*see* in next example).

<u>**Explanation**</u>

Any point lying on the line of intersection of 2 planes will satisfy the equations of both planes.

So, if we multiply one of the equations by a real number, λ and add it to the other equation, then that point will also satisfy the resulting equation, $\vec{r} \cdot (\vec{n}_1 + \lambda\,\vec{n}_2) = D_1 + \lambda\,D_2$.

We observe that it is also an equation of plane, which actually represents family of all planes containing line of intersection of 2 given planes.

<u>**Example**</u>

Find the vector equation of the plane passing through the intersection of two planes:

$\vec{r} \cdot \left(2\hat{\imath} + 2\hat{\jmath} - 3\hat{k}\right) = 7, \quad \vec{r} \cdot \left(2\hat{\imath} + 5\hat{\jmath} + 3\hat{k}\right) = 9$ and through the point $(2, 1, 3)$.

Solution

Two equations of plane are

$$\vec{r} \cdot \left(2\hat{\imath} + 2\hat{\jmath} - 3\hat{k}\right) = 7 \qquad \ldots\ldots\ldots \text{(i)}$$
$$\vec{r} \cdot \left(2\hat{\imath} + 5\hat{\jmath} + 3\hat{k}\right) = 9 \qquad \ldots\ldots\ldots \text{(ii)}$$

Multiply eqn.(ii) by λ, and add to eqn.(i)

$$\vec{r} \cdot \left[\left(2\hat{\imath} + 2\hat{\jmath} - 3\hat{k}\right) + \lambda\left(2\hat{\imath} + 5\hat{\jmath} + 3\hat{k}\right)\right] = 7 + 9\lambda \qquad \ldots\ldots \text{(iii)}$$

This is equation of family of planes passing through the line of intersection of given planes.

We must find the value of λ to find the particular plane passing through $(2, 1, 3)$.

Position vector of this point is $= 2\hat{\imath} + \hat{\jmath} + 3\hat{k}$

Put it in place of $\vec{r}$ in the eqn.(iii), and find the value of λ as follows:

$$\left(2\hat{\imath} + \hat{\jmath} + 3\hat{k}\right) \cdot \left[\left(2\hat{\imath} + 2\hat{\jmath} - 3\hat{k}\right) + \lambda\left(2\hat{\imath} + 5\hat{\jmath} + 3\hat{k}\right)\right] = 7 + 9\lambda$$

$$\Rightarrow \left(2\hat{\imath} + \hat{\jmath} + 3\hat{k}\right) \cdot \left[(2 + 2\lambda)\hat{\imath} + (2 + 5\lambda)\hat{\jmath} + (-3 + 3\lambda)\hat{k}\right] = 7 + 9\lambda$$

$$\Rightarrow 2(2 + 2\lambda) + (2 + 5\lambda) + 3(-3 + 3\lambda) = 7 + 9\lambda$$

$$\Rightarrow 18\lambda - 3 = 7 + 9\lambda$$

$$\Rightarrow \lambda = \frac{10}{9}$$

Put this value of λ in eqn.(iii) to get the required equation of plane as follows:

$$\vec{r} \cdot \left[\left(2\hat{\imath} + 2\hat{\jmath} - 3\hat{k}\right) + \frac{10}{9}\left(2\hat{\imath} + 5\hat{\jmath} + 3\hat{k}\right)\right] = 7 + 9\left(\frac{10}{9}\right)$$

$$\Rightarrow \vec{r} \cdot \left(\frac{38}{9}\hat{\imath} + \frac{68}{9}\hat{\jmath} + \frac{1}{3}\hat{k}\right) = 7 + 9\left(\frac{10}{9}\right)$$

$$\Rightarrow \vec{r} \cdot \left(38\hat{\imath} + 68\hat{\jmath} + 3\hat{k}\right) = 153$$

This is the required equation of plane.

2) <u>**Cartesian Equation:**</u>

Given: Cartesian equations of 2 planes:
$$A_1\, x + B_1\, y + C_1\, z + D_1 = 0$$
$$\text{and} \quad A_2\, x + B_2\, y + C_2\, z + D_2 = 0$$

Required Equation of plane:

$$\boldsymbol{A_1\, x + B_1\, y + C_1\, z + D_1 + \lambda\,(A_2\, x + B_2\, y + C_2\, z + D_2)= 0}$$

- **This will be equation of family of planes** (representing all planes passing through line of intersection of given planes). To find the equation of a particular plane we will be given some information related to that plane and using it, we will be able to find the equation of that plane (see in next example).

<u>**Explanation**</u>

Any point lying on the line of intersection of 2 planes will satisfy the equations of both planes.

So, if we multiply one of the equations by a real number, λ and add it to the other equation, then that point will also satisfy the resulting equation:

$$A_1\, x + B_1\, y + C_1\, z + D_1 + \lambda\,(A_2\, x + B_2\, y + C_2\, z + D_2) = 0$$

It can be written as

$$(A_1 + \lambda A_2)x + (B_1 + \lambda B_2)\, y + (C_1 + \lambda C_2)\, z + (D_1 + \lambda D_2) = 0$$

We observe that it is also an equation of plane, which actually represents family of all planes containing line of intersection of 2 given planes.

<u>**Example**</u>

Find the equation of the plane through the line of intersection of the planes

$x + y + z = 1$ and $2x + 3y + 4z = 5$ which is perpendicular to the plane $x - y + z = 0$.

Solution

Two equations of plane are
$$x + y + z = 1 \qquad \dots\dots\dots \text{(i)}$$
$$2x + 3y + 4z = 5 \qquad \dots\dots\dots \text{(ii)}$$

Multiply eqn.(ii) by λ, and add to eqn.(i)
$$(x + y + z) + \lambda(2x + 3y + 4z) = 1 + 5\lambda$$
$$\Rightarrow (1 + 2\lambda)x + (1 + 3\lambda)y + (1 + 4\lambda)z = 1 + 5\lambda \qquad \dots \text{(iii)}$$

This is equation of family of planes passing through the line of intersection of given planes.

We must find the value of λ to find the particular plane, which is perpendicular to the plane $x - y + z = 0$ $\qquad \dots\dots\dots \text{(iv)}$

DRs of normal to the plane represented by eqn.(iv) are: $1, -1, 1$.

DRs of normal to the plane represented by eqn.(iii) are:

$1 + 2\lambda, \ 1 + 3\lambda, \ 1 + 4\lambda$

$\because$ These 2 planes are perpendicular to each other,

$\therefore$ Their normal are also $\perp$.

And condition for perpendicular lines is: $a_1 a_2 + b_1 b_2 + c_1 c_2 = 0$

where $a_1, \ b_1, \ c_1$ and a_2, b_2, c_2 DRs of two lines respectively.

[*See* 'Conditions for Parallel and Perpendicular Lines' in this chapter]

So, we have $1(1 + 2\lambda) - 1(1 + 3\lambda)y + 1(1 + 4\lambda) = 0$

$\Rightarrow \qquad 3\lambda + 1 = 0$

$\Rightarrow \qquad \lambda = -\dfrac{1}{3}$

Put this value of λ in eqn.(iii) to get the required equation of plane as follows:

$2\left(1 + 2\left(-\tfrac{1}{3}\right)\right)x + \left(1 + 3\left(-\tfrac{1}{3}\right)\right)y + (1 + 4\left(-\tfrac{1}{3}\right))z = 1 + 5\left(-\tfrac{1}{3}\right)$

$\Rightarrow \qquad \tfrac{2}{3}x + 0.\,y + \left(-\tfrac{1}{3}\right)z = -\tfrac{2}{3}$

$\Rightarrow \qquad 2x - z = -2$

This is the required equation of plane.

12 *Coplanarity of 2 lines

Two lines lying in the same plane are called coplanar lines.

1) **<u>Vector Form</u>:**

Given: Vector equations of 2 lines

$$\vec{r} = \vec{a}_1 + \lambda_1 \vec{b}_1 \quad \text{and} \quad \vec{r} = \vec{a}_2 + \lambda_2 \vec{b}_2$$

From these equations, we find their parallel vectors as $\vec{b}_1$ & $\vec{b}_2$ respectively and position vectors $\vec{a}_1$ & $\vec{a}_2$ of points on these lines, respectively.

Condition for coplanarity : $(\vec{a}_2 - \vec{a}_1) \cdot (\vec{b}_1 \times \vec{b}_2) = 0$

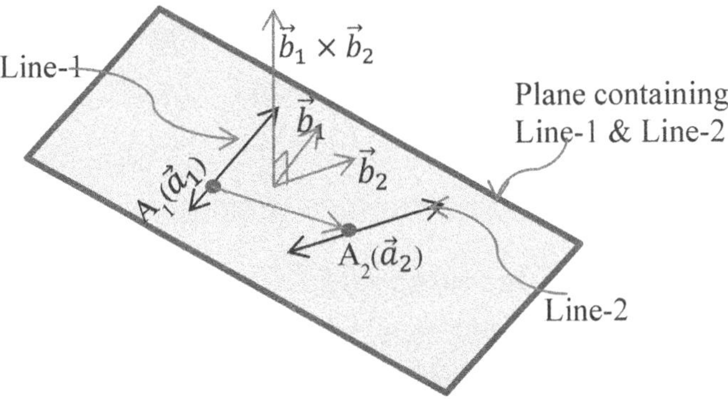

Explanation

From the given equations of lines, we can obtain their parallel vectors $\vec{b_1}$ & $\vec{b_2}$, and position vectors of points, A_1 as ($\vec{a_1}$) & A_2 as ($\vec{a_2}$) lying on them respectively (as shown in above figure).

If the lines are coplanar, then a vector from any point on one line to any point on the other line will also lie in their plane.

i.e., vector $\overrightarrow{A_1 A_2} = \vec{a_2} - \vec{a_1}$ will lie in the plane of the 2 lines.(As shown in the figure)

Also, vector $\vec{b_1} \times \vec{b_2}$ will be perpendicular to both the lines, and hence, perpendicular to their plane.

So, $\overrightarrow{A_1 A_2}$ and $\vec{b_1} \times \vec{b_2}$ are perpendicular

$$\Rightarrow (\overrightarrow{A_1 A_2}) . (\vec{b_1} \times \vec{b_2}) = 0$$

(scalar product of two perpendicular vectors =0)

$$\Rightarrow (\vec{a_2} - \vec{a_1}) . (\vec{b_1} \times \vec{b_2}) = 0$$

It is the required condition for coplanarity of two lines.

Example

Show that the following lines are coplanar

$$\vec{r} = -3\hat{\imath} + \hat{\jmath} + 5\hat{k} + \lambda(-3\hat{\imath} + \hat{\jmath} + 5\hat{k})$$

And $\vec{r} = -\hat{\imath} + 2\hat{\jmath} + 5\hat{k} + \lambda(-\hat{\imath} + 2\hat{\jmath} + 5\hat{k})$

Solution

From the given equations of lines, we can find their parallel vectors and position vectors of points on them. (*see* 'Equation of Line' in this chapter)

Their parallel vectors, respectively, are:

$\vec{b_1} = -3\hat{\imath} + \hat{\jmath} + 5\hat{k}$ and $\vec{b_2} = -\hat{\imath} + 2\hat{\jmath} + 5\hat{k}$.

And the position vectors of points on them, respectively, are

$\vec{a_1} = -3\hat{\imath} + \hat{\jmath} + 5\hat{k}$ and $\vec{a_2} = -\hat{\imath} + 2\hat{\jmath} + 5\hat{k}$

$\vec{a_2} - \vec{a_1} = (-\hat{\imath} + 2\hat{\jmath} + 5\hat{k}) - (-3\hat{\imath} + \hat{\jmath} + 5\hat{k}) = 2\hat{\imath} + \hat{\jmath}$

$$\vec{b_1} \times \vec{b_2} = \begin{vmatrix} \hat{\imath} & \hat{\jmath} & \hat{k} \\ -3 & 1 & 5 \\ -1 & 2 & 5 \end{vmatrix} = -5\hat{\imath} + 10\hat{\jmath} - 5\hat{k}$$. [expanding along 1st row]

For lines to be coplanar, we should have $(\vec{a_2} - \vec{a_1}) . (\vec{b_1} \times \vec{b_2}) = 0$

Here, $(\vec{a_2} - \vec{a_1}) . (\vec{b_1} \times \vec{b_2}) = (2\hat{\imath} + \hat{\jmath}) . (-5\hat{\imath} + 10\hat{\jmath} - 5\hat{k}) = 0$

$\therefore$ The given lines are coplanar.

2) **Cartesian Form:**

Given: Cartesian equations of 2 lines

$$\frac{x - x_1}{a_1} = \frac{y - y_1}{b_1} = \frac{z - z_1}{c_1} \quad \text{and} \quad \frac{x - x_2}{a_2} = \frac{y - y_2}{b_2} = \frac{z - z_2}{c_2}$$

From these equations, we find their DRs as a_1, b_1, c_1 & a_2, b_2, c_2 respectively. Also, we can find coordinates (x_1, y_1, z_1) and (x_2, y_2, z_2) of points lying on these lines respectively.

Condition for coplanarity: $\begin{vmatrix} x_2 - x_1 & y_2 - y_1 & z_2 - z_1 \\ a_1 & b_1 & c_1 \\ a_2 & b_2 & c_2 \end{vmatrix} = 0$

Explanation

From the given equations of lines, we can obtain their DRs as a_1, b_1, c_1 & a_2, b_2, c_2 respectively.

We recall that from DRs, their parallel vectors $\vec{b}_1$ & $\vec{b}_2$ can be written as:

$a_1\hat{\imath} + b_1\hat{\jmath} + c_1\hat{k}$ and $a_2\hat{\imath} + b_2\hat{\jmath} + c_2\hat{k}$, respectively.

Also, we can obtain coordinates of points, A_1 as (x_1, y_1, z_1) and A_2 as (x_2, y_2, z_2) lying on the lines respectively, from their equations. From these coordinates of points, we can write their position vectors as:

$$\vec{a}_1 = x_1\hat{\imath} + y_1\hat{\jmath} + z_1\hat{k} \qquad \& \qquad \vec{a}_2 = x_2\hat{\imath} + y_2\hat{\jmath} + z_2\hat{k}.$$

Now, as explained earlier in the vector form, condition for coplanarity is:

$$(\vec{a}_2 - \vec{a}_1) \cdot (\vec{b}_1 \times \vec{b}_2) = 0$$

i.e., scalar triple product of $(\vec{a}_2 - \vec{a}_1)$, $\vec{b}_1$ & $\vec{b}_2$ is zero.

If we find this scalar triple product, we can obtain the cartesian form of this expression as:

$$\begin{vmatrix} x_2 - x_1 & y_2 - y_1 & z_2 - z_1 \\ a_1 & b_1 & c_1 \\ a_2 & b_2 & c_2 \end{vmatrix} = 0$$

Example

Show that the following lines are coplanar

$$\frac{x+3}{-3} = \frac{y-1}{1} = \frac{z-5}{5} \qquad \text{and} \qquad \frac{x+1}{-1} = \frac{y-2}{2} = \frac{z-5}{5}$$

Solution

From the given equations of lines, we can find their direction ratios and coordinates of points on them. (*see* 'Equation of Line' in this chapter)

Their direction ratios, respectively, are $-3, 1, 5$ and $-1, 2, 5$.

i.e., $a_1 = -3, \ b_1 = 1, c_1 = 5$ and $a_2 = -1, \ b_2 = 2, c_2 = 5$

And the coordinates of points on them, respectively, are:

$(x_1, y_1, z_1) = (-3, 1, 5)$ and $(x_2, y_2, z_2) = (-1, 2, 5)$

For lines to be coplanar, we should have :

$$\begin{vmatrix} x_2 - x_1 & y_2 - y_1 & z_2 - z_1 \\ a_1 & b_1 & c_1 \\ a_2 & b_2 & c_2 \end{vmatrix} = 0$$

Here, $\begin{vmatrix} x_2 - x_1 & y_2 - y_1 & z_2 - z_1 \\ a_1 & b_1 & c_1 \\ a_2 & b_2 & c_2 \end{vmatrix} = \begin{vmatrix} -1+3 & 2-1 & 5-5 \\ -3 & 1 & 5 \\ -1 & 2 & 5 \end{vmatrix}$

$$= \begin{vmatrix} 2 & 1 & 0 \\ -3 & 1 & 5 \\ -1 & 2 & 5 \end{vmatrix}$$

$$= 0$$

$\therefore$ The given lines are coplanar.

13 *Angle between two planes

- If θ is an angle between two planes, then $180° - \theta$ is also an angle between them. One of them is acute, and other is obtuse angle.
- Usually, we take acute angle as the angle between two planes.
- The acute angle between two planes is equal to the acute angle between their normal as shown in figure below.

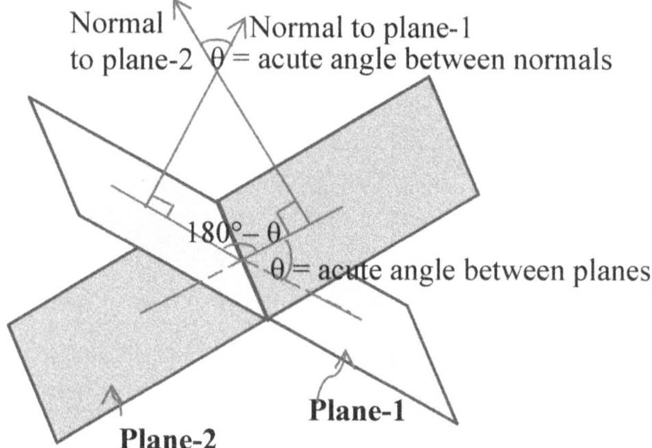

1) **Vector Form:**

Given: Vector equations of 2 planes

$$\vec{r}.\,\vec{n}_1 = D_1 \qquad \text{and} \qquad \vec{r}.\,\vec{n}_2 = D_2$$

From the given equations of planes, we find their normal vectors $\vec{n}_1$ & $\vec{n}_2$, respectively.

If θ = required acute angle, then $\boldsymbol{cos\,\theta} = \dfrac{|\,\vec{n}_1 . \,\vec{n}_2\,|}{|\,\vec{n}_1\,||\,\vec{n}_2\,|}$

Explanation

From the given equations of planes, we can obtain their normal vectors $\vec{n}_1$ & $\vec{n}_2$ respectively.

---

*Asterisk (*) marked article (if any) is **not** in CBSE 2025-26 syllabus.*

As angle between 2 planes will be the same as angle between their normals, so the required acute angle, θ between the planes can be given by:

$$cos\,\theta = \frac{|\vec{n}_1 \cdot \vec{n}_2|}{|\vec{n}_1||\vec{n}_2|}$$

(see 'Angle between two vectors' in chapter - Vector Algebra)

Example

Find the angle between the planes whose vector equations are

$$\vec{r} \cdot (2\hat{\imath} + 2\hat{\jmath} - 3\hat{k}) = 5 \quad \text{and} \quad \vec{r} \cdot (3\hat{\imath} - 3\hat{\jmath} + 5\hat{k}) = 3 \ .$$

Solution

From the given equations of planes, we can find their normal vectors $\vec{n}_1$ & $\vec{n}_2$, respectively (*see* 'Equation of Plane' in this chapter).

Here, we have $\vec{n}_1 = 2\hat{\imath} + 2\hat{\jmath} - 3\hat{k}$ and $\vec{n}_2 = 3\hat{\imath} - 3\hat{\jmath} + 5\hat{k}$

The acute angle θ between the planes is given by $cos\,\theta = \frac{|\vec{n}_1 \cdot \vec{n}_2|}{|\vec{n}_1||\vec{n}_2|}$

$$\therefore\ cos\,\theta = \frac{|(2\hat{\imath}+2\hat{\jmath}-3\hat{k})\cdot(3\hat{\imath}-3\hat{\jmath}+5\hat{k})|}{|2\hat{\imath}+2\hat{\jmath}-3\hat{k}|\ |3\hat{\imath}-3\hat{\jmath}+5\hat{k}|}$$

$$= \frac{|-15|}{\sqrt{(2)^2+(2)^2+(-3)^2}\ \sqrt{(3)^2+(-3)^2+(5)^2}} = \frac{15}{\sqrt{17}\sqrt{43}} = \frac{15}{\sqrt{731}}$$

$$\Rightarrow \theta = cos^{-1}\left(\frac{15}{\sqrt{731}}\right)$$

2) ### Cartesian Form:

Given: Cartesian equations of 2 plane

$$A_1\,x + B_1\,y + C_1\,z + D_1 = 0$$
$$\text{and} \quad A_2\,x + B_2\,y + C_2\,z + D_2 = 0$$

From the given equations of planes, we can obtain DRs of their normals: A_1, B_1, C_1 & A_2, B_2, C_2 respectively.

If θ = required acute angle between the planes, then

$$cos\,\theta = \frac{|\ A_1A_2 + B_1B_2 + C_1C_2\ |}{\sqrt{A_1^2 + B_1^2 + C_1^2}\ \sqrt{A_2^2 + B_2^2 + C_2^2}}$$

Explanation

From the given equations of planes, we can obtain DRs of their normal, as A_1, B_1, C_1 & A_2, B_2, C_2 respectively.

We recall that from DRs, their normal vectors $\vec{n}_1$ & $\vec{n}_2$ can be written as: $A_1\hat{\imath} + B_1\hat{\jmath} + C_1\hat{k}$ and $A_2\hat{\imath} + B_2\hat{\jmath} + C_2\hat{k}$ respectively.

Now, as explained earlier in the vector form, the acute angle θ between the planes can be given by

$$cos\,\theta = \frac{|\vec{n}_1 \cdot \vec{n}_2|}{|\vec{n}_1||\vec{n}_2|}$$

(*see* 'Angle between two vectors' in chapter - Vector Algebra)
If we find scalar product $\vec{n}_1 . \vec{n}_2$ in the numerator and magnitude $|\vec{n}_1|$ & $|\vec{n}_2|$ in the denominator, we can obtain the cartesian form of this expression as:

$$\cos \theta = \frac{\mid A_1A_2 + B_1B_2 + C_1C_2 \mid}{\sqrt{A_1^2 + B_1^2 + C_1^2}\sqrt{A_2^2 + B_2^2 + C_2^2}}$$

Example

Find the angle between the planes whose cartesian equations are:
$$7x + 5y + 6z + 30 = 0 \text{ and } 3x - y - 10z + 4 = 0$$

Solution

From the given equations of planes, we can find DRs of their normal: A_1, B_1, C_1 & A_2, B_2, C_2 respectively. (*see* 'Equation of Plane' in this chapter).

Here, DRs of their normal, respectively, are 7, 5, 6 and 3, −1, −10.

i.e., $A_1 = 7$, $B_1 = 5$, $C_1 = 6$ and $A_2 = 3$, $B_2 = -1$, $C_2 = -10$

The acute angle θ between the planes is given by:

$$\cos \theta = \frac{\mid A_1A_2 + B_1B_2 + C_1C_2 \mid}{\sqrt{A_1^2 + B_1^2 + C_1^2}\sqrt{A_2^2 + B_2^2 + C_2^2}}$$

$$\therefore \cos \theta = \frac{\mid (7)(3) + (5)(-1) + (6)(-10) \mid}{\sqrt{(7)^2 + (5)^2 + (6)^2}\sqrt{(3)^2 + (-1)^2 + (-10)^2}}$$

$$= \frac{\mid -44 \mid}{\sqrt{110}\;\sqrt{110}} = \frac{44}{110} = \frac{2}{5}$$

$$\Rightarrow \theta = \cos^{-1}\left(\frac{2}{5}\right)$$

14 *Distance of a point from a plane

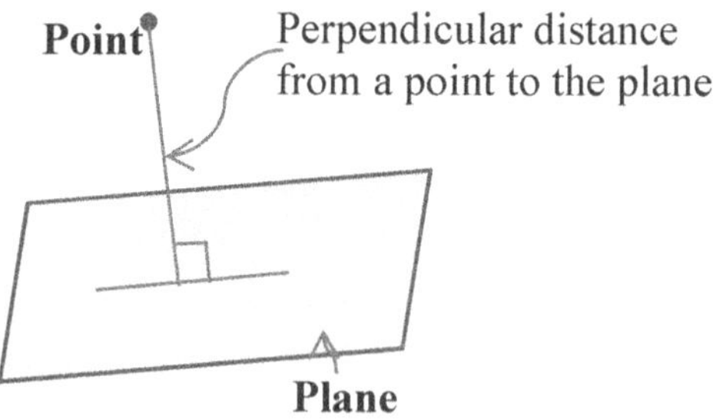

1) **Vector Form:**

Given: (i) $\vec{a}$ = Position Vector of a point

(ii) Vector equation of plane in normal form $\vec{r} . \hat{n} = d$

Or in general form $\vec{r} . \vec{n} = D$

From the given equation of plane, we find unit normal vector ($\hat{n}$) or normal vector ($\vec{n}$) to the plane.

$$\textbf{Required distance} = |\mathbf{d} - \vec{a} \cdot \hat{n}|$$

$$\text{or } \textbf{Required Distance} = \left| \frac{D - \vec{a} \cdot \vec{n}}{|\vec{n}|} \right|$$

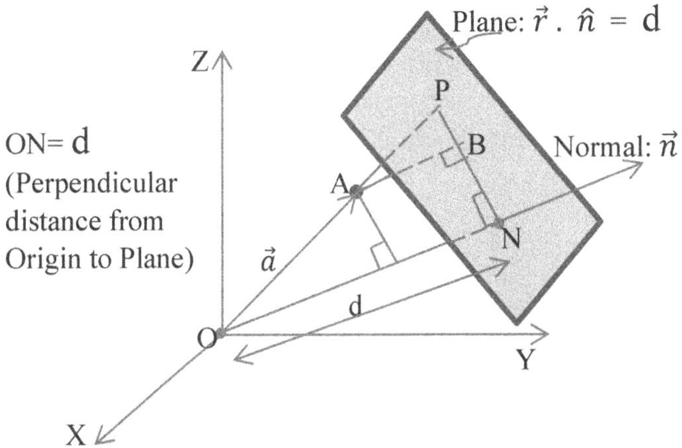

Explanation

Let $\overrightarrow{OA} = \vec{a}$ be position vector of given point, A on the plane (see the above figure).

ON is perpendicular to the plane, and $\vec{n}$ is normal vector to the plane, which will be along ON as shown in the figure above.

d = ON is perpendicular distance from origin to the plane, and it can be obtained from the equation of the plane in normal form.

AB will be the required perpendicular distance of point A from the plane.

OC = Projection of $\vec{a}$ on $\vec{n}$ as shown.

$$= \frac{\vec{a} \cdot \vec{n}}{\vec{n}}$$

(*see* 'Projection of $\vec{a}$ on $\vec{b}$' in chapter – Vector Algebra)

$$= \vec{a} \cdot \hat{n}$$

Now AB = CN = d − OC

$\therefore$ AB = d − $\vec{a} \cdot \hat{n}$

Here, given point A lies between origin and plane.

If A lies beyond the plane, then this expression will come out to be negative.

But distance can't be negative.

$\therefore$ we write AB = $|d - \vec{a} \cdot \hat{n}|$

This formula is applicable for any position of point A in 3D space.

If we are given equation of plane in general form $\vec{r} \cdot \vec{n} = D$,

---

then we can convert it into normal form by dividing the equation by $|\vec{n}|$ as follows:

$$\vec{r} \cdot \vec{n} = D$$

$$\Rightarrow \frac{\vec{r} \cdot \vec{n}}{|\vec{n}|} = \frac{D}{|\vec{n}|}$$

Comparing it with normal form $\vec{r} \cdot \hat{n} = d$, we have

$$\hat{n} = \frac{\vec{n}}{|\vec{n}|} \quad \text{and} \quad d = \frac{D}{|\vec{n}|}$$

$$\therefore AB = |d - \vec{a} \cdot \hat{n}|$$

$$\Rightarrow AB = \left| \frac{D}{|\vec{n}|} - \frac{\vec{a} \cdot \vec{n}}{|\vec{n}|} \right|$$

$$\Rightarrow AB = \left| \frac{D - \vec{a} \cdot \vec{n}}{|\vec{n}|} \right|$$

Example

Find the distance of a point $(3, -2, 1)$ from the plane given by:

$$\vec{r} \cdot (2\hat{i} - \hat{j} + 2\hat{k}) + 3 = 0$$

Solution

The given equation of plane is $\vec{r} \cdot (2\hat{i} - \hat{j} + 2\hat{k}) + 3 = 0$

It can be written as $\vec{r} \cdot (-2\hat{i} + \hat{j} - 2\hat{k}) = 3$

Comparing it with vector equation of plane in general form i.e.,
$\vec{r} \cdot \vec{n} = D$, we find the following:

$$\vec{n} = -2\hat{i} + \hat{j} - 2\hat{k} \quad \text{and} \quad D = 3$$

Position vector of the given point is $\vec{a} = 3\hat{i} - 2\hat{j} + \hat{k}$

Now perpendicular distance of a point from the plane is $= \left| \frac{D - \vec{a} \cdot \vec{n}}{|\vec{n}|} \right|$

$$\therefore \text{Required distance} = \left| \frac{3 - (3\hat{i} - 2\hat{j} + \hat{k}) \cdot (-2\hat{i} + \hat{j} - 2\hat{k})}{|-2\hat{i} + \hat{j} - 2\hat{k}|} \right|$$

$$= \left| \frac{3 - (-6 - 2 - 2)}{\sqrt{(-2)^2 + (1)^2 + (-2)^2}} \right|$$

$$= \frac{13}{3}$$

2) **Cartesian Form:**

Given: (i) Coordinates of a point (x_1, y_1, z_1)

(ii) Cartesian equation of a plane: $A x + B y + C z = D$

From the equation of plane, we find the DRs A, B, C of normal to the plane.

$$\textbf{Required distance} = \frac{\left| A x_1 + B y_1 + C z_1 - D \right|}{\sqrt{A^2 + B^2 + C^2}}$$

<u>**Explanation**</u>

From the given equations of plane, we can obtain DRs of its normal as A, B, C.

We recall that from DRs, its normal vector $\vec{n}$ can be written as $\vec{n} = A\,\hat{\imath} + B\,\hat{\jmath} + C\,\hat{k}$.

Also, the position vector of given point, $A(x_1, y_1, z_1)$ can be written as $\vec{a} = x_1\hat{\imath} + y_1\hat{\jmath} + z_1\hat{k}$

Now, as explained earlier in the vector form, the distance of point A from the plane can be given by

$$\text{Required Distance} = \left| \frac{D - \vec{a}.\vec{n}}{|\vec{n}|} \right|$$

It can also be written as $\left| \dfrac{\vec{a}.\vec{n} - D}{|\vec{n}|} \right|$

Put $\vec{a} = x_1\hat{\imath} + y_1\hat{\jmath} + z_1\hat{k}$ and $\vec{n} = A\,\hat{\imath} + B\,\hat{\jmath} + C\,\hat{k}$ in this expression.

$$\text{Required distance} = \frac{\left|(x_1\hat{\imath} + y_1\hat{\jmath} + z_1\hat{k}).\,(A\,\hat{\imath} + B\,\hat{\jmath} + C\,\hat{k}) - D\right|}{\left|A\,\hat{\imath} + B\,\hat{\jmath} + C\,\hat{k}\right|}$$

$$\Rightarrow \text{Required distance} = \frac{\left|Ax_1 + By_1 + Cz_1 - D\right|}{\sqrt{A^2 + B^2 + C^2}}$$

<u>**Example**</u>

Find the distance of point $(3, -2, 1)$ from the plane $2x - y + 2z + 3 = 0$

Solution

The given equation of plane is $2x - y + 2z + 3 = 0$

Comparing it with cartesian equation of plane in general form

i.e., $x + B\,y + C\,z = D$, we have

$$A = 2, \ B = -1, \ C = 2$$

Coordinates of the given point are $(x_1, y_1, z_1) = (3, -2, 1)$.

Now perpendicular distance of a point from the plane is given by

$$\frac{\left|Ax_1 + By_1 + Cz_1 - D\right|}{\sqrt{A^2 + B^2 + C^2}}$$

$$\therefore \text{Required distance} = \left|\frac{(2)(3) + (-1)(-2) + (2)(1) + 3}{\sqrt{(-2)^2 + (1)^2 + (-2)^2}}\right|$$

$$= \frac{13}{3}$$

15 *Angle between a Line and a plane

Angle between a line and a plane is complimentary angle of the angle between the line and normal to the plane.

i.e., If $\theta = $ angle between line and normal to the plane, then angle between the line and the plane is $\phi = 90° - \theta$ as shown in the figure below.

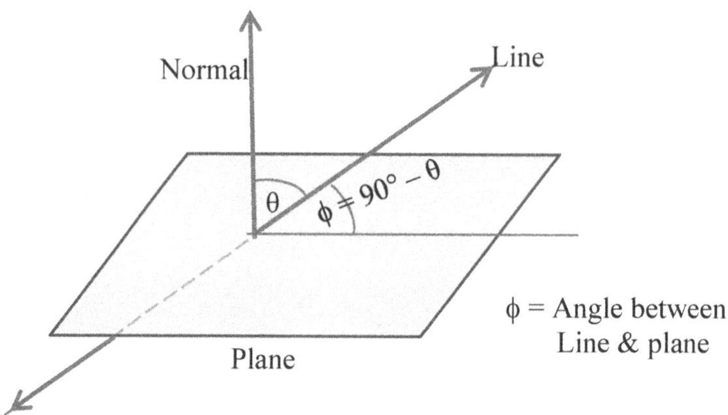

1) **Vector Form:**

Given: Vector equations of a line and a plane

$$\vec{r} = \vec{a} + \lambda\vec{b} \quad \text{and} \quad \vec{r}.\vec{n} = D$$

From the equation of line, we find its parallel vector $(\vec{b})$ and from the equation of plane, we find its normal vector $(\vec{n})$

If ϕ = required angle, then $\boldsymbol{sin\,\phi} = \dfrac{|\vec{b}.\vec{n}|}{|\vec{b}|\,|\vec{n}|}$

Explanation

The angle θ between a line and normal to a plane can be obtained using parallel vector ($\vec{b}$) of line and normal vector ($\vec{n}$) of plane by the expression:

$$cos\,\theta = \dfrac{|\vec{b}.\vec{n}|}{|\vec{b}|\,|\vec{n}|} \quad \ldots\ldots$$

(*see* 'Angle between two vectors' in chapter - Vector Algebra)

Now $\theta = 90° - \phi$ as shown in the figure.

$$\therefore \quad cos(90° - \phi) = \dfrac{|\vec{b}.\vec{n}|}{|\vec{b}|\,|\vec{n}|}$$

$$\Rightarrow \quad sin\,\phi = \dfrac{|\vec{b}.\vec{n}|}{|\vec{b}|\,|\vec{n}|}$$

Example

Find the angle between the line and the plane whose vector equations, respectively, are:

$$\vec{r} = -\hat{\imath} + 3\hat{k} + \lambda(2\hat{\imath} + 3\hat{\jmath} + 6\hat{k}) \quad \text{and} \quad \vec{r}.(10\hat{\imath} + 2\hat{\jmath} - 11\hat{k}) = 3$$

Solution

From the equation of line, we can find its parallel vector,

$$\vec{b} = 2\hat{\imath} + 3\hat{\jmath} + 6\hat{k} \quad \ldots. (\text{see 'Equation of Line' in this chapter})$$

And from the equation of plane, we can find vector normal to it,

$\vec{n} = 10\hat{\imath} + 2\hat{\jmath} - 11\hat{k}$ .... . (*see* 'Equation of Plane' in this chapter)

Acute angle ϕ between line and plane is given by $sin\,\phi = \dfrac{\left|\vec{b}\,.\,\vec{n}\right|}{\left|\vec{b}\right|\left|\vec{n}\right|}$.

Here, $sin\,\phi = \dfrac{\left|(2\hat{\imath}+3\hat{\jmath}+6\hat{k}).(10\hat{\imath}+2\hat{\jmath}-11\hat{k})\right|}{\left|2\hat{\imath}+3\hat{\jmath}+6\hat{k}\right|\,\left|10\hat{\imath}+2\hat{\jmath}-11\hat{k}\right|}$

$\qquad\quad = \dfrac{\left|20+6-66\right|}{\sqrt{(2)^2+(3)^2+(6)^2}\,\sqrt{(10)^2+(2)^2+(-11)^2}} = \dfrac{40}{(7)(15)} = \dfrac{8}{21}$

$\therefore\quad \phi = sin^{-1}\left(\dfrac{8}{21}\right)$

2) **<u>Cartesian Form:</u>**

Given: Cartesian equations of a line and a plane, respectively

$$\frac{x-x_1}{a} = \frac{y-y_1}{b} = \frac{z-z_1}{c} \quad \text{and} \quad A\,x + B\,y + C\,z = D$$

From the equation of line, we find its DRs, a, b, c and from the equation of plane, we find DRs, A, B, C of its normal.

If ϕ = required angle, then

$$sin\,\phi = \frac{\left|\,a\,A + b\,B + c\,C\,\right|}{\sqrt{a^2+b^2+c^2}\,\sqrt{A^2+B^2+C^2}}$$

<u>Explanation</u>

From the given equation of line, we can obtain its DRs as a, b, c. We recall that from DRs, its parallel vectors can be written as $a\,\hat{\imath} + b\,\hat{\jmath} + c\,\hat{k}$.

Also, from the given equation of plane we can obtain DRs of its normal as A, B, C , and hence its normal vector can be written as $A\,\hat{\imath} + B\,\hat{\jmath} + C\,\hat{k}$.

As explained in the vector form, the angle ϕ between the line and the plane can be given by

$$sin\,\phi = \frac{\left|(a\,\hat{\imath} + b\,\hat{\jmath} + c\,\hat{k}).(A\,\hat{\imath} + B\,\hat{\jmath} + C\,\hat{k})\right|}{\left|a\,\hat{\imath} + b\,\hat{\jmath} + c\,\hat{k}\right|\,\left|A\,\hat{\imath} + B\,\hat{\jmath} + C\,\hat{k}\right|}$$

$$sin\,\phi = \frac{\left|\,a\,A + b\,B + c\,C\,\right|}{\sqrt{a^2+b^2+c^2}\,\sqrt{A^2+B^2+C^2}}$$

<u>Example</u>

Find the angle between the line and the plane whose cartesian equations, respectively, are:

$$\frac{x+1}{2} = \frac{y}{3} = \frac{z-3}{6} \quad \text{and} \quad 10\,x + 2\,y - 11\,z = 3.$$

Solution

From the equation of line, we can find its direction ratios: a, b, c.

(see 'Equation of Line' in this chapter)

---

*Asterisk (*) marked article (if any) is **not** in CBSE 2025-26 syllabus.*

Here, $a = 2$, $b = 3$, $c = 6$

And from the equation of plane, we can find DRs of its normal:

A, B, C .   (*see* 'Equation of Plane' in this chapter)

Here, $A = 10$, $B = 2$, $C = -11$

Acute angle ϕ between line and plane is given by

$$\sin \phi = \frac{|\, aA + bB + cC \,|}{\sqrt{a^2 + b^2 + c^2}\ \sqrt{A^2 + B^2 + C^2}} \ .$$

Here, $\sin \phi = \dfrac{|(2)(10)+(3)(2)+(6)(-11)|}{\sqrt{(2)^2+(3)^2+(6)^2}\ \sqrt{(10)^2+(2)^2+(-11)^2}} = \dfrac{40}{(7)(15)} = \dfrac{8}{21}$

$\therefore \quad \phi = \sin^{-1}\left(\dfrac{8}{21}\right)$

Chapter-13   Linear Programming

1   Terminology

1.1   Optimization problem

The problems in which we have to find maximum or minimum value of a quantity like profit, cost, or some resource, etc., under certain conditions (or we say restrictions) are known as **optimization problem**.

- The maximum or minimum value of the quantity is called **optimal value**.

1.2   Mathematical formulation

Representation of an optimization problem mathematically is called **mathematical formulation** *of the problem.*

1.2.1   Objective function

- In mathematical formulation, the quantity to be optimized (maximized or minimized) is represented by a function of two or more variables, and this function is called **objective function**.
- The variables involved in the objective function are called **decision variables**.

1.2.2   Constraints

- The restrictions, under which objective function is to be optimized, are represented by inequalities in terms of decision variables, and these inequalities are called **constraints**.

2   Linear programming problem

An optimization problem is called a **linear programming problem** *if its objective function is a* **linear function,** *and its constraints are* **linear inequalities** *with non-negative variables.*

- Objective function in 2 variables is of the form: $Z = ax + by + c$.
- The variables involved in the objective function are called **decision variables**.

  e.g., in the function $Z = ax + by + c$, x & y are decision variables.
- The constraints are represented by the linear inequalities in terms of decision variables (x and y).
- The conditions that the variables can't be negative are called non-negative constraints.

  i.e., $x \geq 0$ and $y \geq 0$ are non-negative constraints.

---

3   Graphical Solution of Linear Programming

Step-1 From the given context, formulate the LPP mathematically as:

Objective function: $Z = ax + by + c$ to be optimised

(to be maximised or minimised as per the context)

Constraints (some inequalities):   inequality (i)

inequality (ii)

inequality (iii) , etc.

Non-negative constraints: $x \geq 0$ and $y \geq 0$

Step-2 Find feasible region

- Draw the graphs, and find the solution regions for all the individual inequalities (It was learnt in class XI in the chapter - Linear Inequalities. See examples later in this chapter.)

  Solution of each inequality on graph is a different half plane.

  Find and shade the common solutions of all the inequalities and non-negative constraints. This shaded region is known as **feasible region**.

- The feasible region (common shaded portion of the Cartesian plane) can be bounded or unbounded region.

Step-3 Find optimal solution

- **If the feasible region is bounded, then maximum and minimum values of the objective function, both exist, and they occur at the corners (vertex) of this region.**

- **If the feasible region is unbounded, then maximum or minimum value of the objective function may not exist, but if it exists, then it will occur at a corner (vertex) of this region.**

1) Optimal Solution of bounded feasible region:

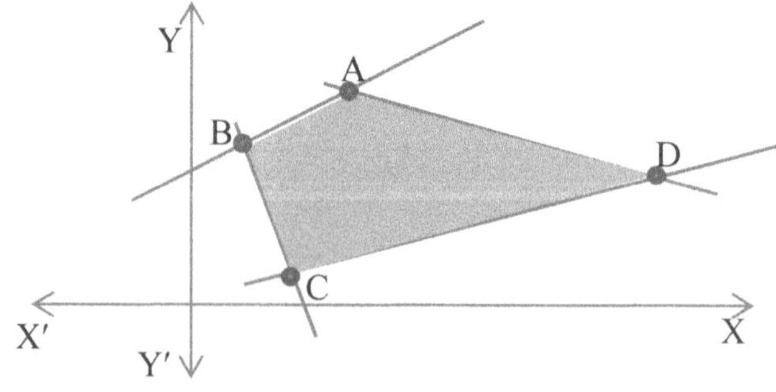

- If the feasible region is bounded as shown by grey shade in the above figure, we write:
  Feasible region is the bounded shaded region ABCDA.
- List the coordinates of vertices (corners) of feasible bounded region, and find the value of objective function ($Z = ax + by + c$) at every vertex. Write them in tabular form as follows:

Corner Points	Value of $Z = ax + by + c$	
A(-,-)	-	
B(p,q)	**- M**	**Maximum**
C(-,-)	-	
D(r,s)	**- m**	**Minimum**

- Mark the row where the value of Z is maximum and the row where it is minimum (as shown in bold letters in the table).

Case 1: Z is maximum (or minimum) at only one corner point

If Z = M is maximum at B(p,q) and Z = m is minimum at D(r,s), then we write:

the maximum value of Z = M is at point (p,q) i.e., at x = p & y = q

And the minimum value of Z = m is at point (r,s) i.e., at x = r and y = s

Case 2: Z is maximum (or minimum) at two corner points

If Z = M is maximum at corner points A & B both, then we write:

the maximum value of Z = M is at every point lying on the line segment joining the points A and B.

If Z = m is minimum at corner points C & D both, then we write:

the minimum value of Z = m is at every point lying on the line segment joining the points C & D.

2) **Optimal Solution of unbounded feasible region:**

- If the feasible region is unbounded as shown by grey shade in the figure below, we write:
  Feasible region is the unbounded shaded region EABCDF.

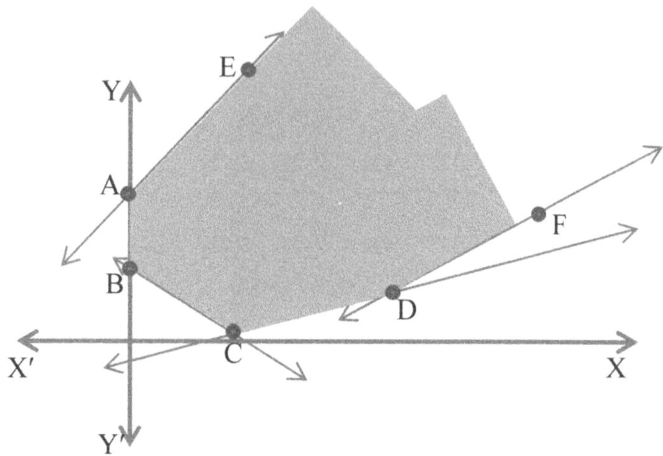

- List the coordinates of vertices (corners) of feasible unbounded region, and find the value of objective function ($Z = ax + by + c$) at every vertex. Write them in tabular form as follows:

Corner Points	Value of $Z = ax + by + c$	
A(-,-)	-	
B(p,q)	- **M**	**Maximum**
C(-,-)	-	
D(r,s)	- **m**	**Minimum**

- Mark the row, where the value of Z is maximum and the row where it is minimum (as shown in bold letters in the table).
  These values of Z may or may not be optimum. To check them we proceed as follows:

(i) **For maximum:**

- If Z = M is maximum at B(p,q), then suppose Z > M. Find the solution region of Z > M (shown by light grey shade in next 2 figures)
  i.e., find the half plane determined by $ax + by + c > M$

Case 1: If the solution region of Z > M overlaps the feasible region (i.e., it has common points with feasible region), then Z has no maximum value. This situation is shown in the following figure:

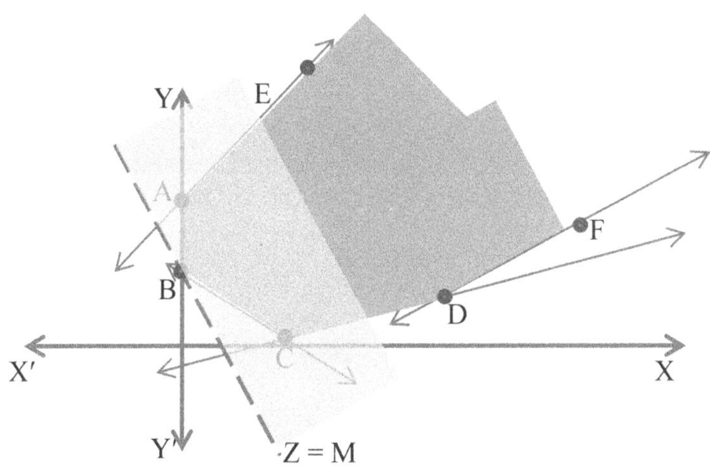

Case 2: If the solution region of Z > M doesn't overlap the feasible region (i.e., no common points with feasible region), then Z = M is the maximum value at B(p,q). This situation is shown in the following figure:

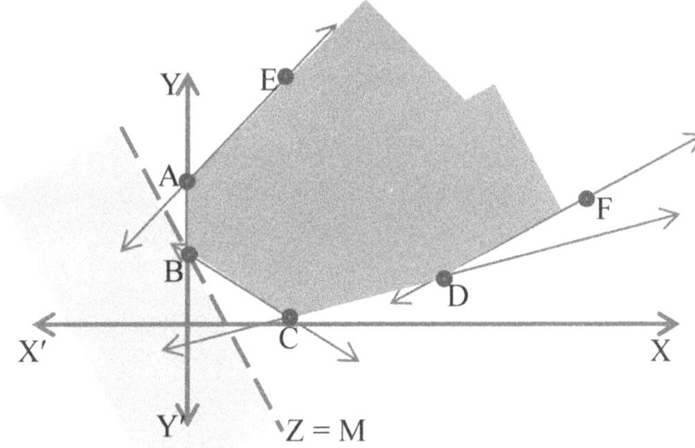

(ii) **For minimum:**

- If Z = m is minimum at D(r,s), then suppose Z < m. Find the solution region of Z < m (shown by light grey shade in the figure)

  i.e., find the half plane determined by $ax + by + c < m$

Case 1: If the solution region of Z < m overlaps the feasible region (i.e., it has common points with feasible region), then Z has no minimum value. This situation is shown in the following figure:

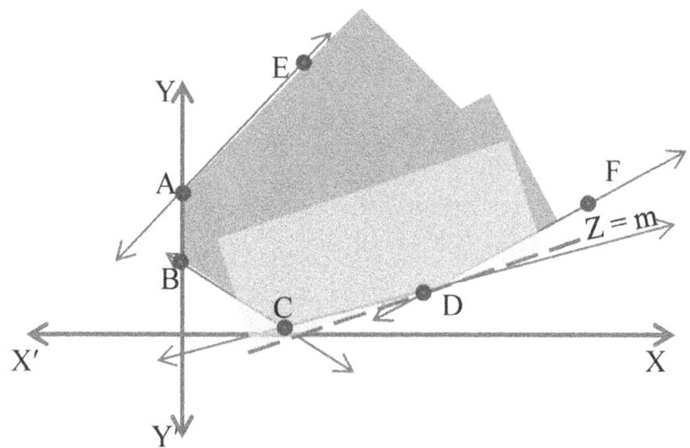

Case 2: If the solution region of Z < m doesn't overlap the feasible region (i.e., it has no point in common with feasible region), then Z = m is the minimum value at D(r,s). This situation is shown in the following figure:

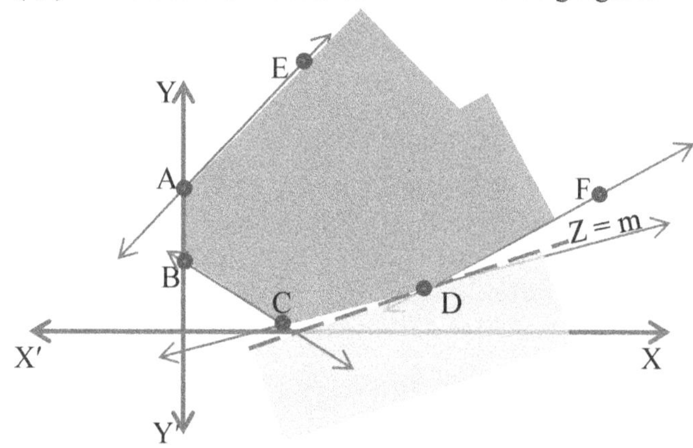

<u>**Example**</u>
Maximise $Z = 3x + 2y$ subject to $x + 2y \leq 10$, $3x + y \leq 15$, $x, y \geq 0$.
Solution
Here, our objective function is $Z = 3x + 2y$, which is to be maximised.
subject to the constraints:

$$x + 2y \leq 10 \qquad \ldots\ldots\ldots\ldots(i)$$
$$3x + y \leq 15 \qquad \ldots\ldots\ldots\ldots(ii)$$
$$x, y \geq 0 \qquad \ldots\ldots\ldots\ldots(iii)$$

We draw graph for each inequality, and obtain its solution region. For inequality (i), draw the graph of $x + 2y = 10$ by taking two points on it as shown in the table below:

---

x	0	10
y	5	0

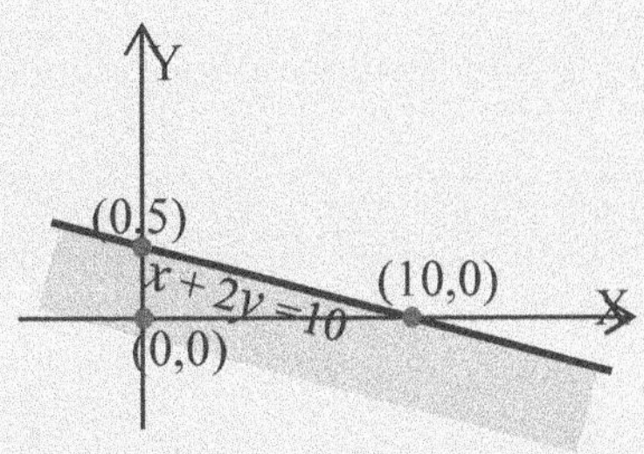

And then check (0,0) in $x + 2y \le 10$.

$\Rightarrow 0 \le 10$ which is true

$\therefore$ Its solution is towards (0,0)

It is shown by light grey shaded region in the above figure.

For inequality (ii), draw the graph of $3x + y = 15$ by taking two points on it as shown in the table below:

x	0	5
y	15	0

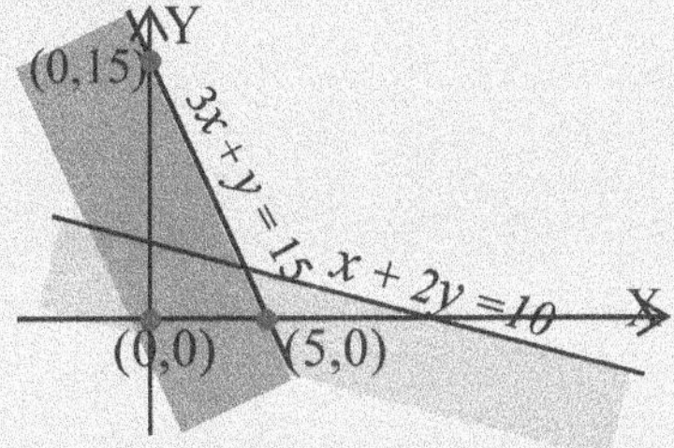

And then check (0,0) in $3x + y \le 15$.

$\Rightarrow 0 \le 15$ which is true

$\therefore$ Its solution is towards (0,0)

It is shown by dark grey shaded region in the above figure.

Also, inequality (iii) is $x, y \ge 0$ which means solution region is in first quadrant.

$\therefore$ Common solution region of all the inequalities is the black shaded region as shown in the next figure.

Hence, feasible region is bounded shaded region OABCO.

We can find the coordinates of corner point B by finding the intersection point of the lines given by the equations : $x + 2y = 10$ and $3x + y = 15$.

Solving these two equations, we find that $x = 4$ and $y = 3$

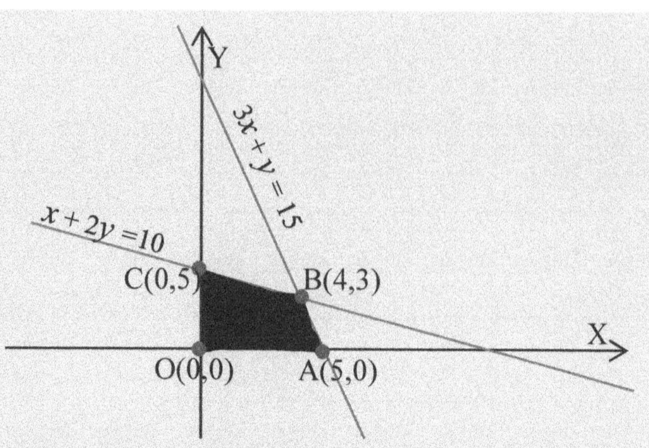

Now we make the table as follows:

Corner Points	Value of $Z = 3x + 2y$	
O(0,0)	0	
A(5,0)	15	
B(4,3)	18	**Maximum**
C(0,5)	10	

So, **Z is maximum at point B(4,3) i.e., at $x = 4$, $y = 3$, and maximum value of Z is 18.**

Note: We needn't draw separate graphs of every inequality. We draw only, the final graph which shows feasible region. (See other examples below)

Example

Minimise and Maximise $Z = 5x + 10y$ subject to the constraints:
$x + 2y \leq 120, x + y \geq 60, x - 2y \leq 0, x, y \geq 0$.

Solution

Here, our objective function is $Z = 5x + 10y$,
subject to the constraints:

$$x + 2y \leq 120 \qquad \ldots\ldots\ldots(i)$$
$$x + y \geq 60 \qquad \ldots\ldots\ldots(ii)$$
$$x - 2y \leq 0 \qquad \ldots\ldots\ldots(iii)$$
$$x, y \geq 0 \qquad \ldots\ldots\ldots(iv)$$

We draw graph for each inequality, and obtain its solution region.

For inequality (i), draw the graph of $x + 2y = 120$ by taking two points on it as shown in the adjacent table.

x	0	120
y	60	0

And then check $(0,0)$ in $x + 2y \leq 120$.

$\Rightarrow 0 \leq 120$ which is true

$\therefore$ Its solution is towards (0,0)

For inequality (ii), draw the graph of $x + y = 60$ by taking two points on it as shown in the adjacent table.

x	0	60
y	60	0

And then check (0,0) in $x + y \geq 60$.

$\Rightarrow 0 \leq 60$ which is false

$\therefore$ Its solution is away from (0,0)

For inequality (iii), draw the graph of $x - 2y = 0$ by taking two points on it as shown in the adjacent table.

x	0	120
y	60	0

And then check (10,0) in $x - 2y \leq 0$.

  (Here, we can't check (0,0) because it lies on this line)

$\Rightarrow 10 \leq 0$ which is false.

$\therefore$ Its solution is away from (10,0)

Also, inequality (iii) is $x, y \geq 0$ which means solution region is in first quadrant.

$\therefore$ Common solution region of all the inequalities is the blue shaded region as shown below.

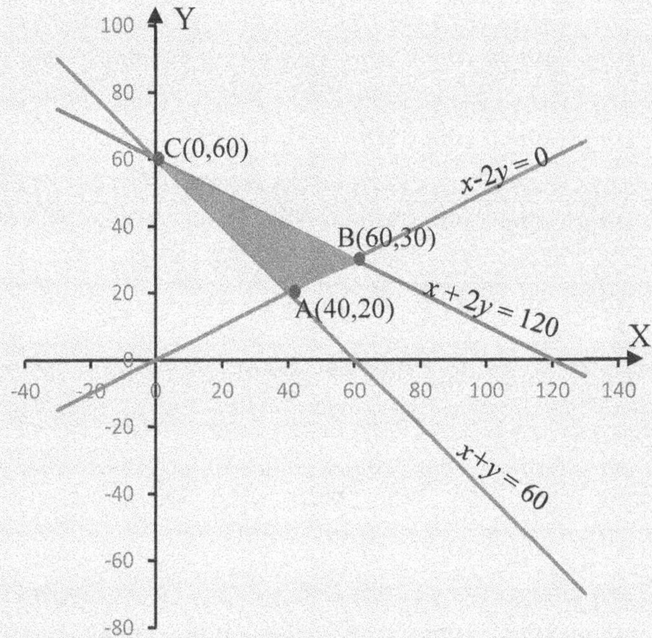

Hence, feasible region is bounded shaded region ABCA.

We can find the coordinates of corner point A by finding the intersection point of the lines given by the equations : $x - 2y = 0$ and $x + y = 60$.

Solving these two equations, we find that $x = 40$ and $y = 20$

To find point B, we solve the equations: $x - 2y = 0$ & $x + 2y = 120$.

On solving them we find that $x = 60$ and $y = 30$

Now we make the table as follows:

Corner Points	Value of Z = 5x + 10y	
A(40,20)	400	**Minimum**
B(60,30)	600	**Maximum**
C(0,60)	600	**Maximum**

So, **Z is minimum at point A(40,20) i.e., at $x = 40$, $y = 20$, and minimum value of Z is 400.**

Also, **Z is maximum at point every point on the line segment BC, and maximum value of Z is 600.**

<u>**Example**</u>

Maximise $Z = -x + 2y$, subject to the constraints:

$x \geq 3, x + y \geq 5, x + 2y \geq 6, y \geq 0.$

Solution

Here, our objective function is $Z = -x + 2y$, which is to be maximised.

subject to the constraints:

$$x \geq 3 \qquad \ldots\ldots\ldots\ldots(i)$$
$$x + y \geq 5 \qquad \ldots\ldots\ldots\ldots(ii)$$
$$x + 2y \geq 6 \qquad \ldots\ldots\ldots\ldots(iii)$$
$$y \geq 0 \qquad \ldots\ldots\ldots\ldots(iv)$$

We draw graph for each inequality, and obtain its solution region.

For inequality (i), draw the graph of $x = 3$ which is vertical straight line passing through $x = 3$.

Solution region of $x \geq 3$ will be towards the right of this line.

For inequality (ii), draw the graph of $x + y = 5$ by taking two points on it as shown in the adjacent table.

x	0	5
y	5	0

And then check (0,0) in $x + y \geq 5$.

$\Rightarrow 0 \geq 5$ which is false

$\therefore$ Its solution is away from (0,0).

For inequality (iii), draw the graph of $x + 2y = 6$ by taking two points on it as shown in the adjacent table.

x	0	6
y	3	0

And then check (0,0) in $x + 2y \geq 6$.

$\Rightarrow 0 \geq 6$ which is false

$\therefore$ Its solution is away from (0,0)

Also, inequality (iv) is $y \geq 0$ which means solution region is above x-axis.

$\therefore$ Common solution region of all the inequalities is the black shaded region as shown below.

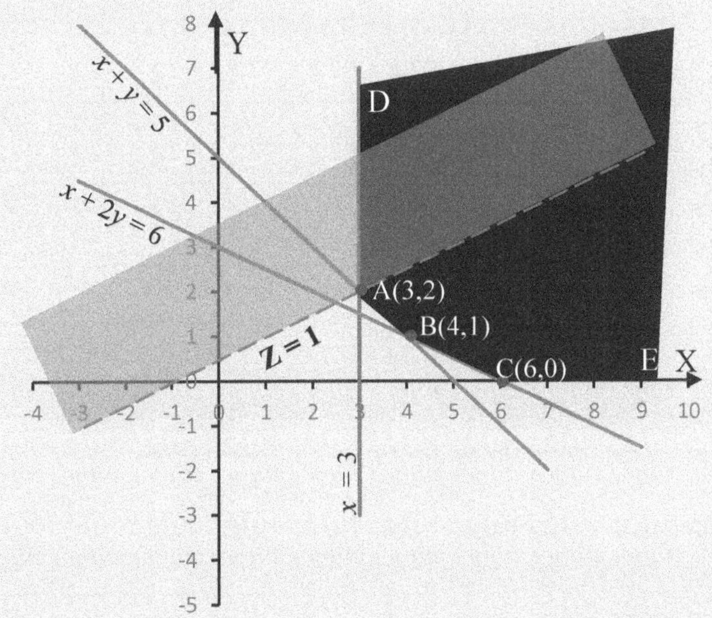

Hence, feasible region is unbounded shaded region DABCE. (**black shade** in the figure)

Corner points can be found by solving the respective equations.

Now we make the table as follows:

Corner Points	Value of $Z = -x + 2y$	
A(3,2)	1	**Maximum**
B(4,1)	–2	
C(6,0)	–6	

In the table, maximum value of $Z = 1$.

But feasible region is unbounded so, we find the solution region of $Z > 1$.

For this, first draw $Z = 1$ i.e., $-x + 2y = 1$ by taking two points on it as shown in the adjacent table.

x	0	–1
y	0.5	0

Here, the line will be drawn in dashes as shown in figure because we are drawing line for $Z > 1$ not for $Z \geq 1$

Check $(0,0)$ in $-x + 2y > 1$

$\Rightarrow 0 > 1$ which is false.

$\therefore$ Its solution is away from $(0,0)$.   . . . . (**grey shade** in the figure).

Since the solution region of $Z > 1$ overlaps the feasible region,

$\therefore$ **Maximum value of Z doesn't exist.**

<u>**Example**</u>

Minimise $Z = 3x + 5y$ such that $x + 3y \geq 3, x + y \geq 2, x, y \geq 0$.

Solution

Here, our objective function is $Z = 3x + 5y$, which is to be minimised.

subject to the constraints:

$\quad x + 3y \geq 3 \qquad \ldots\ldots\ldots\ldots$(i)

$\quad x + y \geq 2 \qquad \ldots\ldots\ldots\ldots$(ii)

$\quad\quad x, y \geq 0 \qquad \ldots\ldots\ldots\ldots$(iii)

We draw graph for each inequality, and obtain its solution region.

For inequality (i), draw the graph of $x + 3y = 3$ by taking two points on it as shown in the adjacent table.

x	0	3
y	1	0

And then check $(0,0)$ in $x + 3y \geq 3$.

$\Rightarrow 0 \geq 3$ which is false.

$\therefore$ Its solution is away from $(0,0)$.

For inequality (ii), draw the graph of $x + y = 2$ by taking two points on it as shown in the adjacent table.

x	0	2
y	2	0

And then check $(0,0)$ in $x + y \geq 2$.

$\Rightarrow 0 \geq 2$ which is false

$\therefore$ Its solution is away from $(0,0)$.

Also, inequality (iii) is $x, y \geq 0$ which means solution region is in first quadrant.

$\therefore$ Common solution region of all the inequalities is the black shaded region in figure drawn on next page.

Here, feasible region is unbounded shaded region DABCE. (**black shade** in the figure)

Corner points can be found by solving the respective equations.

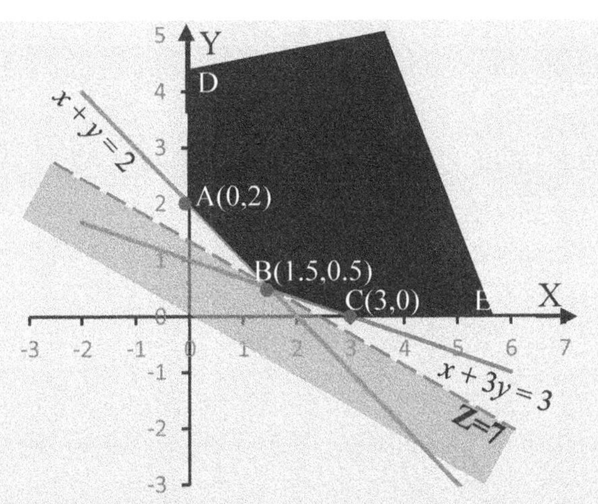

Now we make the table as follows:

Corner Points	Value of $Z = 3x + 5y$	
A(0,2)	10	
B(1.5,0.5)	7	**Minimum**
C(3,0)	9	

In the table, minimum value of $Z = 7$.

But feasible region is unbounded so, we find the solution region of $Z < 7$.

For this, first draw $Z = 7$ i.e., $3x + 5y = 7$ by taking two points on it as shown in the adjacent table.

x	4	–
y	–1	2

Here, the line will be drawn in dashes as shown in figure because we are drawing line for $Z < 7$ not for $Z \le 7$.

Check $(0,0)$ in $3x + 5y < 7$

$\Rightarrow 0 > 1$ which is true.

$\therefore$ Its solution is towards $(0,0)$.   . . . (**grey shade** in the figure).

Since the solution region of $Z < 7$ doesn't overlap the feasible region,

$\therefore$ **Minimum value of $Z = 7$ at B(1.5, 0.5).**

Chapter-14   Probability

1   Basic Formulae (from earlier classes)

- Probability of any event A is written as P(A)
- For equally likely outcomes in the given random experiment,
  Probability of event A is P(A) $= \dfrac{No.\,of\,outcomes\,favourable\,to\,A}{Total\,no.\,of\,outcomes}$
- Maximum probability of an event $= 1$

  (It is known as **Sure Event**)

  Minimum probability of an event $= 0$

  (It is known as **Impossible Event**)

  i.e., $\mathbf{0 \leq P(A) \leq 1}$
- Probability of event '*not A*' $= P(A')$

  $P(A') \ = 1 - P(A)$
- Probability of event 'A and B' $=\ P(A \cap B)$
- Probability of event 'A or B' $=\ P(A \cup B)$

  $P (A \cup B) = P (A) + P (B) - P (A \cap B)$
- Probability of event 'A or B or C' $= P (A \cup B \cup C)$

  $P(A \cup B \cup C) = P(A) + P(B) + P(C) - P(A \cap B) - P(B \cap C)$
  $- P(C \cap A) + P(A \cap B \cap C)$
- For 2 Mutually Exclusive events A and B : $P (A \cap B) = 0$
- For 2 Exhaustive events A and B : $P (A \cup B) = 1$
- For 3 Mutually Exclusive events A , B and C :

  $P (A \cap B) = 0$, $P (B \cap C) = 0$ and $P (C \cap A) = 0$
- For 3 Exhaustive events A, B and C : $P (A \cup B \cup C) = 1$
- De Morgan's Law:

  (i) $P (A \cup B)' = P (A' \cap B')$

  (ii) $P (A \cap B)' = P (A' \cup B')$
- Probability of event 'A but not B'

  $P (A - B) = P (A \cap B') =\ P (A) - P (A \cap B)$
- Probability of event 'B but not A'

  $P (B - A) = P (B \cap A') =\ P (B) - P (A \cap B)$

2   Concept of conditional probability

Suppose a die is rolled. Sample space for the number obtained on it is, S = {1,2,3,4,5,6}.

Let event A be getting an even number.

If it is given that event A has occurred, then we know that the outcomes are only 2,4 and 6.

$\therefore$ For any other event, we can treat A as sample space, and then find the probability of that event.

i.e., we can treat A = {2,4,6} as sample space.

Let event B is getting a number less than 5.

Outcomes favourable to B in A are 2,4.

Number of outcomes favourable to B = 2

And total number of outcomes in A = 3

∴ Probability of B given that A has already occurred

$$= \frac{No.of\ outcomes\ favourable\ to\ B\ in\ A}{Number\ of\ outcomes\ in\ A} \qquad \ldots\ldots\ldots\ldots .(i)$$

$$= \frac{2}{3}$$

It is written as $P(B|A) = \frac{2}{3}$

Here, to find the conditional probability of B given that A has already occurred, we considered A as the sample space.

But event A and B both are from the same sample space,

S = {1,2,3,4,5,6}.

i.e.,　A = {2,4,6}　and　B = {1,2,3,4}

We note that the outcomes favourable to B in A (i.e., 2 and 4) are actually outcomes of A∩B.

i.e., A∩B = {2,4}

$\Rightarrow$　n(A∩B) = 2　　　　……n denotes no. of outcomes

Also, n(A) = 3　　and n(S) = 6

∴ We can convert eqn.(i) as

$$P(B|A) = \frac{No.of\ outcomes\ favourable\ to\ B\ in\ A}{Number\ of\ outcomes\ in\ A}$$

$$= \frac{n(A∩B)}{n(A)}$$

Dividing numerator and denominator both by n(S), we get

$$P(B|A) = \frac{\frac{n(A∩B)}{n(S)}}{\frac{n(A)}{n(S)}}$$

$$P(B|A) = \frac{P(A∩B)}{P(A)}$$

3　Conditional Probability

- The conditional probability of an event B given that the event A has occurred is:

$$P(B|A) = \frac{P(A \cap B)}{P(A)}, \qquad P(A) \neq 0$$

- Probability of event 'not B' given that event A has occurred:

$$P(B'|A) = 1 - P(B|A)$$

- Probability of event 'A or B' given that event C has occurred:

$$P[(A \cup B)|C] = P(A|C) + P(B|C) - P[(A \cap B)|C]$$

<u>**Example**</u>

A pair of dice is rolled, and it is observed that sum of the numbers that come up is 8.

Find the probability that at least one die shows 3.

Solution

Here, sample space for rolling a pair of dice is

$S = \{(1,1),(1,2),(1,3),(1,4),(1,5),(1,6),$
$\qquad (2,1),(2,2),(2,3),(2,4),(2,5),(2,6),$
$\qquad (3,1),(3,2),(3,3),(3,4),(3,5),(3,6),$
$\qquad (4,1),(4,2),(4,3),(4,4),(4,5),(4,6),$
$\qquad (5,1),(5,2),(5,3),(5,4),(5,5),(5,6),$
$\qquad (6,1),(6,2),(6,3),(6,4),(6,5),(6,6)\}$

$n(S) = 36$

Let event A be getting sum of 8.

And event B be 'at least one die shows 3'.

We have to find $P(B|A)$ i.e., probability of B if A has occurred.

To use formula, $P(B|A) = \dfrac{P(A \cap B)}{P(A)}$, we must find $P(A)$ and $P(A \cap B)$

Now $A = \{(2,6),(3,5),(4,4),(5,3),(6,2)\}$

And $B = \{(1,3),(2,3),(3,1),(3,2),(3,3),(3,4),(3,5),(3,6),(4,3),(5,3),(6,3)\}$

$\Rightarrow A \cap B = \{(3,5),(5,3)\}$

$\therefore \; n(A) = 5, \qquad n(B) = 11, \qquad n(A \cap B) = 2$

$\Rightarrow P(A) = \dfrac{n(A)}{n(S)} = \dfrac{5}{36} \qquad$ and $\qquad P(A \cap B) = \dfrac{n(A \cap B)}{n(S)} = \dfrac{2}{36}$

$\therefore \qquad P(B|A) = \dfrac{P(A \cap B)}{(A)} = \dfrac{\frac{2}{36}}{\frac{5}{36}} = \dfrac{2}{5}$

<u>**Example**</u>

A die is rolled, and it is observed that the number which comes up is even number. Find the probability that (i) the number is 4. (ii) the number is not 4.

Solution

Here, sample space is $S = \{1,2,3,4,5,6\}$

Let event A be even number comes up.

i.e., $\quad A = \{2,4,6\}$

(i) Let the event B be the number is 4.

i.e., $\quad B = \{4\}$

Now $\quad A \cap B = \{4\}$

$\therefore \qquad n(A) = 3, \qquad n(B) = 1, \qquad n(A \cap B) = 1$

$\Rightarrow P(A) = \dfrac{n(A)}{n(S)} = \dfrac{3}{6} = \dfrac{1}{2} \qquad$ and $\qquad P(A \cap B) = \dfrac{n(A \cap B)}{n(S)} = \dfrac{1}{6}$

$$\therefore \quad P(B|A) = \frac{P(A \cap B)}{P(A)} = \frac{\frac{1}{6}}{\frac{1}{2}} = \frac{1}{3}.$$

Probability of getting number 4 if even number comes up on the die $= \frac{1}{3}$

(ii) Here the event 'not B' denotes the number is not 4.

So, we have to find $P(B' \mid A)$.

And $\quad P(B' \mid A) = 1 - P(B \mid A)$

$\Rightarrow \quad P(B' \mid A) = 1 - \frac{1}{3} = \frac{2}{3}$

Probability of that the number is not 4 if even number comes up on the die $= \frac{2}{3}$

<u>**Example**</u>

Consider events E = {1,3,5}, F = {2,3} and G = {2,3,4,5} when a fair die is rolled.

Find $P((E \cap F)|G)$, and then using it find $P((E \cup F)|G)$.

Solution

Here, sample space is S = {1,2,3,4,5,6}

And E = {1,3,5}, $\qquad$ F = {2,3}, $\qquad$ G = {2,3,4,5}

$\Rightarrow$ E∩F∩G = {3}

$\Rightarrow n(E) = 3$, $\qquad n(F) = 2$, $\qquad n(G) = 4$, $\qquad n(E \cap F \cap G) = 1$

$\Rightarrow P(E \cap F \cap G) = \frac{n(E \cap F \cap G)}{n(S)} = \frac{1}{6}$ $\quad$ and $\quad$ $P(G) = \frac{n(G)}{n(S)} = \frac{4}{6} = \frac{2}{3}$

$\therefore \quad P((E \cap F)|G) = \frac{P(E \cap F \cap G)}{P(G)} = \frac{\frac{1}{6}}{\frac{2}{3}} = \frac{1}{4}$

Now $\qquad P[(E \cup F) \mid G] = P(E \mid G) + P(F \mid G) - P[(E \cap F) \mid G]$

We must find $P(E \mid G)$ and $P(F \mid G)$ also as follows:

$\quad$ E∩G = {3,5} $\quad$ and $\quad$ F∩G = {2,3}

$\Rightarrow n(E \cap G) = 2$ $\quad$ and $\quad n(F \cap G) = 2$

$\Rightarrow P(E \cap G) = \frac{n(E \cap G)}{n(S)} = \frac{2}{6}$ and $\quad P(F \cap G) = \frac{n(F \cap G)}{n(S)} = \frac{2}{6}$

$\Rightarrow P(E|G) = \frac{P(E \cap G)}{P(G)} = \frac{\frac{2}{6}}{\frac{4}{6}} = \frac{1}{2}$

And $\quad P(F|G) = \frac{P(F \cap G)}{P(G)} = \frac{\frac{2}{6}}{\frac{4}{6}} = \frac{1}{2}$

$\therefore \quad P[(E \cup F) \mid G] = P(E \mid G) + P(F \mid G) - P[(E \cap F) \mid G]$

$$= \frac{1}{2} + \frac{1}{2} - \frac{1}{4}$$

$$= \frac{3}{4}$$

---

*Asterisk (*) marked article (if any) is **not** in CBSE 2025-26 syllabus.*

4 Multiplication Rule of Probability

For two or more events occurring together we use *multiplication rule of probability.*

i.e., to find $P(A \cap B)$, $P(A \cap B \cap C)$, etc., we use this rule. For two events A and B, it can be obtained from the formula of conditional probability

i.e., $P(B \mid A) = \dfrac{P(A \cap B)}{P(A)} \Rightarrow P(A \cap B) = P(A) . P(B \mid A)$

and then we can extend it for more than two events as follows:

(i) $P(A \cap B) = P(A) . P(B \mid A)$, $\qquad P(A) \neq 0$

(ii) $P(A \cap B \cap C) = P(A) . P(B \mid A) . P[C \mid (A \cap B)]$
$$= P(A) . P(B \mid A) . P(C \mid AB)$$

where $P[C \mid (A \cap B)] = P(C \mid AB) =$ probability of event C given that A and B both have already occurred.

Example

Two cards are drawn successively, without replacement from a pack of 52 well shuffled cards. What is the probability that both cards are kings?

Solution

Let the event A be 'first card is king',

and the event B be 'second card is king'.

There are 52 cards, in which 4 are kings before drawing first card.

$\therefore P(A) = \dfrac{4}{52} = \dfrac{1}{13}$

Since card is not replaced after first draw, only 51 cards are left, and there will be 3 kings in it if first was king.

$\therefore$ Probability of B given that A has already occurred is

$$P(B|A) = \dfrac{3}{51} = \dfrac{1}{17}$$

Now probability that both cards are kings is

$$P(A \cap B) = P(A).P(B|A) = \dfrac{1}{13} \times \dfrac{1}{17} = \dfrac{1}{221}$$

Example

Three cards are drawn successively, without replacement from a pack of 52 well shuffled cards. What is the probability that first two cards are kings and the third card drawn is an ace?

Solution

Let the event A be 'first card is king',

the event B be 'second card is king',

and the event C be 'third card is ace'.

There are 52 cards, in which 4 are kings before drawing first card.

$\therefore P(A) = \dfrac{4}{52} = \dfrac{1}{13}$

Since card is not replaced after first draw, only 51 cards are left, and there will be 3 kings in it if first was king.

$\therefore$ Probability of B given that A has already occurred is

$$P(B|A) = \frac{3}{51} = \frac{1}{17}$$

If both two cards drawn are not replaced and both were kings, then total 50 cards are left, and there will be all 4 aces in it.

$\therefore$ Probability of C given that A and B both have already occurred is

$$P(C|AB) = \frac{4}{50} = \frac{2}{25}$$

Now probability that first two cards are kings and the third card drawn is an ace, is

$$P(A \cap B \cap C) = P(A).P(B|A).\,P(C|AB) = \frac{1}{13} \times \frac{1}{17} \times \frac{2}{25} = \frac{2}{5525}$$

5 Independent events

If the occurrence of one event does not affect the probability of the other event, then the events are called **independent events**.

i.e., **For independents events A and B ,**

 P(B|A) = P(B) and P(A|B) = P(A),   (if P (A) $\neq$ 0, P (B) $\neq$ 0)

In that case we find that multiplication rule of probability,

P (A $\cap$ B) = P(A) . P(B | A) will change to P(A $\cap$ B) = P(A) . P (B)

Thus, we can check the independency of two events A and B by the relation:

$$\mathbf{P (A \cap B) = P (A) . P (B)}$$

- We give following relations for independent events:

  (i) For independents events A and B ,

   P (B | A) = P (B), if P (A) $\neq$ 0

  (ii) Two events A and B are *independent events* if

   P (A $\cap$ B) = P (A) . P (B)

  (iii) Three events A, B and C are said to be mutually independent, if

   P (A $\cap$ B) = P (A) . P (B)

   P (A $\cap$ C) = P (A) . P (C)

   P (B $\cap$ C) = P (B) . P (C)

  And P (A $\cap$ B $\cap$ C) = P (A) . P (B) . P (C)

- If two events A and B are independents, then their complementary events 'not A' and 'not B' are also independent.

  i.e., **P (A$'$ $\cap$ B$'$) = P (A$'$) . P (B$'$)**

  also, **P (A $\cap$ B$'$) = P (A) . P (B$'$)**

  and **P (A$'$ $\cap$ B) = P (A$'$) . P (B)**

Example

An unbiased die is thrown twice. Let the event A be 'odd number on the first throw' and B the event 'odd number on the second throw'. Check the independence of the events A and B.

Solution

Here, the sample space is

$S = \{(1,1),(1,2),(1,3),(1,4),(1,5),(1,6),$
$\quad (2,1),(2,2),(2,3),(2,4),(2,5),(2,6),$
$\quad (3,1),(3,2),(3,3),(3,4),(3,5),(3,6),$
$\quad (4,1),(4,2),(4,3),(4,4),(4,5),(4,6),$
$\quad (5,1),(5,2),(5,3),(5,4),(5,5),(5,6),$
$\quad (6,1),(6,2),(6,3),(6,4),(6,5),(6,6)\}$

$n(S) = 36$

Event A is 'odd number on the first throw'.

$\Rightarrow\ A = \{(1,1),(1,2),(1,3),(1,4),(1,5),(1,6),$
$\quad\quad (3,1),(3,2),(3,3),(3,4),(3,5),(3,6),$
$\quad\quad (5,1),(5,2),(5,3),(5,4),(5,5),(5,6)\}$

$\Rightarrow\ n(A) = 18$

$\Rightarrow\ P(A) = \dfrac{n(A)}{n(S)} = \dfrac{18}{36} = \dfrac{1}{2}$

And event B is 'odd number on the second throw'.

$\Rightarrow\ B = \{(1,1),(1,3),(1,5),$
$\quad\quad (2,1),(2,3),(2,5),$
$\quad\quad (3,1),(3,3),(3,5),$
$\quad\quad (4,1),(4,3),(4,5),$
$\quad\quad (5,1),(5,3),(5,5),$
$\quad\quad (6,1),(6,3),(6,5)\}$

$\Rightarrow\ n(B) = 18$

$\Rightarrow\ P(B) = \dfrac{n(B)}{n(S)} = \dfrac{18}{36} = \dfrac{1}{2}$

$A \cap B = \{(1,1),(1,3),(1,5),$
$\quad\quad (3,1),(3,3),(3,5),$
$\quad\quad (5,1),(5,3),(5,5)\}$

$\Rightarrow\ n(A \cap B) = 9$

$\Rightarrow\ P(A \cap B) = \dfrac{n(A \cap B)}{n(S)} = \dfrac{9}{36} = \dfrac{1}{4}$

Since $P(A).\,P(B) = \dfrac{1}{2} \times \dfrac{1}{2} = \dfrac{1}{4}$

$\therefore P(A).\,P(B) = P(A \cap B)$

$\Rightarrow$ A and B are independent events.

Example

An unbiased die is thrown twice. Let the event A be 'odd number on the first throw' , the event B be 'odd number on the second throw' and the event C be 'more than 4 on first throw'. Check the independence of the events A, B and C.

Solution

Here, the sample space is

$$S = \{(1,1),(1,2),(1,3),(1,4),(1,5),(1,6),$$
$$(2,1),(2,2),(2,3),(2,4),(2,5),(2,6),$$
$$(3,1),(3,2),(3,3),(3,4),(3,5),(3,6),$$
$$(4,1),(4,2),(4,3),(4,4),(4,5),(4,6),$$
$$(5,1),(5,2),(5,3),(5,4),(5,5),(5,6),$$
$$(6,1),(6,2),(6,3),(6,4),(6,5),(6,6)\}$$

$n(S) = 36$

Event A is 'odd number on the first throw'.

$\Rightarrow \quad A = \{(1,1),(1,2),(1,3),(1,4),(1,5),(1,6),$
$$(3,1),(3,2),(3,3),(3,4),(3,5),(3,6),$$
$$(5,1),(5,2),(5,3),(5,4),(5,5),(5,6)\}$$

$\Rightarrow \quad n(A) = 18$

$\Rightarrow \quad P(A) = \dfrac{n(A)}{n(S)} = \dfrac{18}{36} = \dfrac{1}{2}$

Event B is 'odd number on the second throw'.

$\Rightarrow \quad B = \{(1,1),(1,3),(1,5),$
$$(2,1),(2,3),(2,5),$$
$$(3,1),(3,3),(3,5),$$
$$(4,1),(4,3),(4,5),$$
$$(5,1),(5,3),(5,5),$$
$$(6,1),(6,3),(6,5)\}$$

$\Rightarrow \quad n(B) = 18$

$\Rightarrow \quad P(B) = \dfrac{n(B)}{n(S)} = \dfrac{18}{36} = \dfrac{1}{2}$

Event C is 'more than 4 on first throw'.

$\Rightarrow \quad C = \{(5,1),(5,2),(5,3),(5,4),(5,5),(5,6),$
$$(6,1),(6,2),(6,3),(6,4),(6,5),(6,6)\}$$

$\Rightarrow \quad n(C) = 12$

$\Rightarrow \quad P(C) = \dfrac{n(C)}{n(S)} = \dfrac{12}{36} = \dfrac{1}{3}$

Now

$A \cap B = \{(1,1),(1,3),(1,5),(3,1),(3,3),(3,5),(5,1),(5,3),(5,5)\}$

$B \cap C = \{(5,1),(5,3),(5,5),(6,1),(6,3),(6,5)\}$

$C \cap A = \{(5,1),(5,2),(5,3),(5,4),(5,5),(5,6)\}$

$A \cap B \cap C = \{(5,1),(5,3),(5,5)\}$

$\Rightarrow n(A \cap B) = 9, \quad n(B \cap C) = 6, \quad n(C \cap A) = 6$ and $n(A \cap B \cap C) = 3$

$\Rightarrow P(A \cap B) = \dfrac{n(A \cap B)}{n(S)} = \dfrac{9}{36} = \dfrac{1}{4}$

$ P(B \cap C) = \dfrac{n(B \cap C)}{n(S)} = \dfrac{6}{36} = \dfrac{1}{6}$

$ P(C \cap A) = \dfrac{n(C \cap A)}{n(S)} = \dfrac{6}{36} = \dfrac{1}{6}$

And $P(A \cap B \cap C) = \dfrac{n(A \cap B \cap C)}{n(S)} = \dfrac{3}{36} = \dfrac{1}{12}$

Since $P(A). P(B) = \dfrac{1}{2} \times \dfrac{1}{2} = \dfrac{1}{4} = P(A \cap B)$

$ P(B). P(C) = \dfrac{1}{2} \times \dfrac{1}{3} = \dfrac{1}{6} = P(B \cap C)$

and $ P(C). P(A) = \dfrac{1}{3} \times \dfrac{1}{2} = \dfrac{1}{6} = P(C \cap A)$

also, $ P(A) .P(B). P(C) = \dfrac{1}{2} \times \dfrac{1}{2} \times \dfrac{1}{3} = \dfrac{1}{12} = P(A \cap B \cap C)$

$\Rightarrow$ A, B and C are independent events.

Example

Probability of solving specific problem independently by A and B are $\dfrac{1}{2}$ and $\dfrac{1}{3}$ respectively. If both try to solve the problem independently, find the probability that the problem is not solved.

Solution

Suppose the event E be 'A solves the problem'
and event F be 'B solves the problem'.

We are given that $P(E) = \dfrac{1}{2}$ and $P(F) = \dfrac{1}{3}$

$\Rightarrow P(\text{not E}) = P(E') = 1 - P(E) = 1 - \dfrac{1}{2} = \dfrac{1}{2}$

And $ P(\text{not F}) = P(F') = 1 - P(F) = 1 - \dfrac{1}{3} = \dfrac{2}{3}$

Since both A and B are trying to solve the problem independently

$\therefore$ Probability of solving the problem by A doesn't depend on whether B solves it or not and vice-versa.

So, E and F are independent events.

 E$'$ and F$'$ will also be independent.

If problem is not solved, it means neither A nor B is able to solve the problem.

$\therefore$ P(problem is not solved) = P(not E and not F)

$$= P(E' \cap F')$$
$$= P(E').P(F')$$
$$= \dfrac{1}{2} \times \dfrac{2}{3} = \dfrac{1}{3}$$

---

6   Partition of Sample Space

The set of events E_1, E_2, . . . , E_n is called **a partition of the sample space S** *if the events E_1, E_2, . . . , E_n are* **mutually exclusive** *and* **exhaustive** *in the sample space S, and all of them have non-zero probabilities.*

i.e., if events E_1, E_2, . . . , E_n in a sample space S are such that

   (i) $E_i \cap E_j = \varphi$, for all $i \neq j$ and $i, j = 1, 2, 3, ..., n$

   (ii) $E_1 \cup E_2 \cup ... \cup E_n = S$ and

   (iii) $P(E_i) > 0$ for all $i = 1, 2, ..., n$, then

   the set of these events form a partition of sample space S.

- Partition of a sample space is not unique.
  There can be many partitions of a sample space.

<u>Example</u>

In rolling a die, the sample space is $S = \{1,2,3,4,5,6\}$.
Consider three events,

$\qquad\qquad$ E_1 : 'getting a number less than 3'

$\qquad\qquad$ E_2 : 'getting a number more than 4'

And $\qquad$ E_3 : 'getting 3 or 4'.

$\Rightarrow\qquad$ $E_1 = \{1,2\}$,$\qquad$ $E_2 = \{5,6\}$ $\qquad$ and $E_3 = \{3,4\}$

Here, $\qquad$ $E_1 \cap E_2 = \phi,$ $\qquad$ $E_2 \cap E_3 = \phi$ $\qquad$ and $E_3 \cap E_1 = \phi$

   It means E_1, E_2, E_3 are mutually exclusive events.

Now $\qquad$ $E_1 \cup E_2 \cup E_3 = \{1,2,3,4,5,6\} = S$

   It means E_1, E_2, E_3 are exhaustive events.

Also, $\qquad$ $P(E_1) = \dfrac{2}{6} = \dfrac{1}{3}$, $P(E_2) = \dfrac{2}{6} = \dfrac{1}{3}$, $\qquad\qquad$ $P(E_3) = \dfrac{2}{6} = \dfrac{1}{3}$

   It means $P(E_1) = P(E_2) = P(E_3) = \dfrac{1}{3} > 0$

   E_1, E_2 and E_3 are mutually exclusive and exhaustive events with each having a non-zero probability.

$\therefore$ They form a partition of sample space S.

We can have more partitions of this sample space.

e.g., consider events, $\qquad$ E_1 : 'getting an even number'

and $\qquad\qquad\qquad\qquad$ E_2 : 'getting an odd number'

i.e., $\qquad$ $E_1 = \{2,4,6\}$ and $E_2 = \{1,3,5\}$

We can easily check that they are also mutually exclusive and exhaustive events with non-zero probabilities.

$\therefore$ They also form partition of S.

---

7   Theorem of Total Probability

If the events $E_1, E_2, \ldots, E_n$ form a partition of the sample space S such that each of the events $E_1, E_2, \ldots, E_n$ has non-zero probability of occurrence, and A is any event associated with S, then

$$\mathbf{P(A) = P(E_1).P(A \mid E_1) + P(E_2).P(A \mid E_2) + \ldots + P(E_n).P(A \mid E_n)}$$

<u>**Example**</u>

A bag contains 4 red and 4 black balls, another bag contains 2 red and 6 black balls. One of the two bags is selected at random, and a ball is drawn from the bag. Find the probability that the ball is drawn red.

Solution

Let events E_1 be 'first bag is selected'

and events E_2 be 'second bag is selected'.

Here, both these events will be mutually exclusive and exhaustive, and hence form partition of sample space.

Let event A be 'red ball is drawn'.

Probability of selecting any of the bag out of given two bags $= \dfrac{1}{2}$

i.e., $P(E_1) = \dfrac{1}{2}$ and $P(E_2) = \dfrac{1}{2}$

Now probability of red ball from the first bag is $= \dfrac{4}{8} = \dfrac{1}{2}$

$$[\because \text{ First Bag contains 4 red out of total 8 balls}]$$

and probability of red ball from the second bag is $= \dfrac{2}{8} = \dfrac{1}{4}$

$$[\because \text{ Second Bag contains 2 red out of total 8 balls}]$$

Symbolically, we write these probabilities as

$$P(A|E_1) = \dfrac{1}{2} \quad \text{and} \quad P(A|E_2) = \dfrac{1}{4}$$

Now probability that red ball is drawn, is given by theorem of total probability:

$$P(A) = P(E_1). \; P(A|E_1) + P(E_2). \; P(A|E_2)$$

$$\Rightarrow \qquad P(A) = \dfrac{1}{2} \times \dfrac{1}{2} + \dfrac{1}{2} \times \dfrac{1}{4} = \dfrac{3}{8}$$

8   Bayes' Theorem

If $\{E_1, E_2, \ldots, E_n\}$ is a partition of the sample space S such that each of the events $E_1, E_2, \ldots, E_n$ has non-zero probability of occurrence, and A is any event associated with S and it is known that event A has occurred, then the probability that A has occurred from part $E_1, E_2, \ldots, E_n$ respectively, is found by the formulae:

$$P(E_1 \mid A) = \frac{P(E_1) . P(A \mid E_1)}{P(E_1).P(A \mid E_1) + P(E_2).P(A \mid E_2) + \ldots + P(E_n).P(A \mid E_n)}$$

$$P(E_2 \mid A) = \frac{P(E_2) . P(A \mid E_2)}{P(E_1).P(A \mid E_1) + P(E_2).P(A \mid E_2) + \ldots + P(E_n).P(A \mid E_n)}$$

. . .   . . .

. . .   . . .

$$P(E_n \mid A) = \frac{P(E_n) . P(A \mid E_n)}{P(E_1).P(A \mid E_1) + P(E_2).P(A \mid E_2) + \ldots + P(E_n).P(A \mid E_n)}$$

- The events $E_1, E_2, \ldots, E_n$ are called *hypotheses*.
- The probability $P(E_i)$ is called the *priori probability* of the hypothesis E_i.
- The conditional probability $P(E_i \mid A)$ is called *a posteriori probability* of the hypothesis E_i.

Example

A bag contains 4 red and 4 black balls, another bag contains 2 red and 6 black balls. One of the two bags is selected at random, and a ball is drawn from the bag which is found to be red. Find the probability that the ball is drawn from the first bag.

Solution

In the same way as in the previous example, we proceed as follows:

Let events E_1 be 'first bag is selected'

and events E_2 be 'second bag is selected'.

Let event A be 'red ball is drawn'.

$$P(E_1) = \frac{1}{2} \qquad \text{and} \qquad P(E_2) = \frac{1}{2}$$

$$P(A|E_1) = \frac{1}{2} \qquad \text{and} \qquad P(A|E_2) = \frac{1}{4}$$

We know that red ball comes out from the bag.

$\therefore$ We have to find the probability that the ball is drawn from first bag if the ball is red.

i.e., we have to find $P(E_1|A)$

It can be found by Bayes' theorem:

$$P(E_1|A) = \frac{P(E_1) . P(A|E_1)}{P(E_1).P(A|E_1) + P(E_2).P(A|E_2)}$$

$$\Rightarrow \qquad P(E_1|A) = \frac{\frac{1}{2} \times \frac{1}{2}}{\frac{1}{2} \times \frac{1}{2} + \frac{1}{2} \times \frac{1}{4}} = \frac{\frac{1}{4}}{\frac{3}{8}} = \frac{2}{3}$$

$\therefore$ The probability that the red ball comes out from first bag is $\frac{2}{3}$

---

9 Random Variable

A random variable is a real valued function whose domain is the sample space of a random experiment.

- A random variable X assigns a real value to each outcome of given sample space.

Example

Consider a random experiment of tossing a coin thrice, and we count the number of times the heads is obtained.

Here, the sample space is S = {HHH, HHT, HTH, HTT, THH, THT, TTH, TTT}

If X is a variable which denotes number of times heads is obtained, then the value of X for outcome HHH is 3, for HHT is 2, and so on.

For each outcome in the sample space, we write it as

$$X(HHH) = 3, \quad X(HHT) = 2, \quad X(HTH) = 2, \quad X(HTT) = 1$$
$$X(THH) = 2, \quad X(THT) = 1, \quad X(TTH) = 1, \quad X(TTT) = 0$$

Since variable X has a real value for each and every outcome of sample space, we say that X is a random variable.

It can be represented in the form of a function as $X: S \rightarrow R$, where S is sample space, and R is set of real number and its range is {0,1,2,3}

9.1 Probability distribution of random variable

A description which gives the values of random variable along with their corresponding probabilities is called as probability distribution of random variable

Let X be a random variable defined on the sample space S, and it can take the values as $x_1, x_2, x_3, x_4, \ldots, x_n$ with

their corresponding probabilities as $p_1, p_2, p_3, p_4, \ldots, p_n$.

Its probability distribution table is written as:

X	p_i
x_1	p_1
x_2	p_2
x_3	p_3
.	.
.	.
x_n	p_n

Example

In a random experiment of tossing a coin thrice, find the probability distribution of number of times heads is obtained.

Solution

Here, the sample space is S = {HHH, HHT, HTH, HTT, THH, THT, TTH, TTT}

Let random variable, X denotes number of times heads is obtained. We can obtain heads 0, 1, 2 or 3 times in tossing a coin thrice,

$\therefore$ X can take the values as 0, 1, 2, 3

Now

$$P(X=0) = P(TTT) = \frac{1}{8}$$

$$P(X=1) = P(HTT,THT,TTH) = \frac{3}{8}$$

$$P(X=2) = P(HHT,HTH,THH) = \frac{3}{8}$$

$$P(X=1) = P(HHH) = \frac{1}{8}$$

Its probability distribution table is written as:

X	p_i
0	$\frac{1}{8}$
1	$\frac{3}{8}$
2	$\frac{3}{8}$
3	$\frac{1}{8}$

9.2 Mean and variance of random variable

If all possible values of the random variable X are:

$x_1, x_2, x_3, x_4, \ldots, x_n$, and their corresponding probabilities are

$p_1, p_2, p_3, p_4, \ldots, p_n$, then

- Mean is : $\mu = \sum p_i x_i$

  i.e., $\mu = p_1 x_1 + p_2 x_2 + p_3 x_3 + \ldots + p_n x_n$

- Variance is : $\sigma^2 = \sum p_i x_i^2 - \mu^2$

  i.e., $\sigma^2 = (p_1 x_1^2 + p_2 x_2^2 + p_3 x_3^2 + \ldots + p_n x_n^2) - \mu^2$

Procedure

Step-1 Find probabilities of all values of $X = x_1, x_2, x_3, x_4, \ldots, x_n$

Step-2 Write the values $x_1, x_2, x_3, x_4, \ldots, x_n$ in 1st column (**headed as x_i**) of the table and their probabilities $p_1, p_2, p_3, p_4, \ldots, p_n$ in 2nd column (**headed as p_i**).

(*See table on next page*)

Step-3 In the 3rd column, find the product of values of X and their corresponding probabilities ((**headed as $p_i x_i$**)

Step-4 In the 4th column, multiply $p_i\,x_i$ with x_i to get $p_i\,x_i^2$.

We get the table as shown below:

x_i	p_i	$p_i\,x_i$	$p_i\,x_i^2$
x_1	p_1	$p_1\,x_1$	$p_1\,x_1^{\,2}$
x_2	p_2	$p_2\,x_2$	$p_2\,x_2^{\,2}$
x_3	p_3	$p_3\,x_3$	$p_3\,x_3^{\,2}$
.	.	.	.
.	.	.	.
x_n	p_n	$p_n\,x_n$	$p_n\,x_n^{\,2}$
		$\sum p_i\,x_i = {-}\,{-}$	$\sum p_i\,x_i^2 = {-}\,{-}$

Step-5 Add entries in 3rd column to obtain mean as $\mu = \sum p_i\,x_i$

Step-6 Add entries in 4th column to obtain $\sum p_i\,x_i^2$

Step-7 Find variance as $\sigma^2 = \sum p_i\,x_i^2 - \mu^2$

<u>**Example**</u>

In a random experiment of tossing a coin thrice, find the mean and variance of number of times heads is obtained.

Solution

Here, the sample space is

S = {HHH, HHT, HTH, HTT, THH, THT, TTH, TTT}

Let random variable, X denotes number of times heads is obtained.

We can obtain heads 0, 1, 2 or 3 times in tossing a coin thrice,

$\therefore$ X can take the values as 0, 1, 2, 3

Now $P(X=0) = P(TTT) = \dfrac{1}{8}$

$P(X=1) = P(HTT, THT, TTH) = \dfrac{3}{8}$

$P(X=2) = P(HHT, HTH, THH) = \dfrac{3}{8}$

$P(X=1) = P(HHH) = \dfrac{1}{8}$

Its probability distribution table is written as:

x_i	p_i	$p_i\,x_i$	$p_i\,x_i^2$
0	$\dfrac{1}{8}$	0	0
1	$\dfrac{3}{8}$	$\dfrac{3}{8}$	$\dfrac{3}{8}$
2	$\dfrac{3}{8}$	$\dfrac{6}{8}$	$\dfrac{12}{8}$
3	$\dfrac{1}{8}$	$\dfrac{3}{8}$	$\dfrac{9}{8}$
		$\sum p_i\,x_i = \dfrac{12}{8} = \dfrac{3}{2}$	$\sum p_i\,x_i^2 = \dfrac{24}{8} = 3$

$\therefore$ Mean of the number of heads is,

$$\mu = \sum p_i\, x_i = \frac{3}{2} = 1.5$$

and variance of the number of heads is,

$$\sigma^2 = \sum p_i\, x_i^2 - \mu^2$$

$$= 3 - \left(\frac{3}{2}\right)^2 = \frac{3}{4} = 0.75$$

10 *Bernoulli Trials and Binomial Distribution

- Performing same activity, a number of times in a random experiment is known as a trial of the experiment.
- *Trials of a random experiment are called* **Bernoulli trials**, *if they satisfy the following conditions :*
  (i) *There should be a* **finite number of trials**.
  (ii) *The trials should be* **independent**.
  (iii) *Each trial has exactly* **two outcomes : success or failure**.
  (iv) *The* **probability of success remains the same** *in each trial*.
- For Bernoulli trials, random variable X denotes the number of successes.
- If n is the number of trials, then X can take any integral value from 0 to n.
- Probability distribution of number of successes in Bernoulli trials can be found by **Binomial distribution**.

Example

From an urn containing 7 red and 9 black balls, three balls are drawn successively with replacement after each draw.

Here, we observe the following points.

(i) There are **finite number of trials** (no. of trials are 3).

(ii) Since balls are replaced after every draw, the probability of an event remains same in every trial. So, **trials are independent**.

(iii) Each trial can have exactly two outcomes: **success or failure.**
   If drawing red ball is success, then drawing non-red ball will be failure.
   If drawing black ball is success, then drawing non-black ball will be failure.

(iv) Also, **probability of success remains the same** *in each trial*.
   It is because probability of red ball or probability of black ball in every trial is same.

$\therefore$ Drawing of the balls in this case are Bernoulli trials.

<u>**Example**</u>

From an urn containing 7 red and 9 black balls, three balls are drawn successively without replacing the ball after the draws.
 Since balls are not replaced after the draws, the probability of an event will not remain same in every trial. So, **trials are not independent.**
 Neither probability of red ball nor probability of black ball is same in every trial.
 $\therefore$ **Probability of success can't be same** *in each trial.*
So, drawing of the balls in this case are not Bernoulli trials.

10.1 *Binomial Distribution

If a random experiment consists of Bernoulli trials, then the probability of a given number of successes can be found by Binomial Distribution.

- Probability of $X = r$ (i.e., r successes) is found as

$$P (X = r) = {}^{n}C_r \; p^r \, q^{n-r}$$

   where C denotes *combination*
   p = probability of success in each trial
   q = probability of failure in each trial

- Remember ${}^{n}C_r = \dfrac{n!}{r!(n-r)!}$

   [*see* chapter – 'Permutations and Combinations' of class XI]

- Sum of probabilities of success and failure in each trial is equal to 1
   i.e., $p + q = 1$

- If the number of successes $= r$,
   then the number of failures $= n - r$.

- Probability of r successes $=$ probability of $n - r$ failures

- A binomial distribution with **n**-Bernoulli trials and probability of success in each trial as **p**, is denoted by **B (n, p)**.

- Mean: $\mu = np$

- Variance: $\sigma^2 = npq$

Procedure to solve questions on Binomial distribution

Step-1 Define success in a trial.

Step-2 Find the probability of success in a trial as $p = - - -$
   and the probability of failure in a trial as $q = 1 - p$
   $= - - - - -$

Step-3 Note down the number of trials as $n = - - - - -$

Step-4 Let the random variable X denotes the number of successes, and note down all the possible values of X as: $X = 0, 1, 2, \ldots, n$

Step-5 Now we can find the probability of any number (r) of successes using the formula $P(X = r) = {}^nC_r\, p^r\, q^{n-r}$

Example

Five cards are drawn successively with replacement from a well-shuffled deck of 52 cards. What is the probability that (i) all the five cards are spades? (ii) only 3 cards are spades?

Solution

Let the success be 'getting a spade in a trial'.

There are 13 spades in a deck of 52 cards.

Probability of success in a trial is $p = \dfrac{13}{52} = \dfrac{1}{4}$

Probability of failure in a trial is $q = 1 - p$

$$= 1 - \frac{1}{4} = \frac{3}{4}$$

Number of trials, $n = 5$

Let X denotes the number of successes.

And all the possible values of X are $0, 1, 2, 3, 4, 5$.

We can find probability of any number of successes using Binomial distribution:

$$P(X = r) = {}^nC_r\, p^r\, q^{n-r}$$

(i) If all the five cards are spades, then we must find the probability of 5 successes.

$$\therefore P(X=5) = {}^5C_5\, p^5\, q^{5-5} = (1)\left(\frac{1}{4}\right)^5 \left(\frac{3}{4}\right)^0 = \left(\frac{1}{4}\right)^5 = \frac{1}{1024}$$

(ii) If we get only 3 spades, then we must find the probability of 3 successes.

$$\therefore P(X=3) = {}^5C_3\, p^3\, q^{5-3} = \frac{5!}{3!(5-3)!}\left(\frac{1}{4}\right)^3 \left(\frac{3}{4}\right)^2 = (10)\frac{9}{1024} = \frac{45}{512}$$